B2

STUDENT'S BOOK

BEYOND

MACMILLAN

Robert Campbell
Rob Metcalf
Rebecca Robb Benne

	LISTENING & VOCABULARY	GRAMMAR (2)	LANGUAGE & BEYOND	SPEAKING	WRITING
	I remember your name ***Take clear notes*** **Vocabulary (2):** Word families	Articles and other determiners ***Show what thing you're talking about***	Know yourself: ***Work on your weaknesses***	That's interesting! ***Make conversation*** Tell me more	Report back (*report*) ***Present statistical information***
	The written word ***Follow the speaker's argument*** **Vocabulary (2):** Character adjectives	*Used to* and *would* ***Talk about habits and states in the past***	Get thinking: ***Consider the consequences of your actions***	What happened? ***Describe an experience*** Where was I?	My fantasy story (*story*) ***Avoid repetition***
	The cabin project ***Understand referring words*** **Vocabulary (2):** Adjective + preposition, verb + noun + preposition	Future continuous and future perfect ***Talk about what will be happening and what will have happened***	Get organised: ***Set achievable goals***	Anything's possible ***Express certainty, probability and doubt*** Absolutely	Dear Sir or Madam (*formal letter or email*) ***Write a formal letter or email***
	No regrets ***Recognise imaginary situations*** PRONOUNCE Sentence stress and meaning **Vocabulary (2):** Abstract nouns	Wishes and regrets: *I wish/If only* ***Talk about wishes and regrets***	Know yourself: ***Learn from your mistakes***	What do you reckon? ***Express and react to opinions*** The way I see it	My trip advice (*review*) ***Contrast ideas***
	An unusual journey ***Deal with new vocabulary when you listen*** **Vocabulary (2):** Verbs to describe change	Comparisons ***Compare people, things and actions***	Get thinking: ***Understand how adverts try to sell to you***	Wait a second ***Interact with other people in a conversation*** By the way	Something different (*article*) ***Write an article***

LISTENING & VOCABULARY	GRAMMAR (2)	LANGUAGE & BEYOND	SPEAKING	WRITING
Teen tips for parents ***Follow a conversation*** **Vocabulary (2):** Three-word phrasal verbs	*-ing* and *-ed* clauses ***Use clauses that start with -ing or -ed***	Respect others: ***See things from another person's perspective***	I was wondering … ***Ask polite questions*** Do you mind?	Seen from the outside (*description*) ***Give impressions in a description***
The greatest films never made ***Understand purpose and intention*** **Vocabulary (2):** Adjective + noun collocations	Future in the past ***Talk about future events seen from the past***	Respect others: ***Respect rules and social boundaries***	It was awesome! ***Express likes and dislikes*** It's not my cup of tea	The perfect choice (*website post*) ***Make suggestions and express preferences***
Customer service ***Recognise a speaker's attitude and feelings*** **Vocabulary (2):** Buying and selling	Modal verbs of speculation and expectation ***Give possible explanations for things***	Get organised: ***Make a budget and stick to it***	Let's discuss it ***Take part in a debate*** Shall I start?	On balance … (*essay*) ***Develop an argument***
The elephant in the room ***Infer meaning*** **Vocabulary (2):** Idioms	Question tags ***Ask questions and confirm ideas using question tags*** PRONOUNCE Weak forms and simplifications in natural speech	Communicate & cooperate: ***Prepare for an interview***	I've got some bad news ***Soften what you say*** Better luck next time	Old friends (*informal email*) ***Write an informal email***
Speech day ***Be an active listener*** **Vocabulary (2):** Colloquial phrases	Inversion ***Add emphasis to what you write and say*** PRONOUNCE Word groups and stressed words	Communicate & cooperate: ***Be a successful non-native speaker***	Centre stage ***Describe a picture*** From one side to the other	Frankly, it's unacceptable (*email*) ***Express strong views***

IRREGULAR VERBS page 140 **EXTRAS** pages 141–142 **PROJECTS** page 143

UNIT 1

WHAT'S IN A NAME?

IN THE PICTURE Names

»» Talk about names and naming traditions

RECALL AND READ

1 Work in pairs. Discuss what the names below mean.

family name   given name   first name   middle name   surname

2 a Read the curious facts in the fact file below and check your answers to Exercise 1.

b Work in pairs. Discuss the facts. Which ones are new to you? Which do you find surprising? Why?

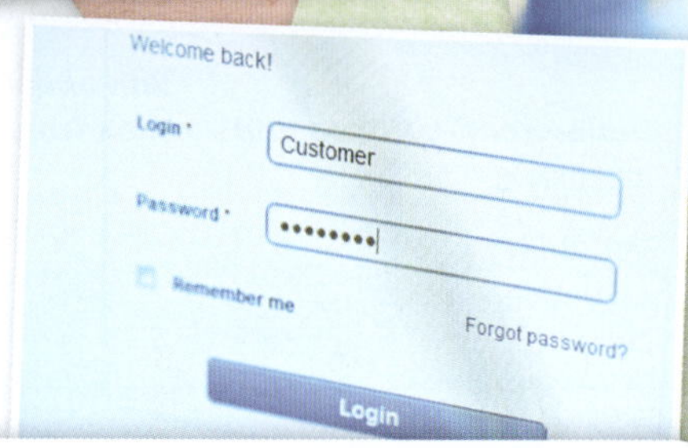

WORK WITH WORDS

3 a Work in pairs. Find real examples of three types of name below in the fact file. Think of another example of each one.

alias	assumed name	brand name
domain name	household name	initials
maiden name	nickname	pen name/pseudonym
stage name	title	username

b Look at the other types of name in the box. What do you think they are?

c Match the other types of name to the definitions.

1 A name used to log on to an online account.
2 A fictitious name used by an author.
3 A word or abbreviation that shows a person's job, status, etc.
4 A woman's original surname if she adopts her husband's surname when she gets married.
5 The first letters of a person's names, written in capitals.
6 An address on the internet.
7 A person or brand that's very well known.
8 A name someone uses or is called instead of their real name.
9 A name used to hide a person's real identity.

4 ▶1.01 Listen and repeat the words in Exercise 3a.

5 ▶1.02 Listen to six scenes. What type of name are the people talking about in each one?

6 Work in pairs. Find examples of the names in Exercise 3a in the collage.

Curious facts about names

- In most Western countries, your given (or first) name comes before your surname (or family name). In many Asian countries, your surname comes first.
- Many English speakers have a middle name – a second given name.
- Most Spanish speakers use two surnames: their father and mother's first surnames.
- Surnames were first used in China around 5,000 years ago to identify tribe members. Children were given their mother's surname.
- Iceland uses the patronymic system for creating a surname based on the father's first name. For example, Jon Sigurðsson's son and daughter will have the surnames Jonsson and Jonsdóttir respectively. However, matronymic surnames based on the mother's first name are becoming increasingly popular.
- In parts of Indonesia and India, mononyms (single names) are still used. In Western cultures, mononyms are only used for famous people, like the legendary footballer Pelé (his nickname) or the singer Beyoncé (her stage name).
- Some countries have rules about naming. In Denmark, parents have to choose from a list of acceptable given names. In the USA, anything goes – you can make up baby names. In the 2000s it became fashionable to give babies brand names like Armani ... and Pepsi!

Real name:
Charles Lutwidge Dodgson

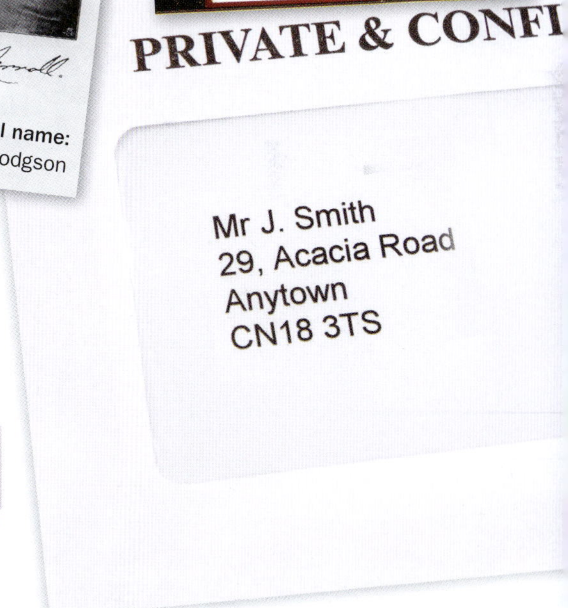

7 a 1.03 PRONOUNCE **Listen and repeat the words, focusing on the unvoiced and voiced sounds.**

	Unvoiced	Voiced
1	/f/ first name	/v/ given name
2	/s/ surname	/z/ username
3	/ʃ/ initials	/ʒ/ Asian
4	/tʃ/ China	/dʒ/ stage name

b Find another example of each sound on page 6.

8 THE MOVING PICTURE **Watch the video. What different types of names do the people talk about? What do they say about them?**

EXTEND

9 Read the sentences on the right. What do the expressions in purple mean? Check your ideas in a dictionary.

'My parents **named** me **after** my grandmother.'
'**Calling people names** is a type of bullying.'
'Imran's dad's **a big name in** the music business.'
'Your behaviour is **giving** the school **a bad name**!'

SPEAK

10 Work in pairs. Do one or both of the tasks.

- Compare the naming traditions and trends in the fact file with those in your country. What are the pros and cons of each one?
- Discuss the questions from the Moving Picture video.
  1 What's the story behind your full name?
  2 Do you have any nicknames? Tell us about them.
  3 Are you completely happy with your name? Why?/Why not?

GO BEYOND

Do the Words & Beyond exercises on page 130.

Workbook, page 4

READING Katrina

»» Find information efficiently

SPEAK AND READ

1 Work in pairs. Answer the questions.

1 Have there been any big storms in the news recently? Where?
2 What do you know about hurricanes? Make notes.

2 a Read the tips in the HOW TO box.

b ▶1.04 Find answers to the questions in the text.

1 What's the origin of the word 'hurricane'?
2 Where do hurricanes form?
3 Were there more hurricanes in the years following Katrina?
4 What's a 'storm surge'?
5 How long have men's names been used for hurricanes?
6 What do you call the centre of a hurricane?

HOW TO

find information efficiently

- ☐ Identify the text type. Look at headings, images, layout and other types of text (links, footnotes, etc).
- ☐ Think about the structure. How is information usually organised in this text type?
- ☐ Identify sections that might have the information you need.
- ☐ Don't read every word. Look for words connected to the information you need.

HOT TOPICS | IMAGES & VIDEOS | QUIZ ZONE | SEARCH

HURRICANE
Contents

OVERVIEW

A hurricane is a powerful tropical cyclone with sustained wind speeds of 119kph or higher. Hurricanes form in the north Atlantic or north-east Pacific. Similar storms are known as typhoons in the north-west Pacific and cyclones in the south Pacific and Indian Ocean.

WORD ORIGIN

'Hurricane' comes from the Spanish word 'huracán', which Spanish explorers copied from the indigenous people of the Caribbean. The word probably has its roots in *Hurakan*, the name of an ancient Mayan storm god.

FORMATION

Hurricanes form over warm waters when enormous amounts of moist air rise into the atmosphere and winds start to circle around the storm's 'eye'. As long as temperatures on the sea's surface remain at 26°C or above, the storm can continue to grow stronger. These storms, which sometimes start near the coast of Africa, can take days or weeks to strengthen into hurricanes.

INTENSITY AND DAMAGE

The intensity of a hurricane is categorised according to its wind speed. There are five categories, which describe the damage its wind speeds are likely to cause. However, where it reaches the coast can be equally important, as some areas are more vulnerable to storm surges – increases in sea level caused by strong winds. In 2005, a hurricane called Katrina became the costliest hurricane in US history despite only being a Category 3 storm when it made landfall.

NAMING

Hurricanes' names are taken from lists of names compiled by the World Meteorological Organization. Each name starts with a different letter of the alphabet but doesn't include the letters Q, U, X, Y or Z. Six lists are used in rotation, so the list for 2015 will be used again in 2021. However, if a storm is particularly destructive, its name is retired. The current system has been used since 1953, although originally only women's names were used. Men's names were added to the lists in 1979 as a result of pressure from feminist groups.

TRENDS

In 2005 a record five hurricane names were retired – Dennis, Katrina, Rita, Stan and Wilma. This led to speculation that hurricane activity was increasing as a result of climate change. The years following Katrina did not support that theory and the connection between hurricane activity and climate change is hotly debated.

3 Which tips in the HOW TO box did you use for help with Exercise 2b? Tick (✓) them.

4 Work in pairs. Write two more questions about hurricanes. Then pass them to another pair to answer.

REACT

5 Work in pairs. Compare what you've learned about hurricanes.

GO BEYOND

What's the connection between hurricanes and these words: *sustained*, *indigenous*, *moist*, *landfall* and *retired*? Look in the text and make notes.

»» Workbook, page 5

GRAMMAR Present tenses review

>>> Talk about things in or connected to the present

READ

1 Put the news updates in chronological order.

Home | Profile | Messages | #Carol

.... **Atlantic News** We're having serious problems. Hurricanes always cause damage, but the emergency services have received over 100 calls since **#Carol** arrived.

.... **Jake Reid** Still no hurricanes! Have we ever had a season like this? We were told to expect a big one, but they're always changing their minds!

.... **Coast Radio** The worst is over. The NWS has just downgraded **#Carol** to a tropical storm.

.... **Atlantic News** Tropical cyclone **#Carol**'s been growing in strength since Monday. It's now predicted to make landfall as a Category 2 hurricane.

.... **Megan Brookes** **#Carol**'s coming! The wind's getting stronger. Surfers are leaving the beach. We've been preparing all morning, but it's still scary!

STUDY

2 Read the explanations. Then underline one example of each verb tense use in Exercise 1.

Present tenses review

Present simple

Use: For habits, routines and facts.

Present continuous

Use (1): For things in progress now or around now.
Use (2): For temporary or changing situations.
Use (3): With *always* to criticise someone's habits.

Present perfect simple

Use (1): For past actions when you don't say an exact time (with *ever*, *never*, etc).
Use (2): For recently completed actions (with *just*, *already*, *so far*, *yet*, etc).
Use (3): For actions in a period that started in the past and continues to now (with *for* or *since*).

Present perfect continuous

Use (1): For actions in progress recently (with *recently*, *lately*, *all day*, etc).
Use (2): For actions in progress from a time in the past until now (with *for* or *since*).

State verbs

You can use a continuous form with a state verb if it describes an action: *thinking* (= considering), *having* (= eating), *being* (= behaving), etc.

See GRAMMAR DATABASE, page 120.

Workbook, pages 6–7

PRACTISE

3 Choose the correct option.

TRENDING TOPICS

NAMES IN THE NEWS

- Some people (1) ***never give* / *are never giving*** up. British social worker **Andy Bear** has finally (2) ***passed* / *been passing*** his driving test – after a record 53 attempts.
- Police (3) ***question* / *are questioning*** IT billionaire Alan Smith, alias **Kit Conman**. Governments worldwide claim that ever since his online business was set up he has (4) ***use* / *been using*** it to spy on them.
- **Carlos Suarez** (5) ***doesn't make* / *isn't making*** many films, but they are always well received. His latest work has just (6) ***won* / *been winning*** the Golden Moon Award for best documentary.
- The Australian weather service (7) ***doesn't say* / *isn't saying*** much about cyclone **Brenda**, perhaps due to the general belief that weather forecasters (8) ***always get* / *are always getting*** things wrong lately.

4 Complete each question with the simple or continuous form of the present or present perfect. More than one answer may be possible.

1 what stories / be / in the news recently?
2 what / learn / about in your other classes at the moment?
3 what / you / do / in your free time over the last few days?
4 what effect / climate change / have / on local weather conditions?
5 what / think / about internet piracy?
6 in what ways / you / change / since you became a teenager?

5 Decide if the verbs describe actions or states. Then write them in the correct simple or continuous form. Which question in Exercise 4 is being answered?

'I (1) .... (**not have**) a lot of time for anything except schoolwork at the moment. Right now my teachers (2) .... (**be**) really demanding. Normally I (3) .... (**like**) to answer messages and update my page in the evening, but I (4) .... (**not be**) online much this week yet. I (5) .... (**think**) about the weekend all the time, though. It's not far off now, and I (6) .... (**really / want**) to switch off and relax.'

SPEAK

6 Work in groups. Ask and answer the questions in Exercise 4.

Take clear notes

SPEAK AND LISTEN

1 Work in pairs. Answer the questions.

1 How good is your memory? Give examples.
2 Would you go to the talk in the poster? Why?/Why not?

2 a Read the tips in the HOW TO box.

b You're going to attend the talk in the poster and take notes. Think about how to organise your notes.

c 1.05 Listen and take notes. Then work in pairs. Compare your notes and discuss any differences.

3 Which tips in the HOW TO box did you use for help with Exercises 2b and 2c? Tick (✓) them.

4 1.05 Complete the sentences using your notes. Then listen again and check your answers.

1 The speaker sees memory training as key to a student's ______ .
2 He thinks that a bad memory is just an ______ one.
3 The first step to remembering something is to ______ on it.
4 The most important memory technique is ______ .
5 To remember names, it's a good idea to associate a person's name with their ______ .
6 The speaker also talks about the benefits of enough ______ .

HOW TO
take clear notes

- ☐ Know why you need your notes. Focus on relevant information.
- ☐ Decide how to organise your notes: headings and bullet points, or a network or a mind map?
- ☐ Leave space to add further information.
- ☐ Only write words and short phrases. Use abbreviations: *ie*, eg, >, =, etc.
- ☐ Check your notes while your memory's fresh.

REACT

5 Work in pairs. Discuss the talk. Which ways to improve your memory do you already use? Which would you consider using?

WORK WITH WORDS

6 a Work in pairs. Look at the ways to build word families. Then complete the table.

Nouns:
verb + *-tion* / *-ance* / *-ment* / *-y* / *-ing*
adjective + *-ness*

Adjectives:
noun + *-al* / *-ful* / *-ive* / *-able* / *-y*
verb + *-ed*

Verbs:
noun + *-ise* / *-en*

Verb	Noun	Adjective
appear		apparent
exaggerate		
forget		
imagine		
improve		
mean		
memorise		
practise	practice	
sleep		
strengthen		strong
succeed	success	
train		

b 1.06 Listen and check. Then listen and repeat the words.

7 a Complete the sentence below with one of the word families in Exercise 6a.

To remember what a new word ______ , look up its ______ in a dictionary, then write a sentence which uses it in a ______ way.

b Work in pairs. Think of a sentence that uses the words in another family. Write the sentence with gaps for those words. Can another pair complete it?

GO BEYOND
Do the Words & Beyond exercise on page 130.

Workbook, pages 8–9

GRAMMAR Articles and other determiners

1

››› Show what thing you're talking about

READ AND LISTEN

1 1.07 **Read and listen to the conversation. Do you know the name Oscar couldn't remember?**

Anne: Have you got a **good memory**?
Oscar: I remember most things.
Anne: OK, I'll test you. We studied all these things last week. Who invented **paper**?
Oscar: **The Chinese**.
Anne: Who were **the first men** on **the moon**?
Oscar: Neil Armstrong and ...
Anne: Few people remember both names. What's **the capital** of **South Africa**?
Oscar: I'm not sure. **Cape Town**? **Pretoria**?
Anne: Either answer's correct. It's got **a third capital** too – **Bloemfontein**. In which year did **the United States** abolish **slavery**?
Oscar: In 1865. So ... how did I do?
Anne: Not bad. You couldn't answer every question. But you answered most of them!

STUDY

2 Read the explanations. Which example of an article + noun isn't included in Exercise 1?

Articles

Use: To show if you're referring to something specific or general.

Form:

a(*n*) +	one example of a thing
the +	a specific thing: *the next question* a unique thing: *the moon*, *the sky* plural names of people and places rivers, oceans, seas, deserts a group or type: *the English*; *the car*
no article +	plural and uncountable nouns with a general reference abstract ideas: *love, privacy* singular place names, streets, parks

See GRAMMAR DATABASE, page 120.

3 Complete the explanations with *singular* and *plural*. Use Exercise 1 to help you.

Other determiners

Use: To show which things you're referring to.

Form:
Before ______ and uncountable nouns:
all, most, some, no
Before ______ nouns:
both, many, a few, few (= a very small number)
Before ______ countable nouns:
no, either, neither
each (= two or more things separately)
every (= three or more things together)

See GRAMMAR DATABASE, page 120.

PRACTISE

4 Complete the questions with *a*(*n*), *the* or – if no article's needed. Then answer the questions.

1 Which was ___ first country to democratically elect ___ female leader?
a The UK b Sri Lanka c Argentina
2 ___ spiders are ___ type of arthropod. What type?
a arachnids b insects c crustaceans
3 Who was ___ inventor of ___ telephone?
a Berners-Lee b Marconi c Graham Bell
4 Which city in ___ America is considered to be ___ birthplace of ___ jazz music?
a New Orleans b New York c Chicago
5 Which of ___ continents are ___ Galápagos Islands nearest to?
a South America b Antarctica c Africa
6 Which Russian author wrote ___ novel ___ *War and Peace*?
a Nabokov b Tolstoy c Dostoyevsky
7 Which is ___ world's driest and ___ largest desert?
a the Antarctic b the Sahara c the Gobi
8 Where was ___ paper money first used?
a India b Egypt c China

5 Complete the report with the correct options.

Report by Olga and David
(1) *Each* / *Every* of us asked 15 students the question 'How much do you know about mammals?' (2) *Either* / *Both* of us knew that (3) *all* / *every* baby mammals drink their mother's milk and (4) *each* / *every* other student in the class knew that too.
(5) *Many* / *Most* students (18 out of 30) also knew that mammals are warm-blooded. (6) Very *few* / *a few* students (2 out of 30) knew that almost all mammals have at least some hair on their bodies and (7) *either* / *neither* of us knew that before we did our research.
(8) *Some* / *Most* students (27 out of 30) knew that mammals give birth to live young, but when we asked if there are any exceptions, there were (9) *no* / *none* correct answers. (10) *No* / *None* of us knew that there are five mammals that lay eggs.

WRITE AND SPEAK

6 a Work in pairs. Choose a set of survey questions – A or B.

A Where's [country]? What's the capital city? Who's the president or prime minister?
B Where was [person] born? In what year? Why is he/she famous?

b Conduct a survey. Ask other students your questions and note their answers.

c Write notes for a report on your survey. Then tell other students the results.

››› Workbook, page 10

LANGUAGE & BEYOND

I'm *quiet* / *talkative* .
I tend to be *pessimistic* / *optimistic* .
I'm / *I'm not* a perfectionist.
I'm *good* / *bad* at working in a team.
I find it *easy* / *hard* to make decisions.
I'm a *good* / *bad* listener.
I'm *easy-going* / *bad-tempered* .
I *can* / *can't* accept criticism.
I'm *lazy* / *hardworking* .
I *like* / *don't like* taking risks.

»» Work on your weaknesses

SPEAK AND READ

1 Work in pairs. Look at the pictures. What do they show? How do the people feel?

PHRASE BYTES

I think what's happening is ...
I reckon he/she'd like to ... but ...
The boy/girl in ... looks really ...

2 a Choose the options that are true for you in the text above.

b Work in pairs. Look at the options. Decide which ones are definitely strengths or weaknesses and which ones can be a strength or a weakness depending on the situation.

PHRASE BYTES

If you're ... that's clearly a ...
Yes, but doesn't it depend on ... ?
I'm not sure I agree.
OK, I see what you mean.

DO

3 Read and follow the tips in the article.

4 Work in pairs. Do you think the tips are a good way to identify and work on your weaknesses? Why?/Why not?

WORK ON YOUR WEAKNESSES

1 **MAKE A LIST**
Write down all the things you consider to be weaknesses.

2 **KEEP THINGS IN PERSPECTIVE**
Nobody's perfect. Perfection isn't a realistic aim. Circle the weaknesses that you'd *really* like to work on.

3 **ESTABLISH PRIORITIES**
Choose one weakness – the one with the biggest negative impact on your daily life and hopes for the future.

4 **TAKE THINGS ONE STEP AT A TIME**
Make a plan. Think of one situation in which your chosen weakness is a problem. Next time you're in that situation, behave or think like someone who doesn't have your weakness. And be positive. If you expect failure, you'll probably fail.

5 **DON'T GIVE UP**
If your plan didn't work the first time, try again. Real change always takes time.

REFLECT

5 Discuss these questions with your class. Do you agree with the REFLECTION POINT?

1 It's sometimes said that everyone has weaknesses. Do you think that's true? Give reasons for your answer.
2 Do you have any weaknesses that can also be seen as a strength? Explain why.
3 Do most of you think the tips in Exercise 3 are helpful? If not, why not?

REFLECTION POINT

To work on your weaknesses, you first need to identify them. You then need to make a plan that allows you to focus on improving one thing. At the same time, it's important to remember that we all have weaknesses and that nobody's 'perfect'.

EXTEND

6 Work in pairs. Each think of a weakness related to your schoolwork. Follow the tips in Exercise 3 together and help each other to make a plan. Then record your progress.

KNOW YOURSELF

»» Workbook, page 13

SPEAKING That's interesting!

>>> Make conversation

SPEAK

1 **Work in pairs. Make a list of the things people typically talk about when they meet somebody for the first time.**

WATCH OR LISTEN

2 1.08 **Watch or listen to the scene. Which things on your list in Exercise 1 do they talk about?**

George: Hi. Is anyone sitting here?
Sophie: No. Go ahead.
George: It's warm in here.
Sophie: Yes.
George: You're Sophie, aren't you?
Sophie: That's right.
George: I'm George. I'm a friend of Naomi's.
Sophie: Oh, right. (1) .... How is Naomi?
George: She's fine. She couldn't come to the talk so I said I'd take notes for her.
Sophie: Have you ... ?
George: Naomi said that ... Sorry. (2) ....
Sophie: No. (3) ....
George: I was just going to say that Naomi was really upset she couldn't come. (4) ....
Sophie: It wasn't anything important. What brings you to this talk anyway – apart from taking notes for Naomi?
George: I'm hoping to study psychology eventually.
Sophie: Really? (5) ....
George: There's not a lot to tell. I just have a passion for understanding how people work.
Sophie: (6) .... So do I. (7) ....
George: George.
Sophie: I'm really forgetful when it comes to people's names.

3 **a** **Match the sentence halves. Then complete the conversation in Exercise 2 with the sentences.**

1 After	a interesting.
2 Go	b your name again?
3 Nice to	c you.
4 Tell me	d more.
5 That's	e you going to say?
6 What was	f meet you.
7 What were	g on.

b 1.08 **Watch or listen again to check your answers.**

4 1.09 **Listen and repeat the expressions, paying attention to intonation.**

ACT

5 **a** **Work in pairs. Role-play the situation below and make conversation. Then swap roles.**

It's the beginning of the school year. You're in the school canteen. One of you is eating and reading a book. The other is looking for somewhere to sit.

b **Repeat the activity with a new partner.**

PHRASEBOOK 1.10

MAKE CONVERSATION

Introductions

You're ... , aren't you?
I'm ... I'm a friend of ...
Nice to meet you.
What was your name again?

Invite someone to talk

Go on.
After you.
What were you going to say?

Show interest

Oh, right.
Really?
Tell me more.
That's interesting.

>>> Workbook, page 11

WRITING Report back

Present statistical information

SPEAK AND READ

1 Work in pairs. Who or what are these things normally named after where you live?

streets/roads
schools/colleges
sports/leisure centres
museums/libraries
towers/tall buildings

2 Read the report. What do its writers want to happen? How do they support their suggestion?

TO: The Town Council
FROM: The Old Town Youth Group
SUBJECT: Naming the new square

INTRODUCTION
Ever since the new square was created, local residents have been campaigning for the right to choose its name. We are a youth group based near the square and we would also like to be consulted.

OUR SURVEY
We have carried out a survey at the youth club to find out how many of us would like to help choose a name and to gather possible ideas.

THE RESULTS
The majority of us – over 90 per cent – want to be consulted about the square's name. When we asked about the type of name, just over half of us said we wanted it named after someone important from the neighbourhood – a writer or artist, for example. Approximately a third said they preferred the name of someone who represents positive values, like Nelson Mandela. A small minority (about one in ten people) suggested an abstract name like Peace Square.

CONCLUSION
Given the overwhelming support for us helping to name the square, we suggest that the council organises a public vote to choose a name.

STUDY

3 a Read the tips in the HOW TO box.

HOW TO
present statistical information

- Use percentages – *30% (of)* or *30 per cent (of)*.
- Use fractions – *a quarter (of)*, *half (of)*, *three quarters (of)*.
- Use expressions like *one in five people*.
- Use adjectives/adverbs: *almost*, *approximately* and prepositions: *(just) over*, *under* with the expressions above.
- Use *the (vast) majority (of)* and *a/the minority (of)*.

b Underline examples of the words and expressions in the report.

PRACTISE

4 Rewrite each sentence using the words/numbers in brackets.

1 We asked all of the students in the class. (100)
We asked 100 per cent of the students in the class.
2 95 per cent of us want the sports centre to be given a name. (vast)
3 One in three of us wants to name it after a local sportsperson. (third)
4 10% of students think it should be called *The Sports Place*. (one)
5 27% of us suggest naming it after a sporting legend. (quarter)

PLAN, WRITE AND CHECK

5 You're going to write a report with your class's suggestion for (re)naming something in or near your school.

- Use one of the ideas in Exercise 1, or another place or building.
- Either invent the statistics, or carry out a survey to discover your classmates' opinions and suggestions.
- Use the report above to help you organise your ideas.

6 Write your report. Use the tips from the HOW TO box to help you present its statistical information. Then check it.

SHARE AND REVIEW

7 Swap your report with a partner. Read your partner's report and review it. Did your partner make a strong case for the class suggestion?

Workbook, pages 12–13

VOCABULARY Names

1 Complete the text with the words/phrases in the box. There are two words/phrases you don't need to use.

alias | assumed name | brand name | domain name | household name | initials | maiden name | nickname | pseudonym | stage name | title | username

WELCOME TO NEBRASKA NAMING SERVICES (NNS)

NEBRASKA NAMING SERVICES

Are you a star in need of a (1) ______ or (2) ______ that will help make you a (3) ______? Or a writer in need of a pen name or (4) ______? Do you need a (5) ______ or (6) ______ to hide your real identity? Are you a woman who wants to return to her (7) ______? Or are you a company looking for a great (8) ______ and internet (9) ______, or a safe system for setting up a customer's online account (10) ______? Look no further! You have just found the world's best naming service.

___ /10

Word families

2 Complete the text with the correct form of the words in brackets.

NAME TRAINING COURSES

NEBRASKA NAMING SERVICES

At the NNS we're very (1) ______ (**imagine**) with names. But we also know how (2) ______ (**forget**) people can be. It is no (3) ______ (**exaggerate**) to say that an (4) ______ (**improve**) in your ability to remember names is the most important key to (5) ______ (**succeed**). It helps (6) ______ (**strong**) the bonds between people and build (7) ______ (**mean**) relationships. That's why we run special (8) ______ (**train**) courses to give (9) ______ (**practise**) advice on how to (10) ______ (**memory**) names.

___ /10

GRAMMAR Present tenses review

3 Complete the interview. Use the present or present perfect tense of the verbs, simple or continuous forms.

READ AN INTERVIEW WITH OUR FOUNDER!

Q: How long (1) ______ (**NNS / be**) in business?

A: We (2) ______ (**invent**) names for almost five years now.

Q: Who (3) ______ (**need**) to use a service like NNS?

A: A lot of our customers (4) ______ (**be**) companies that (5) ______ (**have**) problems finding an original name. But we (6) ______ (**come**) up with a number of well-known stage names too over the last five years.

Q: What about your courses?

A: They're still very new, but our courses (7) ______ (**become**) more and more popular.

___ /14

Articles and other determiners

4 Complete the text with the words in the box or –.

a(n) | all | both | every | neither | the

TESTIMONIALS

NEBRASKA NAMING SERVICES

'We spent months trying to think of a name for our company, but (1) ______ name we thought of had been used before. Initially, we wanted to use our surnames, but (2) ______ was suitable. NNS came up with two names and (3) ______ were fantastic. It was definitely (4) ______ money well spent.' *Abigail and Mason*

'I used to be terrible at remembering (5) ______ names, but doing NNS's name-training course changed that. (6) ______ course taught me to recall (7) ______ person's name after hearing it just once. (8) ______ of the other people on the course were just as satisfied as I was.' *Alex*

___ /16

Your score: ___ /50

SKILLS CHECK

✓✓✓ Yes, I can. No problem!
✓✓ Yes, I can. But I need a bit of help.
✓ Yes, I can. But I need a lot of help.

I can find information efficiently. ______
I can take clear notes. ______
I can work on my weaknesses. ______
I can make conversation. ______
I can present statistical information. ______

Workbook, pages 14–15

UNIT 2 THE WHOLE STORY

IN THE PICTURE Types of story

>>> Talk about stories

RECALL AND READ

1 Work in pairs. Do the tasks.

1 Find five of the types of book in the pictures.

children's book	comic book	e-book
encyclopaedia	guidebook	novel

2 Write five more types of book.
thesaurus …

2 Read the leaflet. What different forms have stories had over the years?

WORK WITH WORDS

3 a Complete the definitions with the words in the box.

fable	fairy tale	folk tale	tale
tall story (UK)/tall tale (US)			

1 ……………… : a traditional children's story in which magical things happen
2 ……………… : an old traditional story that was originally told orally
3 ……………… : a traditional story, typically about animals, that teaches a moral lesson
4 ……………… : a story about imaginary events or people
5 ……………… : a story that someone invents in order to deceive other people

b 1.11 Listen to the exhibition curator to check your answers.

4 1.12 Listen to the curator answer a question. Match the words/phrases in the box to the stories.

epic	legend	myth	saga	urban legend/myth

1 *Star Wars* ………………
2 Crocodiles in the sewers of New York ………………
3 King Arthur and the Knights of the Round Table ………………
4 Gilgamesh ………………
5 The Minotaur ………………

5 1.13 Listen and repeat the words in Exercises 3a and 4.

THE STORY OF THE STORY

Join us as we explore the world of storytelling from prehistoric drawings and paintings, through folk tales told by our ancestors, to the interactive digital storytelling of today.

From the exhibition curator

There are said to be over one million books in the new Library of Birmingham but storytelling didn't start with the written word. It originated with pictures and then the spoken word. Drawings of animals, people and symbols on cave walls were early forms of communication and storytelling. Then, as we developed the power to speak, stories began to be told orally. *The Epic of Gilgamesh* is probably the earliest example of a written story. It described the adventures of the King of Uruk and was written on 12 clay tablets in Mesopotamia around 5,000 years ago.

A lot has happened in the time between the creation of those primitive tablets and the super-fast digital tablets we use today. But one thing hasn't changed. From the very beginning, we have used storytelling to help explain and understand the world around us.

The Story of the Story is a unique opportunity to enter the world of ancient myths and legends, revisit the fairy tales of your childhood, and explore the digital worlds of gaming and interactive storytelling.

TYPES OF BOOKS

2

6 **Work in pairs. Match some of the words in Exercises 3a and 4 to the pictures (a–e). Which of the stories in the pictures do you know?**

7 1.14 PRONOUNCE **Listen and write the words in the table according to their long vowel sounds. Then listen and repeat all the words.**

encyclopaedia saga tall true urban

/iː/ e-book	/ɜː/ word	/uː/ do	/ɔː/ story	/ɑː/ start

8 THE MOVING PICTURE **Watch the video about the Library of Birmingham. What are its unique features?**

EXTEND

9 a **Work in pairs. Complete the story expressions with the words in the box. Use a dictionary to help you.**

likely long old sob

A: You're late again. It's always the same (1) .... story. What happened this time?
B: It's a (2) .... story.
A: I haven't got time. Anyway, I don't want to hear another of your depressing (3) .... stories.
B: I met a prince.
A: Hah! That's a (4) .... story.

b **Which story in the pictures does the conversation come from?**

SPEAK

10 **Work in pairs. Choose one of the story types in Exercises 3a and 4 and think of a famous story. Tell the story to your partner. Can your partner identify the story and the story type?**

GO BEYOND

Do the Words & Beyond exercises on page 131.

Workbook, page 16

READING Kamishibai

>>> Deal with new vocabulary when you read

SPEAK AND READ

1 a Work in pairs. Kamishibai is a form of storytelling. Look at the photo of the Kamishibai storyteller. How did he tell his stories?

b 1.15 Read the introduction to the Kamishibai story and check your answer.

MANGA COMICS first became popular in Japan in the 1950s. Many of the most famous manga artists of the period had learned their trade as Kamishibai storytellers. Kamishibai (the name means 'paper drama') is a form of Japanese storytelling that originated in the 12th century.

The Kamishibai storyteller travelled from village to village by bicycle. On the back of his bicycle, he had a wooden stage. While he was telling his story, he inserted pictures into the stage that depicted the scenes he was describing. The storyteller could bring his story to life by moving the pictures.

The storyteller often told his stories in serial format, presenting a new episode or chapter on each visit to the village. Many of the stories were based on Japanese tales such as the one below.

URASHIMA TARO

A long time ago, long before you were born, a young fisherman named Urashima Taro lived in a small coastal fishing village in the back of beyond.

One day, while he was walking along the seashore, Taro saw a group of children shouting and running like savages around something on the sand. When he came closer, he could see that they were kicking and throwing stones at a small turtle.

As soon as he saw what was happening, Taro told the children to stop being cruel. He offered them money if they left the turtle in peace and, of course, they took him up on his offer.

Once the children had gone, he took the turtle to the water's edge and set it free. The turtle started swimming out to sea and soon Taro lost sight of it.

After a few days, Taro was fishing by the seashore when suddenly a big turtle appeared from out of the waves. It was the same turtle whose life he had saved. However, now the turtle was much larger and older.

To his amazement, the turtle began to speak. 'Hello, Taro-san!' the turtle said with a voice as deep as the sea. 'I would like to reward you for your kindness and take you to the beautiful Coral Palace at the bottom of the ocean. Will you come with me?'

What happened next? Did Taro go with the turtle? Find out in the next episode of *Urashima Taro*.

2 Read the story of Urashima Taro. Then answer the questions.

1 Where's the story set and who are the main characters?
2 What are the main points in the plot?

3 a Read the tips in the HOW TO box.

b Work in pairs. Read the story again and complete the tasks.

1 Underline any new words, phrases, similes and idioms. Which ones could you work out the meaning of as you read? Which weren't important for overall understanding?
2 Try to work out the meaning of any words and phrases you still don't know.

4 Which tips in the HOW TO box did you use for help with Exercise 3b? Tick (✓) them.

HOW TO

deal with new vocabulary when you read

- ☐ Use the immediate and general context to try and work out meaning.
- ☐ Look at a word's parts. Is it the verb, noun or adjective form of a word you know?
- ☐ Identify similes: comparisons with *as … as* and *like*. Think about the qualities the two things share.
- ☐ Identify idioms: expressions whose meaning isn't obvious. Think about the image they create.
- ☐ If necessary, use a dictionary.

REACT

5 Work in pairs. Answer the question and complete the tasks.

What do you think happens in the rest of the story?

- Student A: look at page 141. Student B: look at page 142.
- Read your part of the story and make notes.
- Retell your part of the story without looking at the text.

GO BEYOND

Look for time expressions in the story. In what way are they used to help tell the story?

Workbook, page 17

GRAMMAR Narrative tenses review

»» To describe events in the past

READ AND LISTEN

1 (1.16) **Read and listen to the story. What kind of story do you think it is – a true story, a ghost story or an urban legend?**

IN CONGRESS, JULY 4, 1776.
A DECLARATION
BY THE REPRESENTATIVES OF THE
UNITED STATES OF AMERICA,
IN GENERAL CONGRESS ASSEMBLED.

A few years ago, a financial analyst from Philadelphia was walking round a flea market when he saw an old picture of a country scene. He paid $4 for the picture, thinking he could use the frame for something else. After he'd removed the painting from the frame, he found an old document behind it. He showed it to a friend who collected Civil War memorabilia. The document, which had been hiding behind the painting for many years, turned out to be one of 500 official copies of the 1776 Declaration of Independence. There were only 24 other copies known to exist, and this one was in excellent condition. It sold at auction for $2.42 million.

STUDY

2 **Read the explanations. Then underline an example of each tense in Exercise 1.**

Narrative tenses review

Past simple

Use: For completed actions in the past.

Past continuous

Use: For actions in progress in the past, often interrupted by events in the past simple.

Past perfect simple

Use (1): For an action that happened before another action or time in the past. Use the past simple for the other action.
Expressions: *before*, *after*, *by the time*; *just*, *yet*, *already*, etc
Use (2): With *because* to give an explanation.

Form: *had/hadn't* + past participle

Past perfect continuous

Use: For actions in progress up to a time in the past.
Expressions: *all morning/day*; *for*, *since*

Form: *had/hadn't been* + verb + *-ing*
Irregular past simple and participles: see page 140.

See GRAMMAR DATABASE, page 121.

PRACTISE

3 **Complete the urban legend with the words in the box. There are two words you don't need.**

after	before	for	just	since	soon
until	when	while	yet		

Did you hear the story about the publishing company employee who died at his desk (1) ______ he was working and remained there (2) ______ five days (3) ______ anyone noticed something was wrong? His name was George Turklebaum and he'd been working for the company (4) ______ the 1990s. (5) ______ he'd died, the other 23 office workers had continued working around him without realising what had happened. The alarm wasn't raised (6) ______ the following weekend (7) ______ a cleaner found him. He'd (8) ______ turned 51 and he'd died of a heart attack.

4 (1.17) **Complete the ghost story using the past simple/continuous and past perfect simple/continuous. Then listen and check.**

Jen: (1) ______ (tell / ever) you about my friend Paul?
Tom: No, I don't think so. What (2) ______ (happen)?
Jen: Well, at the time of 'the incident', he (3) ______ (live) in a house outside a small village. He (4) ______ (walk) home one night when he (5) ______ (see) someone outside his house. The man (6) ______ (wear) strange old-fashioned clothes. He said he (7) ______ (be) in an accident and (8) ______ (need) help.
Tom: What (9) ______ (happen) to him?
Jen: He (10) ______ (stay) at a house on the hill and (11) ______ (wake up) to discover that the house (12) ______ (be) on fire. By the time he (13) ______ (manage) to get out, the house (14) ______ (be) almost completely destroyed.
Tom: How (15) ______ (react / Paul)?
Jen: He (16) ______ (take) out his phone to call for help but when he (17) ______ (look up), the man (18) ______ (go). Apparently, there was no house on the hill. The house that (19) ______ (be) there (20) ______ (burn down) a hundred years ago.

WRITE AND SPEAK

5 **Work in pairs. What are the ingredients of a good urban legend or ghost story? Do you know any? Write one story using narrative tenses. Then read it to the class.**

»» Workbook, pages 18–19

LISTENING AND VOCABULARY The written word

>>> Follow the speaker's argument

SPEAK AND LISTEN

1 **Work in pairs. Describe the three handwriting samples.**

a
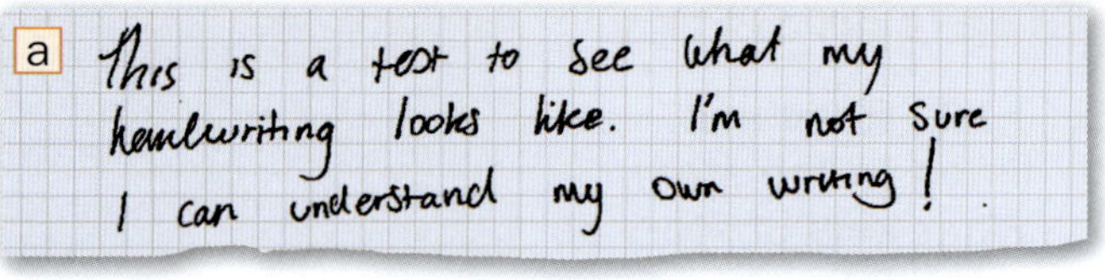

b

c
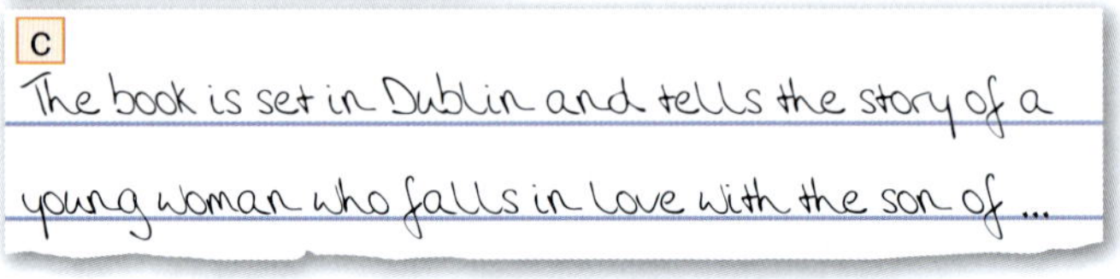

2 **1.18 Listen to Gregory's podcast and match the people to the handwriting samples.**

Gregory

Linda

Louis

3 a **Read the tips in the HOW TO box.**

b **1.18 Listen again and complete each sentence with the correct name in the box.**

Greg   Linda   Louis   Mr Bryant (teacher)
Harvey (graphologist)

1 .... changes his opinion about handwriting.
2 .... thinks writing by hand is more personal.
3 .... thinks handwriting is important.
4 .... rarely writes anything by hand.
5 .... makes reference to a study to help make a point.

4 **Which tips in the HOW TO box did you use for help with Exercise 3b? Tick (✓) them.**

REACT

5 **Work in pairs. Answer the questions.**

1 Do you write by hand outside the classroom?
2 Is it possible to analyse someone's character from their handwriting?

WORK WITH WORDS

6 a **Match the character adjectives to the definitions.**

creative   inventive   open   outgoing   practical
reserved   sensible   sensitive   tactful   temperamental

1 is friendly and enjoys meeting and talking to people ....
2 has a lot of imagination and ideas ....
3 is honest and doesn't keep things secret ....
4 makes good everyday decisions and choices ....
5 tends not to talk about or show their feelings ....
6 is likely to become angry or upset easily ....
7 is good at thinking of new and original methods ....
8 changes from one mood to another very quickly ....
9 is logical and down-to-earth ....
10 is careful about what they say to not upset other people ....

b **1.19 Listen and check. Then listen and repeat.**

7 **Write three sentences about yourself using adjectives from Exercise 6a.**

8 **Work in pairs. Complete the tasks.**

- Show your partner an example of your handwriting.
- Describe your partner's handwriting and analyse their character.
- Compare the results with the sentences you wrote in Exercise 7.

PHRASE BYTES

This writing's neat/tidy/untidy ...
It's easy/difficult to read.
The writer uses capital/cursive (joined-up) letters.
This person's handwriting slopes to the left/right.

HOW TO

follow the speaker's argument

Listen for words and phrases that:

- ☐ express the speaker's opinion (*I think, personally, in my opinion*).
- ☐ add similar or contrasting ideas (*similarly, in the same way; however, on the other hand*).
- ☐ add emphasis or give examples (*in fact, especially; for example/instance*).
- ☐ show reasons and results (*because, on account of; so, therefore*).
- ☐ list or summarise ideas (*firstly, to summarise*).

GO BEYOND

Do the Words & Beyond exercise on page 131.

Workbook, pages 20–21

GRAMMAR *Used to* and *would*

Talk about habits and states in the past

READ

1 Read the article. What was responsible for making communication a lot faster?

In today's world of instant communication, it's easy to forget that messages used to take days or weeks to reach their destination. The sender would then have to wait for a response which wouldn't arrive for many days or weeks. How did we use to get things done?
In Ancient Persia, messages used to be handwritten on papyrus and delivered by messengers on horseback. On good roads, they would travel around 200 miles a day, changing horses at a series of 'posts' on the way.
This system for delivering messages didn't change for centuries. But even with the introduction of the railway and motor car, people didn't use to expect a response for several days. It was the growth of the internet that was responsible for really speeding up communication.

STUDY

2 Complete the explanations with examples from Exercise 1.

Used to

Use: To talk about habits and states in the past.

Form:
Positive and negative
.... / *didn't use to* + infinitive
Questions and short answers
did + *I/you*, etc + ... + infinitive
Yes, I did. / *No, they* ....

Note: *used to* doesn't have a present form. For present habits, use the present simple.

Would

Use: To talk about habits (NOT states) in the past.

Form: *would/wouldn't* + infinitive (without *to*)

Note: *would* is more common in written descriptions than in speech.

See GRAMMAR DATABASE, page 121.

Get it right

There **used to** be a post office here.
NOT There ~~would be~~ a post office here.

PRACTISE

3 Complete the Q&A with the correct form of *used to*.

Q: How (1) .... (read / people) books before printing was invented?

A: Johannes Gutenberg invented his famous printing press in 1448. Before that, ordinary people (2) .... (not read) a lot. In medieval times, people called scribes (3) .... (copy) books by hand in monasteries. Curiously, before the ninth century, they (4) .... (not leave) any spaces between words sothetextwouldlookabitlikethis! The scribe (5) .... (not add) titles or capital letters either. Someone called a rubricator (6) .... (do) this.

4 Match and join the sentence halves with *would* or *wouldn't*.

1 Printing books ....
2 Sometimes the typesetters ....
3 That's because the text ....
4 Luckily, the letters ....
5 They ....

a be thrown away after printing.
b be assembled letter by letter.
c be used again to make the text for another page.
d need a whole day to create a page.
e take a long time with Gutenberg's printing process.

5 Choose the correct option. If more than one option is possible, choose both.

Exhibit 5H42 is a rare example of a primitive device that (1) *used to* / *would* be popular in the first half of the 21st century. People (2) *used to* / *would* purchase and download books from primitive websites. They (3) *used to* / *would* then read the books in text format on a device like this. These devices (4) *used to* / *would* be powered by rechargeable batteries.

WRITE AND SPEAK

6 Work in pairs. Do the tasks.

- Imagine it is the year 2115. How has life changed? Write a description of an object that people used to use or an activity that people used to do in the first decades of the 21st century. Don't write the name of the object or activity.
- Read your description to the class. Can they name the object or activity?

LANGUAGE & BEYOND

>>> Consider the consequences of your actions

MY BLOG ABOUT ME | CONTACT

I used to go out with a boy at school. Let's call him Leo.

He'd write me love poems that were really nice. I wanted to write him a poem but I'm not very creative, so I copied one from the internet. He said it was amazing, so I told him I'd written it. I later discovered that he'd thought it was so good, he'd shown it to his English teacher. The teacher had recognised the poem instantly and, not being very tactful, told Leo. Leo told me he didn't want to go out with someone he couldn't trust, so we broke up. I was upset, so I told a 'friend' at school. My friend's a bit temperamental and started saying bad things about me online. I got really sad and my schoolwork suffered. Then the school got in touch with my parents to tell them what had happened. Now my parents probably think I'm a liar.

posted by anonymous 17th Apr

SPEAK AND READ

1 **Work in pairs. Describe the photos. What do you think the story is about?**

2 **Read Alison's story to check your answer to Exercise 1.**

PHRASE BYTES

He/She looks like ...

Maybe they've had an argument / broken up ...

I think the man's calling ...

DO

3 a **Work in pairs. Answer the questions about the events in Alison's story. What was the consequence in each case?**

1 Why did Alison say she'd written the poem?
2 What did the teacher tell Leo?
3 Why did Alison tell a friend what had happened?
4 How did Alison feel?
5 How did the school react?

b **Look at the events in Alison's story again. Could she have predicted any of the people's reactions? Discuss what you think Alison should and shouldn't have done.**

4 **Work in groups. Read each situation and consider the possible consequences. What would you do in each case?**

1 You're riding a bicycle when your phone rings. You want to answer but you don't want to stop cycling.
2 A friend who went to a party without their parents' permission wants you to say that he or she spent the evening studying at your house if anyone asks.

REFLECT

5 **Discuss these questions with your class. Do you agree with the REFLECTION POINT?**

1 Why is it important to consider the consequences of an action?
2 Why do we often do things without considering all the consequences?
3 How easy is it to predict all of the consequences of an action?

REFLECTION POINT

The decisions we make and actions we take affect what happens in the future. We often make decisions or do things without considering all the consequences, especially when they have positive short-term consequences. We can't predict all eventualities but it's important to think about long-term consequences before we act.

EXTEND

6 **Work in groups. Complete the task.**

Look at the situations in Exercise 4. Think of another situation in which someone has to consider the consequences of their actions. Make a list of the possible consequences and the consequences of each consequence. How many consequences can you think of?

Workbook, page 25

SPEAKING What happened?

Describe an experience

SPEAK

1 a **Make notes about something that happened to you in the past that was exciting, funny or frightening.**

Where did it happen? Who was involved? What happened?

b **Work in pairs. Tell your partner about what happened.**

WATCH OR LISTEN

2 1.20 **Watch or listen to the scene. Then answer the three questions in Exercise 1a.**

Naomi: Are you all right? You look really pale.
Al: I've just been robbed.
Kalu: What? When? Where?
Al: Just now. In the High Street on my way here.
Naomi: (1) ....
Al: (2) .... I'd just been to the chemist's to get something for my headache and ...
Kalu: Go on.
Al: What? Oh. (3) .... Right. So I was standing in the High Street waiting for the lights to change when I felt someone bump into me. I had this feeling. I don't know how to describe it. (4) .... like something wasn't right. Do you know what I mean?
Kalu: (5) ....
Al: I felt for my wallet and it wasn't there. So then I realised what had happened.
Naomi: (6) ....
Al: Hang on. I haven't finished. I ran after them.
Kalu: Really? You're kidding.
Al: I know. I know. I should've thought about what might've happened. But it happened so fast.
Naomi: Did you catch them?
Al: (7) .... I was running and shouting. I must've scared them because they dropped the wallet.
Naomi: You were lucky. They could've hurt you.

PHRASEBOOK 1.22

Tell a story

It was really amazing/funny/strange.

I don't know how to describe it.

I felt frightened/good/odd.

Do you know what I mean?

This is the best/interesting/worst part.

Hang on. I haven't finished.

I've forgotten what I was saying. / What was I saying? / Where was I?

Ask questions about the story

What happened?

How did it happen / you feel / you react?

So what did you do/say/think?

React to a story

Go on.

Wow. That's incredible/interesting/scary.

You're joking/kidding.

Really?

You were lucky.

3 **Choose the correct options. Then write each phrase in the conversation.**

a I felt *frightened* / *good* / *odd* .
b How did *it happen* / *you feel* / *you react* ?
c This is the *best* / *interesting* / *worst* part.
d *I've forgotten what I was saying*. / *What was I saying*? / *Where was I*?
e So what did you *do* / *say* / *think* ?
f It was really *amazing* / *funny* / *strange* .
g Wow. That's *incredible* / *interesting* / *scary* .

4 a 1.20 **Watch or listen again to check your answers to Exercise 3.**

b 1.21 **Listen and repeat the phrases, paying attention to intonation.**

ACT

5 **Work in pairs. Prepare a conversation about the event you made notes on in Exercise 1. Explain what happened using phrases from the PHRASEBOOK. You can make the event more dramatic if you want.**

Workbook, page 23

WRITING My fantasy story

Avoid repetition

SPEAK AND READ

1 Work in pairs. Ask and answer the questions.

1 If you could be anyone else in the world, who would you like to be? Why?
2 What other dreams or ambitions do teenagers often have?

2 Read the extract from a story. Who's telling the story? What's the situation?

My phone alarm beeped. I took a last look at myself in the hotel mirror. 'Who are you?' I thought, hardly recognising the odd, pale figure staring back at me. Harry was waiting in the corridor. Angie had warned us to avoid the reception area so we took the lift straight down to the car park. While we were waiting for the limousine, a couple of fans crept out from the darkness. For a moment I thought they'd spotted me but then they walked straight past us. Before I had time to congratulate myself on my inventive new disguise, the limo had pulled up in front of us and Angie was inside, handing me the guest list, as practical as always. 'The President's daughters are coming to see you tonight,' she said. 'I'll dedicate a song to them', I replied as the black stretch limo cruised down the city streets like a spacecraft from my favourite science fiction film, heading for the mother ship. 'Break a leg,' Angie laughed when we arrived at the stadium. It was going to be a good show.

Get it right

I looked at ~~me~~ myself in the mirror.

I congratulated ~~self~~ myself.

STUDY

3 a Read the tips in the HOW TO box.

HOW TO

avoid repetition

- Use pronouns and adverbs to avoid repeating nouns and names (*he*, *her*, *there* ...).
- Use synonyms (*recognise*, *identify*, *know*), similar words (*notice*, *spot*) or different forms of the same word (*recognition*). Use a thesaurus to help you.
- Use a variety of time conjunctions (*when*, *while*, *as*, *as soon as* ...).
- Join short sentences with conjunctions to avoid repeating the subject (*and*, *but*, *so* ...).

b Read the story again and complete the tasks.

1 Highlight the pronouns in the first three sentences.
2 Write the different ways the writer describes the car.
3 Write the words the writer uses instead of *walked*, *stopped* and *drove*.
4 Circle conjunctions that join two phrases.
5 Underline time conjunctions.
6 Draw a rectangle around a simile and an idiom.

PRACTISE

4 Read the paragraph and identify the examples of repetition. Then rewrite it avoiding repetition. Use the HOW TO box to help you.

Angie phoned me two days later. Angie phoned me to say that *Rolling Stone* magazine wanted to interview me. The *Rolling Stone* magazine reporter came to my house one day later in a car. A photographer came with the female reporter. The reporter, photographer and I walked in the garden. The photographer took photos of me in the garden. Then we had lunch. Then the reporter asked me questions.

PLAN, WRITE AND CHECK

5 You're going to write an extract from your own fantasy story. Who are you – a sports star, an actor, a world leader ... ? What's the situation? Make notes. Use Exercise 2 to help you.

6 Write your extract. Use the tips from the HOW TO box and avoid repetition. Then check it.

SHARE AND REVIEW

7 Swap your story with a partner. Read your partner's story and review it. Did your partner manage to avoid repetition?

Workbook, pages 24–25

VOCABULARY Types of story

1 Complete the types of story.

INSTANT STORY GENERATOR

STEP ONE: Choose your story type.

1 _ p _ c
2 f _ b l _
3 f _ _ r _ t _ l _
4 f _ l k t _ l _
5 l _ g _ n d
6 m _ t h
7 s _ g _
8 t _ l _
9 t _ l l st _ ry
10 _ r b _ n l _ g _ n d

___ /10

Character adjectives

2 Match the adjectives to the questions.

STEP TWO: Create your main characters.

___ creative ___ inventive ___ open ___ outgoing
___ practical ___ reserved ___ sensible ___ sensitive
___ tactful ___ temperamental

Who are the main characters in your story? What are they like?

1 Are they very honest?
2 Or are their feelings easily hurt?
3 Do their moods change very easily?
4 Are they good at coming up with new ideas and methods?
5 Are they quiet and reluctant to show their feelings?
6 Do they like being sociable?
7 Are they good at making and fixing things?
8 Are they very imaginative?
9 Are they down-to-earth, practical people?
10 Are they careful about what they say to avoid hurting other people?

___ /10

GRAMMAR Narrative tenses review

3 Write the verbs in the past simple/continuous or past perfect simple/continuous.

STEP THREE: Choose the start of your story.

It was a Monday. I (1) ______ (walk) along the road when suddenly I (2) ______ (hear) a loud crash behind me. While I (3) ______ (look) round to see what (4) ______ (make) the noise, I (5) ______ (feel) a sudden blast of hot air.

The day before the murder, Janet (6) ______ (visit) the doctor. She (7) ______ (not feel) well for a few weeks and the time (8) ______ (come) to do something about it.

___ /16

Used to and *would*

4 Complete the sentences with *would/wouldn't* or the correct form of *used to*.

STEP FOUR: Create a backstory for your main character.

Janet was a very reserved person. She (1) ______ (not talk) much about her past. When people asked 'What (2) ______ (do) before you became famous?' she (3) ______ (smile) and change the subject.

I have, however, discovered a few things about her. She (4) ______ (not call) herself Janet, for example. It's an alias. And she (5) ______ (live) in New York. Her apartment was near Central Park so she (6) ______ (go running) every morning. And it was while she was running that she (7) ______ (think) about her future.

___ /14

Your score: ___ /50

SKILLS CHECK

✓✓✓ Yes, I can. No problem!
✓✓ Yes, I can. But I need a bit of help.
✓ Yes, I can. But I need a lot of help.

I can deal with new vocabulary. ______
I can follow the speaker's argument when I listen. ______
I can consider the consequences of my actions. ______
I can describe an experience. ______
I can avoid repetition. ______

Workbook, pages 26–27

READ AND COMPLETE

1 **Read the book review. Five sentences have been removed from the report. Choose from sentences A–F to fill each gap (1–5). There's one extra sentence you don't need to use.**

LIFE OF PI

Life of Pi is the epic tale of one boy's struggle to survive at sea after a storm destroys the cargo ship on which he and his family are travelling from India to Canada. (**1**) ____ Written by the Canadian author Yann Martel, the book was published in 2001, winning the Man Booker Prize for Fiction the following year. Since it was published, it has sold more than nine million copies around the world.

The book's protagonist is a 16-year-old Indian boy called Piscine Molitor. His parents named him after a swimming pool in Paris but when his school classmates give him an unfortunate nickname, Piscine shortens his name to 'Pi'.

The book is divided into three sections. In the first we learn about Pi's childhood in India where his father owns a zoo. (**2**) ____ We also discover that Pi is interested in religion but not just one religion – he follows several. It is a time of political change in India, which is why his father decides to move his family and animals to Canada. The whole of the second part takes place at sea where Pi, who is a highly intelligent, imaginative and inventive young man, is forced to train the tiger in order to become its master. (**3**) ____

I don't want to reveal what happens in the final part of the book but it makes you question everything that you have read beforehand. (**4**) ____ Sometimes memories force us to exaggerate or change our stories to make them more meaningful. We often prefer to hear an invented version of a story rather than the true one because it works better as a piece of fiction or because we'd rather not face up to the truth.

Life of Pi is part adventure story and part fable. It's a reflection on storytelling itself as well as on the importance of belief. After it was published, most people agreed that it would be impossible to adapt it for the cinema. The director Ang Lee thought otherwise and managed to create a memorable 3-D film version. The film's producers were initially unsure of how the public would react to the film. (**5**) ____ The film's depiction of surviving a storm, therefore, echoed events that were still fresh in the minds of many people. Another example of how close fact and fiction can often come.

I've enjoyed sharing Pi's journey and while it has left me with many unanswered questions, I thoroughly recommend the book to anyone who enjoys a good meaningful story.

A According to its author, life is a story and we can choose our own story.
B Pi quickly develops the strength and skills he needs to survive at sea with his unusual companion.
C Born in Salamanca, Spain, to French-speaking Canadian parents, *Life of Pi* was the author's third novel.
D The shipwreck leaves him sharing a lifeboat with several animals, including a Bengal tiger named Richard Parker.
E Its release came soon after the devastation caused by Hurricane Sandy that left hundreds dead in several countries including the United States.
F It is here that the boy learns how dangerous wild animals can be.

Reading and completing: ______ /10

EXAM TIPS

do a gapped text exercise

- Read the title and the whole text.
- Read all the removed sentences. Which part of the text do they refer to? Don't forget that there's one sentence you don't need.
- Look at the sentences before and after each gap in the text. Which sentence fits the gap?
- Read the whole paragraph with your sentence in it. Does it make sense?
- Check that the extra sentence doesn't fit any of the gaps.

find information efficiently
See page 8.

deal with new vocabulary when you read
See page 18.

LISTEN

2 1.23 **You will hear a young woman called Nicola talking about telling jokes. Complete the sentences with no more than three words.**

1 Nicola says the longest word in the English language is ________ .
2 Some of her favourite jokes are ________ ones.
3 Nicola's problem is that she isn't good at ________ .
4 She says the first thing people want to do when they hear a good joke is ________ about it.
5 She describes herself as being a very ________ person.
6 Nicola assumes V F Harry is a ________ name.
7 The initials V F stand for ________ .
8 On the website there's a section with tips for ________ .
9 V F Harry's second tip is to make notes in order to ________ your own.
10 In her final joke, Nicola says a person gets robbed ________ in the United States.

Listening: ________ /10

WRITE

3 In your class you've been talking about books and reading. Now your teacher has asked you to write the essay below for homework. Write your essay (140–190 words) using all the notes and giving reasons for your opinion.

> The way we read books has changed dramatically over recent years. Is this a good or a bad thing?

Notes
Write about:
1 how we used to read compared with today
2 the consequences of this change
3 ________ (your own idea)

Writing: ________ /10

Progress check score ________ /30

EXAM TIPS

listen and complete notes

- Read the sentences carefully before you listen.
- Think about what type of information is missing.
- Listen for the words before and after the missing information.
- Write the exact words that you hear (1–3 words).

take clear notes
See page 10.

follow the speaker's argument
See page 20.

EXAM TIPS

write an opinion essay

- Read the task carefully. What's the essay about? Are there any ideas that you have to include?
- Start with an introduction. Say what your opinion is.
- Use a new paragraph for each new idea.
- Give reasons for your opinions: facts, examples or personal experiences.
- Use appropriate expressions to organise your ideas and make them easy to follow.
- Finish with a summary of your opinion.

present statistical information
See page 14.

avoid repetition
See page 24.

UNIT 3

FUTURE LIFE GOALS

IN THE PICTURE Setting goals

»» Talk about short- and long-term goals

RECALL AND READ

1 Work in pairs. Complete each phrase with a different verb.

achieve	aim	dream	set	succeed

1 .... of doing something
2 .... in doing something
3 .... to do something
4 .... something
5 .... goals

2 a Work in pairs. Look at the pictures and make a list of Ed's personal goals. Use phrases from Exercise 1.

b Which of his goals are short term and which are long term?

3 Read Ed's class assignment. Which of his goals did you correctly identify?

WORK WITH WORDS

4 a Match the phrasal verbs to the words in bold in the text. Use a dictionary to help you.

1 carry on ....
2 come up with ....
3 get round to ....
4 give back ....
5 give up ....
6 miss out on ....
7 put off ....
8 sign up for ....
9 start up ....
10 take over ....
11 take up ....
12 work out ....

b 1.24 Listen and check. Then listen and repeat.

5 1.25 Complete the conversation between Ed and his sister. Write the correct form of the phrasal verbs in Exercise 4. Then listen and check.

Marta: Ed? Have you got my tablet?
Ed: Yes. Sorry. I needed it to (1) .... the club e-newsletter.
Marta: You're always taking things. Sometimes in life you have to (2) .... something .... in return. That reminds me! Have you (3) .... an idea for the party invitation yet?
Ed: No. I haven't had time.
Marta: If you keep (4) .... it ...., then you'll never do it.
Ed: I'll (5) .... it soon, I promise. When I finish this game.
Marta: You always say the same thing. I'm going to (6) .... asking you soon.
Ed: I need to (7) .... how to use the design program first.
Marta: I thought you wanted to (8) .... a design company and (9) .... the world!
Ed: If you (10) .... being annoying, I won't design your invitation.
Marta: Then you'll (11) .... your first paid job.
Ed: Maybe I'll (12) .... designing video games instead.

MY PERSONAL GOALS

I think it's important to set goals in life. They help you see where you're going and the steps you need to take to get there. Here are some of my short- and long-term goals.

MY SHORT-TERM GOALS

To achieve some of my goals, I need more free time. So my first goal is to **stop** playing video games (at least for a month!). They're addictive and I don't want to **lose the opportunity to do** other things. I want to **start** playing chess (it can't be *that* difficult!) so that's my second goal. I aim to be more organised in the future. I always **postpone** tidying my room. So I'll **finally do** that. And I'll **continue** being nice to my sister.

MY LONG-TERM GOALS

I aim to have a business one day so I want to **join** the Teen Entrepreneurs Club. Then I need to **think of** a great idea for a business. I need to **discover** how to put the idea into practice. Eventually I'll **create** a company. I'll employ people and **return** something to the community. It's all part of my ultimate goal to **control** the world! 😉

6 **Do you think Ed has achieved any of his original goals? Give reasons for your answer.**

7 a ▶1.26 PRONOUNCE **When one word ends in a consonant sound and the next word starts with a vowel sound or the same consonant, speakers often join the words together. Listen to the sentence.**

Did you come up with the right idea?

b ▶1.27 **Listen and write the sentences you hear.**

8 THE MOVING PICTURE ▶ **Watch Jeri-Lee, Shamaiya and Ryan talk about life goals. What are their short- and long-term goals?**

Phrasal verbs with objects

Three-word phrasal verbs are transitive and **inseparable**. The object must come after the verb:

Have you ________ ***a plan*** *for taking over the world yet?*
I've been too busy, but I'll ________ ***it*** *soon!*

Two-word phrasal verbs can be transitive or intransitive. Most transitive verbs are **separable**. The object can come between or after the two words:

I'm going to ________ ***a business.***
I'm going to ________ ***a business*** ________ .

Pronouns must go between the two words:

I'm going to ________ **one** ________ .

EXTEND

9 **Complete the sentences on the right with phrasal verbs from Exercise 4.**

SPEAK

10 **Work in pairs. Complete the tasks.**

- Each student writes three short-term and three long-term goals on separate pieces of paper.
- Place the pieces of paper face down on a flat surface.
- Take it in turns to turn over a piece of paper. Ask each other about your goals.
- Tell the class about two of your partner's goals.

GO BEYOND

Do the Words & Beyond exercise on page 132.

Workbook, page 28

READING Inventing the future

>>> Assess a text

SPEAK AND READ

1 Work in pairs. Which of the names do you recognise? What do they all have in common?

Steve Jobs Mark Zuckerberg Bill Gates

2 a Read the tips in the HOW TO box.

b 1.28 Read the text quickly and answer the questions.

1 What type of text is it? Who's it for?
2 In which order do the following topics appear?
___ competition ___ website design ___ meeting ___ friends

3 Which tips in the HOW TO box did you use for help with Exercise 2b? Tick (✓) them.

HOW TO
assess a text

- ☐ Identify the text type (*leaflet*, *article* ...). Look at headings, images, layout, etc.
- ☐ Read the first few lines. Identify who the text was written for and why.
- ☐ Read the 'topic sentence' at or near the start of each section/paragraph. It tells you what it's about.
- ☐ Decide which parts of the text to read in detail.

TEC INVENTING THE FUTURE

Hi Everyone,

There's lots to read in this month's newsletter, so let's get started with our question of the month: What do Mark Zuckerberg, Steve Jobs and Bill Gates all have in common? You'll find the answer at the end of this newsletter.

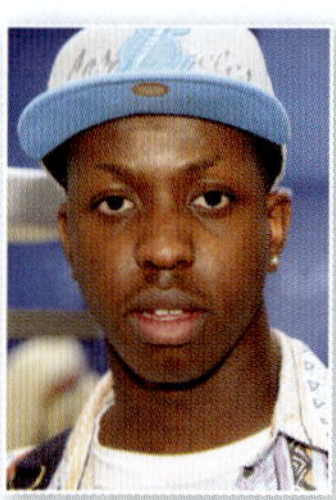

At the next TEC meeting, our special guest will be Jamal Edwards. I'm sure many of you already know Jamal's inspiring story from filming his pet dog on his phone camera, aged 14, to becoming the creative force behind SB.TV, the internet music channel, at the age of 16. At the meeting, he'll share some of the lessons he's learned from building up an internet business from scratch. Don't miss out – it'll be fun!

Here's some good news. Our sponsor, Creative City Prospects, wants to encourage new start-ups and is organising a competition for young entrepreneurs. To enter, all you need to do is come up with a new business idea. Pitch your idea on video and send it to Creative. One lucky winner will be picked by a panel of investors who'll take the winning idea to the next stage of development.

We need new members! Spread the word and get your friends to sign up. *Why should they?* Because starting up a business means you won't have to look for a job in the future and you'll hopefully be able to give other people jobs too.

Finally, as some of you know, Abi is leaving school at the end of the academic year, so we're going to need someone to take over the running of our website. The TEC website is our shop window, so we're looking for someone with design flair combined with a good general knowledge of web design and coding. You won't have to write any of the content, so don't worry about being a great writer. If you're interested, let me know. We'll miss you, Abi!

Answer to the question of the month: They all started businesses and/or met their future business partners while they were still at school.

That's it for now. Carry on creating and don't forget: 'Stay hungry, stay foolish.'

JT

4 Read the sentences and decide if they are true (*T*) or false (*F*). Correct the false sentences.

1 At the next meeting, Jamal will explain how he started his business. T/F
2 You need to present your competition idea at the Creative offices. T/F
3 The competition is an opportunity to win money. T/F
4 You have to be able to write code to run the club's website. T/F

REACT

5 Work in pairs. Read the newsletter again. Then answer the questions.

1 Would you like to join a club like TEC? Why?/Why not?
2 Do you think starting a business while you're at school is a good thing to do? Why?/Why not?

GO BEYOND

Read the text again and underline the phrasal verbs. Then find a noun with the same form as one of the phrasal verbs. What does it mean? Use a dictionary to help you.

Workbook, page 29

GRAMMAR Futures review

Talk about the future in different ways

READ AND LISTEN

1 1.29 **Read and listen to Beth's competition presentation. Who's she meeting next week?**

'My name's Beth and today I'm going to tell you about our new app called *Goal!* The app, which launches next month, is designed to help young people achieve their goals. It's likely to be most popular with young people. I'll give you an example ... Jordi has been getting bad grades at school and he's going to fail his final exams unless he improves. *Goal!* will suggest the steps he needs to take in order to achieve his goal. Users will be able to enter short-term and long-term goals. There's already interest in the app. Next week I'm meeting a major start-up investor who'll almost definitely get involved. And we're about to start work on developing version 2.0.'

STUDY

2 Read the explanations. Then underline an example of each use in Exercise 1.

Futures review

Use: Different forms express different ways of talking about the future.

Form:	Use:
Present simple	timetables, schedules
Present continuous	arrangements
be going to (1)	plans, intentions
be going to (2)	predictions based on present evidence
will (1)	facts
will (2)	predictions, often with *probably/ definitely*
will (3)	promises, immediate decisions
be likely to	things that will probably happen
be about to	things that will happen very soon
will be able to	future ability

See GRAMMAR DATABASE, page 122.

PRACTISE

3 Read Phil's presentation and choose the correct options.

'Imagine the situation. You're at home. It's 1 o'clock and the next bus (1) ____ in 20 minutes. (2) ____ some friends in town to go to the cinema at 4.30 but it looks like you're (3) ____ late. What can you do? With my motorised high-speed skateboard, (4) ____ late again. But why am I talking about it? I've got a better idea. (5) ____ you how it works. Ladies and gentlemen, (6) ____ see the first ever demonstration of the *Ultra-S-board*!'

1 **A** will leave **B** leaves
2 **A** You're meeting **B** You'll meet
3 **A** being **B** going to be
4 **A** you'll never be **B** you're never being
5 **A** I show **B** I'll show
6 **A** you'll **B** you're about to

4 Read Amber and Raul's presentation. Write the verbs in the correct form of the future.

Amber: Based on current statistics, all of us (1) ____ (**live**) longer in the future. This means there (2) ____ (**be**) more old people in the world, including you one day. When you're 60, you (3) ____ (**probably try**) to keep in touch with your friends. However, older people (4) ____ (**not be likely / use**) the same social networking sites as young people in the future. 60NET is an idea for a social networking site for people aged 60 and over.

Raul: So how (5) ____ (**60NET / be**) different? Well, here's our plan. We (6) ____ (**make**) the site easy for older people to use. When you're 60, you (7) ____ (**can't see**) as well as you can now. So the size of the letters (8) ____ (**be**) bigger and there (9) ____ (**not be**) any ads. 60NET (10) ____ (**definitely be**) the answer to all your needs when you're older. Thank you.

5 Write complete questions.

1 which of the three ideas / win / probably / the competition ?
2 any of them / be likely to / make money ?
3 do you think you / be / an entrepreneur / in the future ?

WRITE AND SPEAK

6 Work in pairs. Ask and answer the questions in Exercise 5. Then think of a business idea for the competition and write a presentation using different future forms. Present your idea to the rest of the class.

Workbook, pages 30–31

LISTENING AND VOCABULARY The cabin project

»» Understand referring words

SPEAK AND LISTEN

1 Work in pairs. Answer the questions.

1 What's the difference between a day and boarding school?
2 What are the advantages and disadvantages of each one?
3 What's different about the boarding school in the photo?

2 1.30 Listen to the radio report. What are the cabins used for and why?

3 a Read the tips in the HOW TO box.

b 1.30 Listen again and choose the correct answer (A, B or C).

1 The cabin project helps students to …
A develop as individuals.
B do their best academically.
C recognise discipline problems.

2 Why are the students encouraged to buy and cook their own meals?
A to eat food of their own choice
B to get on with each other
C to prepare them for university life

3 How many pupils are there in each cabin?
A one B three C six

4 What are the students in the library doing now?
A taking charge of the library
B designing their curriculum
C writing a novel

4 Work in pairs. What do the words in bold refer to?

1 'So can you tell **us** something about the thinking behind the cabin project?'
2 'We're very proud of **them**.'
3 'We'll be adding **more** over the next 12 months.'
4 'Each **one** has three twin-bedded bedrooms.'
5 '**These** students will have been following a secondary curriculum for five years.'
6 'And I'm pretty sure **that**'s what they're doing now.'

5 Which tips in the HOW TO box did you use for help with Exercises 3b and 4? Tick (✓) them.

HOW TO

understand referring words

- ☐ Pronouns, relative pronouns, *one/ones* and *there* refer back to people, things or places.
- ☐ *Not many*, *none*, *more*, etc can also refer back to something: *We invited 100 people, but not many came.*
- ☐ *This/that* and *which* can refer back to part or the whole of the previous sentence.
- ☐ *Do/did* and *so* can refer back to a verb phrase: *We did the same. I hope so.*
- ☐ *Here/there* and *this/that*, etc can refer to what speakers see around them.

REACT

6 Work in pairs. What do you think of the cabin project? Do you think students should be able to help design their curriculum?

WORK WITH WORDS

7 Complete the pupil's sentences with the phrases in the table.

1 I think we're all ______ how lucky we are to be here.
2 Living like this helps us to ______ when we leave school.
3 In life I think it's important to ______ your actions.
4 The school's ______ other things too – like its rugby team.
5 I won this medal in the school games. I'm very ______ it.
6 It feels good when they let us ______ how and what we learn.
7 I get ______ my roommate when he can't stop talking!
8 The house staff ______ us to make sure we don't misbehave.
9 I have a younger brother here and I feel ______ looking after him.
10 Our parents ______ us when we do well.

Adjective + preposition	Verb + adjective/ noun + preposition
annoyed with	get ready for
aware of	keep an eye on
famous for	take charge of
proud of	take pride in
responsible for	take responsibility for

8 1.31 Listen and check. Then listen and repeat.

9 Work in pairs. Write sentences about you and your school using some of the words in Exercise 7.

GO BEYOND

Do the Words & Beyond exercise on page 132.

Workbook, pages 32–33

GRAMMAR Future continuous and future perfect

>>> Talk about what will be happening and what will have happened

READ AND LISTEN

1 1.32 **Read and listen to the conversation. How does Hal know so much about the future?**

Hal: What do you think you'll be doing in six years' time?
Inma: If my parents have their way, I'll be working in the family business. What about you?
Hal: Let's see … I'll have finished university by then and I'll have been running my own business for a couple of years. So I'll have built up my fortune and we'll be living in Los Angeles.
Inma: *We*?
Hal: No, you're right. I won't have got married by then. That's the year after.
Inma: You seem to have your whole life planned.
Hal: I've been using this new app called *Goal!* You should try it. It helps you plan and achieve your goals.

STUDY

2 Read the explanations. Then underline an example of each tense in Exercise 1.

Future continuous and future perfect
Future continuous
Use: For actions in progress at a time in the future.
Form: *will* + *be* + verb + *-ing*
Future perfect simple
Use: For actions completed before a time in the future, often with *by*.
Form: *will* + *have* + past participle
Future perfect continuous
Use: For actions in progress before a time in the future, often with *for* and *since*.
Form: *will* + *have* + *been* + verb + *-ing*
See GRAMMAR DATABASE, page 122.

PRACTISE

3 a Write sentences using the future perfect continuous.

At the end of this year …
1 Inma / study / English / for six years .
2 Hal / play / the piano / for three years .
3 Inma and Hal / live / here / for 15 years .
4 they / go / to the same school / for five years .

b Make the sentences true for you.

At the end of this year I'll have been studying English for …

4 a Write questions using the future continuous, future perfect or future perfect continuous.

1 what / Hal / do / in 2019 ?
2 what / he / achieve / by then ?
3 how long / he / live / in Los Angeles in 2022 ?
4 what / he / do / by the time he moves to Los Angeles ?
5 when / he / buy / an apartment by ?
6 what / he / write / in 2023 ?

b Look at the app information and write the answers to the questions in Exercise 4a.

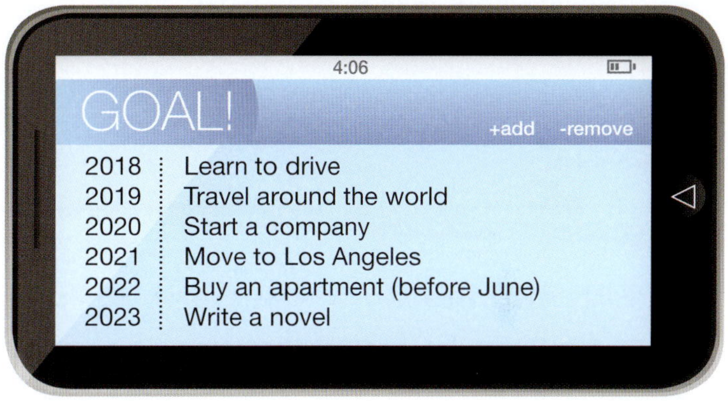

5 Read Inma's letter to Hal and write the verbs in the future continuous, future perfect or future perfect continuous.

Berlin, 16th April 2023

Dear Hal,
How are you? I (1) ________ (**visit**) New York next month on tour with the group. We (2) ________ (**not stay**) for long but I'd love to see you. By the time we get there, we (3) ________ (**tour**) for seven months and we (4) ________ (**perform**) in 15 different countries! Remember when we talked about the future? It's hard to imagine that six years (5) ________ (**pass**) by the time we see each other. (6) ________ (**you / achieve**) all your goals by then? Who'd have thought that I'd become an international rock star?!
Inma

WRITE AND SPEAK

6 a Make notes about the future. What would you like to happen?

2018 ________ 2021 ________
2019 ________ 2022 ________
2020 ________ 2023 ________

b Work in pairs. Ask questions about the different years to find out about your partner's future. Then write three sentences using the future continuous, future perfect and future perfect continuous.

What will you be doing in 2018?
I'll be travelling around the world.
What will you have done by 2020?
I'll have …

>>> Workbook, page 34

LANGUAGE & BEYOND

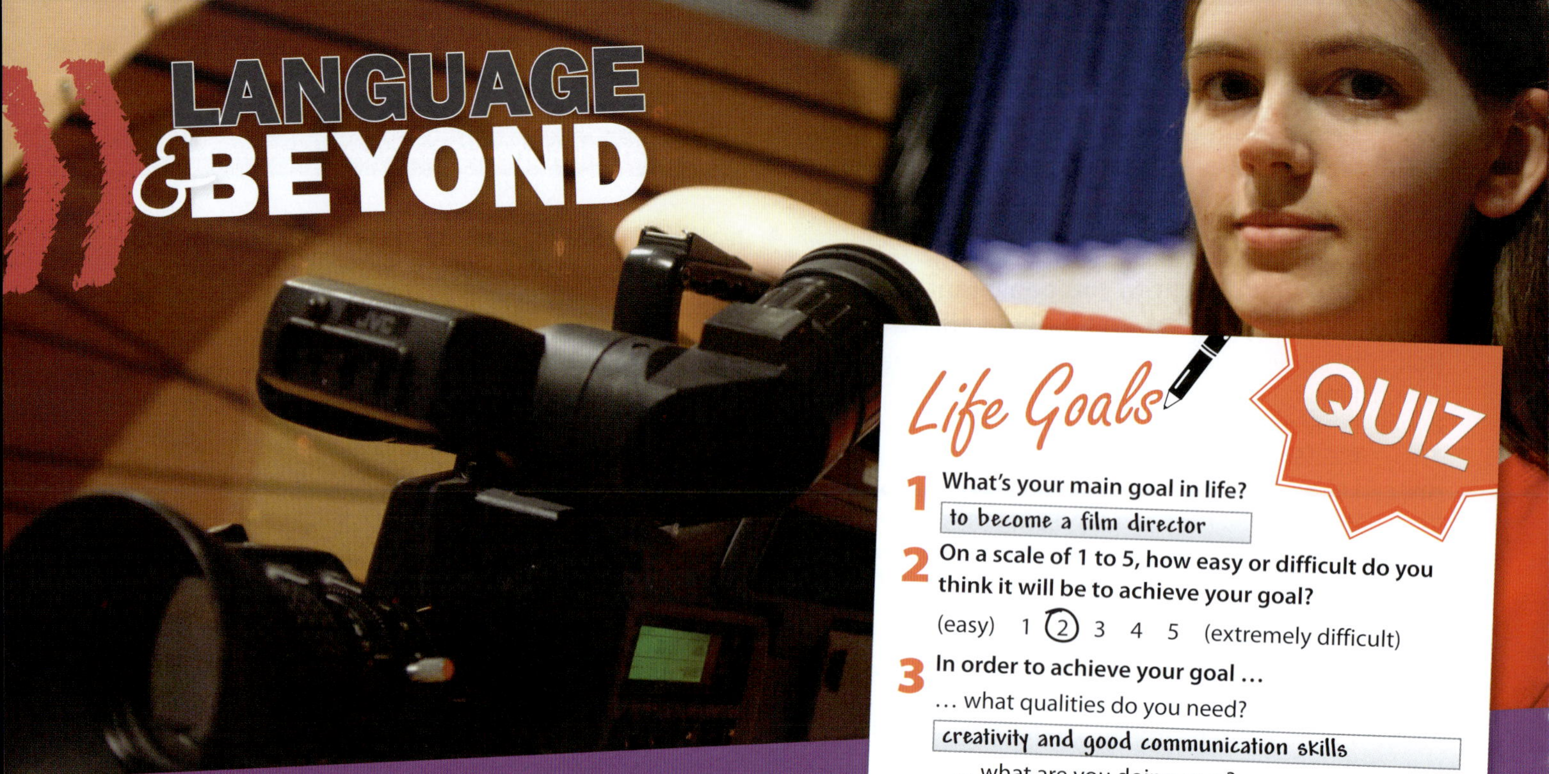

Life Goals QUIZ

1 What's your main goal in life?

to become a film director

2 On a scale of 1 to 5, how easy or difficult do you think it will be to achieve your goal?

(easy) 1 (2) 3 4 5 (extremely difficult)

3 In order to achieve your goal …

… what qualities do you need?

creativity and good communication skills

… what are you doing now?

making short films with my phone
going to see as many films as I can
reading about the history of cinema

… what steps can you take after leaving school?

go to film school, enter competitions
get some work experience

4 How certain are you that you'll achieve your goal?

I'm quite certain: 80%!

5 What will you do if you don't achieve your goal?

find another job related to cinema or photography

>>> Set achievable goals

SPEAK AND READ

1 **Work in pairs. Look at the photo. What do you think Hannah's ambition is? How easy do you think it will be for her to achieve it?**

2 **Read the questionnaire that Hannah completed. Compare your answers to exercise 1.**

3 **Which adjectives best describe Hannah? Give reasons for your choices.**

ambitious creative practical realistic reserved unrealistic

PHRASE BYTES

I think her ambition is …

It'll be quite difficult/easy for her … because …

DO

4 **Look at the goals and steps on the right. Which of the steps would you need to take to achieve each goal? Add more steps of your own.**

5 **Do the questionnaire in Exercise 2. Describe your own goal or one of the goals from Exercise 4. Then compare your answers with a partner. Is their goal realistic? Why?/Why not?**

GOALS

- start a business
- become an actor
- design furniture
- teach in other countries
- be a fashion designer

STEPS

- do an apprenticeship …
- get work experience …
- go to university …
- learn a skill …
- raise money …

REFLECT

6 **Discuss these questions with your class. Do you agree with the REFLECTION POINT?**

1 Why is it important to have goals in life?
2 How can planning ahead improve your chances of achieving your goal?
3 What are the dangers of having unrealistic goals?

REFLECTION POINT

Having goals in life can help you achieve what you want to do. In order to achieve your goals, you need to plan the steps you need to take and then work towards taking each step. It's important to have realistic goals; otherwise you may never achieve them and become frustrated.

EXTEND

7 **Work in groups. Make a list of things you'd like to achieve before the end of the school term or year. Choose one goal and plan the steps you need to take to achieve it.**

Workbook, page 37

SPEAKING Anything's possible

»» Express certainty, probability and doubt

SPEAK

1 Work in pairs. Complete the sentences about next weekend so they are true for both of you.

1 We're both definitely going to / not going to ...
2 We'll both probably ...
3 We doubt if we'll ...

WATCH OR LISTEN

2 1.33 Watch or listen to the scenes. How does Liam's attitude change? Why do you think it changes?

1

Megan: Hi Liam. We're thinking of starting a film club.
Liam: That's a good idea.
Megan: Do you think so?
Liam: Definitely.
Connor: So, if it goes ahead, will you join?
Liam: (1) ....
Connor: We'll probably meet on Thursdays after school. Is that a good time for you?
Liam: That's perfect.
Megan: Really? Are you sure?
Liam: Yes. (2) ....

2

Connor: The film club starts next week. You'll be there, right?
Liam: (3) .... When is it?
Connor: On Thursday after school.
Liam: Then (4) .... be able to make it.
Megan: Why not?
Liam: I'll be swimming.
Megan: But you said Thursdays were perfect.
Liam: That's impossible. I always go swimming on Thursdays. Listen. I'll try to come but (5) ....

3

Connor: So will there be a meeting?
Megan: (6) .... We'll probably be the only people there.
Connor: If we start meeting regularly, then people will start coming.
Megan: Are you certain?
Connor: (7) ....
Megan: I don't know. I doubt it'll make any difference. But anything's possible, I guess.

3 a Write the phrases in the conversation.

a I definitely won't
b I doubt it
c I'm certain ... absolutely
d I'm not sure
e I'm positive
f it's very unlikely
g Of course

b 1.33 Watch or listen again to check your answers.

4 1.34 Listen and repeat the phrases, paying attention to intonation.

5 Rewrite the sentences using phrases from Exercise 4 to give your opinions.

1 The Earth is round.
2 I'll start a business.
3 Life exists on other planets.
4 I'll become famous.

ACT

6 Work in pairs. Complete the tasks.

- Think of an after-school club you'd like to start. Agree on a regular time and place to meet.
- Tell another pair about your club and ask them if they'd like to join.
- Listen to their idea for a club. React to their idea using the phrases in the PHRASEBOOK.

PHRASEBOOK 1.35

Express certainty
Absolutely
Definitely
Of course
I'm sure/certain/positive.

Express probability
Probably
It's (very) likely/unlikely ...
It's possible/impossible.

Express doubt
I doubt it.
I doubt ...
I'm not sure.

Workbook, page 35

WRITING Dear Sir or Madam

»» Write a formal letter or email

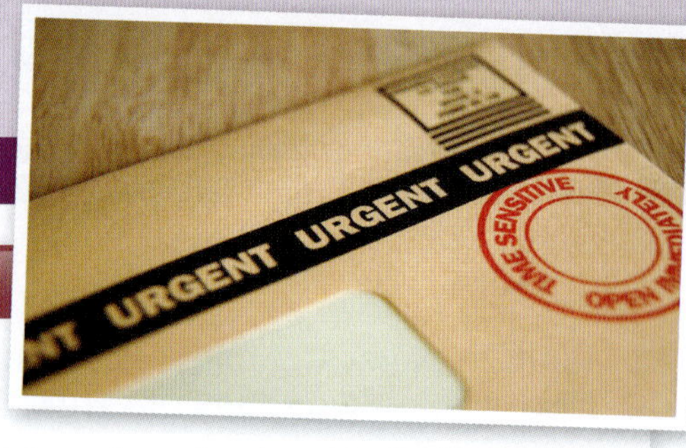

SPEAK AND READ

1 Work in pairs. Ask and answer the questions.

1 On what occasions do people write formal letters or email messages?
2 Have you ever written or received a formal letter or email? If so, when?
3 What are the main differences between a formal and informal letter?

2 Read the email message. Who's Mr Davies? What do the writers want to know?

New mail ← Reply →

Dear Mr Davies,

We are writing to ask your permission to start up a computer club at the school and to find out if it would be possible to use the computer room for our meetings.

There are two main reasons why we are certain that a computer club will be popular. Firstly, learning how computers work and being able to write code are key skills in today's world and will be useful to us in the future. Secondly, video games and apps are great fun to use. We think other pupils at the school will want to learn how to create them too.

To begin with, the club would meet twice a month but it is likely that we would want to meet more often once everything is set up and running.

We are very aware that the equipment in the computer room is valuable. We would like to assure you that we will be responsible for making sure that nothing is damaged.

We hope you will consider our request and allow us to start the club. We look forward to hearing from you.

Yours sincerely,

Edward Carter and Maria Martin

STUDY

3 a Read the tips in the HOW TO box. Which point(s) only apply to a letter?

HOW TO

write a formal letter or email

- ☐ Write full forms not contractions. Use formal words and phrases whenever possible.
- ☐ Write your address at the top right with the date underneath. Write the name and address of the person you are writing to underneath on the left.
- ☐ Start with Dear Mr/Mrs/Ms [+ surname], if you know the person's name, or Dear Sir or Madam, if you don't.
- ☐ Begin by stating your reason for writing. Finish by saying what you hope will happen next.
- ☐ At the end write 'Yours sincerely' or 'Yours faithfully' and type or sign your name underneath.

b Which of the points did Edward and Maria follow in their message? Tick (✓) them.

4 The subject line is important in a formal email. It should clearly explain the purpose of the message in as few words as possible. Choose the best subject line for Edward and Maria's message.

a We'd like permission to set up a club
b Why we'd like to start a computer club
c Request to start a computer club

PRACTISE

5 Use the phrases below to replace phrases in the message with the same meaning.

1 The purpose of this message is to
2 To begin with,
3 Furthermore,
4 Initially,
5 We appreciate
6 We hope to receive a reply from you soon.

PLAN, WRITE AND CHECK

6 You're going to write a letter to the school principal, asking permission to start a new club.

- Think of a club you'd like to start (dance, film, science ...) and where to meet.
- Make a note of why you think the school needs your club.
- Use the message above to help you organise your ideas.

7 Write your letter. Use the tips from the HOW TO box to help you make your letter formal. Then check it.

SHARE AND REVIEW

8 Swap your letter with a partner. Read your partner's letter and review it. Whose club proposal is most interesting?

»» Workbook, pages 36–37

VOCABULARY Phrasal verbs: goals and achievements

1 Complete the New Year resolutions with the phrasal verbs.

get round to give back give up put off sign up for take up

Next year I'm going to ...

1 ________ eating junk food. (I have to stop!)
2 ________ a new sport.
3 ________ the school trip.
4 ________ something to Mum and Dad. They've helped me a lot recently.
5 ________ fixing my bike. I can't (6) ________ doing it for much longer!

carry on come up with miss out on start up take over work out

I'm not going to ...

7 ________ going to the theme park again.
8 ________ being lazy in my history class.
9 ________ another excuse for not phoning Kate. I just have to (10) ________ what to say to her!
11 ________ another club. I'm too busy. That reminds me – I need to find someone to (12) ________ the cookery club – what a disaster!

___ /12

Adjective + preposition, verb + noun + preposition

2 Write the correct preposition.

6 March

I failed my history exam! I'm so annoyed (1) ________ myself. Mum and Dad aren't very proud (2) ________ me. Our teacher is famous (3) ________ setting hard exams. I should've been aware (4) ________ the dangers of not revising. I'm the only one responsible (5) ________ failing.

12 May

Get ready (6) ________ some good news! Today I take pride (7) ________ being able to announce that I finally spoke to Kate!! I can't take responsibility (8) ________ what happened. Ed took charge (9) ________ the situation and called Kate. Keep an eye (10) ________ this space to see what happens.

___ /10

GRAMMAR Futures review

3 Choose the correct options.

8 August

It's 6am and I'm (1) ***about to / likely to*** leave home to go on the school trip. The coach (2) ***leaves / will leave*** at 6.45, so (3) ***we'll probably meet / we're meeting*** outside the school in 40 minutes. (4) ***We spend / We're going to spend*** five days in the mountains. According to my weather app, it's (5) ***being / going to be*** sunny and hot, so (6) ***we'll be able to / we're about to*** do outdoor sports. I've promised myself that (7) ***I'm trying / I'll try*** rock climbing. Ed says (8) ***we probably stay / we'll probably stay*** in log cabins. He also says (9) ***we're seeing / we're likely to see*** some bears. Can't wait!

___ /18

Future continuous and future perfect

4 Write the verbs in the correct future form.

31 October

In two months we (1) ________ (**celebrate**) the end of the year. I wonder how many of this year's resolutions I (2) ________ (**complete**) by then. I (3) ________ (**not go**) to a theme park but I don't care. Next week I (4) ________ (**go out**) with Kate for four months. I hope we (5) ________ (**go out / still**) this time next year.

___ /10

SKILLS CHECK

✓✓✓ Yes, I can. No problem!
✓✓ Yes, I can. But I need a bit of help.
✓ Yes, I can. But I need a lot of help.

I can assess a text. ________
I can understand referring words when I listen. ________
I can set achievable goals. ________
I can express certainty, probability and doubt. ________
I can write a formal letter or email. ________

Workbook, pages 38–39

UNIT 4

LEARNING FROM THE PAST

IN THE PICTURE Buildings past and present

>>> Talk about buildings and architecture

1

RECALL AND READ

1 **Work in pairs. Unscramble the letters to make the names of buildings. You have two minutes.**

1 e-m-m-s-u-u
2 e-r-o-t-w
3 a-e-e-h-r-t-t
4 a-d-i-m-s-t-u
5 a-i-n-o-s-t-t
6 a-c-e-l-s-t
7 r-a-t a-e-g-l-l-r-y
8 c-c-e-n-o-r-t a-h-l-l

2 **Read the travel brochure. Match the photos (1–5) to the descriptions (A–E).**

AMAzing Tours

Ancient and Modern Architecture

Here's a sample of some of our amazing tours.

A ....
From the blue and white columned façade of Catherine Palace in St Petersburg to the blue and white Vorobyovy Gory tower blocks in Moscow, Russia's a great place to see classic and contemporary architecture on a grand scale.

B ....
Climb the steps of the Kukulkán Pyramid to view the awe-inspiring ancient Mayan city of Chichén Itzá. Then travel to Mexico City to discover imaginative modern-day buildings like the Calakmul office block, known as the Washing Machine.

C ....
A mad mix of the old and new, our tour takes you to see the great castles of central Spain, like the Alcázar in Segovia, and modern masterpieces like the Guggenheim Museum in Bilbao. Is this the world's most famous art gallery?

D ....
One of the great civilisations gives us ancient masterpieces like the Temple of Heaven complex in Beijing, whose first buildings date from the early 15th century, and minimalist 21st century buildings like the futuristic Beijing Opera House.

E ....
Walk around Oxford, with the domes, arches, windows and 'dreaming spires' of its ancient university buildings, then head down to London to take in cutting-edge inner-city wonders like the emblematic Shard, one of Europe's tallest skyscrapers.

WORK WITH WORDS

3 1.36 **Match the words to the definitions. Listen and check. Then listen and repeat.**

arch column dome façade office block palace pyramid skyscraper spire steps temple tower block

Types of building

1 .... : a very tall building containing offices or flats
2 .... : a tall building with flats or offices on each floor. The American word is high-rise
3 .... : a large building with offices in it
4 .... : a building used for worship in some religions
5 .... : a large stone structure with a square base and sides that meet at a point at the top
6 .... : a very large building that's the home of a royal family, president or other leader

Parts of buildings

7 .... : flat pieces of wood or stone that go up or down to a different level
8 .... : a thick post used for supporting a roof or decorating a building
9 .... : a curved structure at the top of a window or door
10 .... : the pointed top of a tower or part of a building
11 .... : a roof shaped like the top half of a ball
12 .... : the front of a large or impressive building

4 a Work in pairs. Use the words in Exercise 3 to describe the buildings in the photos.

b Think of examples of each type of building in your country. Describe them.

PHRASE BYTES

This building's a(n) …

This part of the building could be …

That's definitely a …

Would you say these are … ?

5 THE MOVING PICTURE Watch the clues about six well-known buildings. See if you can write the name and location of each one and the century in which it was completed.

EXTEND

6 Work in pairs. What do you think the idioms mean? Choose an option.

1 Hugh looks happy, but it's **just a façade**.
   a it's just the way his face is
   b he's hiding his real feelings

2 When I told Dad I'd broken the video camera, he **hit the roof**.
   a was really angry
   b was so surprised he jumped in the air

3 Carter and Maya are very different but, surprisingly, they **get on like a house on fire**.
   a are really close friends
   b have lots of arguments

SPEAK

7 Work in pairs. Do one or both of the tasks. Give reasons for your answers.

- Discuss the buildings in the photos. What do you think of each one? Which ones would you like to go and see? Which other buildings around the world would you like to see?
- Discuss modern architecture. Do you like it? Is it as good as architecture from the past? Will people still like it 100 years from now?

GO BEYOND

Do the Words & Beyond exercises on page 133.

Workbook, page 40

READING Lessons from the past

»» Understand opinions

SPEAK AND READ

1 Work in pairs. Answer the questions.

1 How often do you watch documentaries on television?
2 What types of documentaries do you like watching?

2 1.37 Read the TV review. Tick (✓) the topics that the documentary covers.

____ Anthropology ____ Geology ____ Environment ____ Geography ____ History

DID YOU SEE ... ?

Past and present (documentary) **Reviewed by Lisa Dunton**

Episode 6: Lessons from the past (DTV 9pm) ★★★★☆

In the last episode of his series about how ancient civilisations have shaped the modern world, Dr Aidan Swift looked at why some of the most successful societies from the past collapsed and ended with a warning: We'll suffer the same fate unless we learn from their mistakes.

No expense had been spared as Dr Swift, with his mad professor haircut, was flown to exotic locations around the globe to gather evidence for his theories. From the majestic columns and temples of the Mayan city of Chichén Itzá in Mexico, we were taken to Easter Island, with its iconic moai statues, and then to the barren beauty of Greenland, where a Norse population survived for over four centuries. What caused the downfall of these once great civilisations? Overpopulation, disease and war all played a part, according to Dr Swift, but it was damage to the environment that really finished them off. Given the evidence, it was hard to disagree with his conclusions.

In the case of the Easter Islanders, they apparently had to cut down so many trees to move those enormous statues around that eventually none were left, leaving them without their main source of food and transport. Diseases brought by European settlers are then thought to have wiped out most of those who had survived the consequences of deforestation.

Dr Swift's message was that these societies might have survived if they'd respected their environment. He has said he believes we're on the edge of a similar disaster and that if we stopped destroying the environment immediately, we might just prevent our own downfall. But he wasn't optimistic, arguing that if we really understood the dangers, we'd have taken action already.

On the whole, I found the programme extremely thought-provoking. It was beautifully filmed, though at times it would have been nice to see more of the site and less of Dr Swift in his 1970s safari suit (did they make cuts in the costume department to pay for all that travelling?). Personally, I'd have preferred less diversity and more detail too. I found myself wanting to know more about those lost civilisations. Yet despite this, it's well worth watching online if you missed this episode. You'll enjoy it – as long as you're not expecting a happy ending!

3 a Read the tips in the HOW TO box.

b Read the review again. Who expresses an opinion about these things – Lisa Dunton (*LD*), Dr Swift (*DS*) or both (*B*)? Are the opinions positive or negative? Explain why.

1 Our future ____
2 The locations ____
3 Why civilisations collapse ____
4 Dr Swift's clothes ____
5 The amount of information ____
6 The documentary in general ____

4 Which tips in the HOW TO box did you use for help with Exercise 3b? Tick (✓) them.

REACT

5 Work in pairs. Discuss your reactions to the fourth paragraph. Do you agree with Dr Swift?

HOW TO
understand opinions

Look for words/phrases that:

- ☐ introduce opinions: *think*, *believe*, *find*; *personally*.
- ☐ evaluate something: *fascinating*; *worth doing*.
- ☐ make comparisons: *more*, *less*; *I'd have preferred ...*
- ☐ introduce other people's opinions: *claim*, *argue*; *according to*; *apparently*.

GO BEYOND

Underline the adjectives in the review. What do they mean? Check in your dictionary.

Workbook, page 41

GRAMMAR Conditionals

»» Talk about the consequences of possible or imaginary situations

READ AND LISTEN

1 ▶1.38 **Read and listen to the conversation. Why didn't Dom do well in his history test?**

Liv: How was your history test?
Dom: Not good. I couldn't remember anything about the Maya. My teacher says I'm going to fail the subject unless I do better. But I might pass providing I get a good mark for the project. I'm so busy, though. If I wasn't so busy, I'd have done better.
Liv: If you didn't have so many rehearsals for the school play, you'd have loads of time.
Dom: Yeah, it's hard work. I wouldn't have accepted the leading role if I'd known.
Liv: But if you hadn't got the leading role, you wouldn't be the school superstar!

STUDY

2 Complete the explanations with examples from Exercise 1.

Conditionals

First conditional

Use: For possible future situations.

Form: present + *will*

Note (1): Other modals (*might, must,* etc), other future forms (*going to*, etc) and imperatives can replace *will*.

....

....

Note (2): *unless, as/so long as, providing/provided* (*that*) can replace *if*.

Second conditional

Use: For unlikely or imaginary situations in the present or future.

Form: past + *would*

....

Third conditional

Use: For imaginary situations in the past.

Form: past perfect + *would have*

....

Note: Other modals can replace *would*.

Mixed conditionals

Use: Mix second and third conditionals to connect the past with the present.
If I wasn't so busy, I'd have done better.

See GRAMMAR DATABASE, page 123.

PRACTISE

3 Rewrite the underlined part of the sentences using the word in brackets and no more than three other words.

History project: The Aztecs. Deadline: Thursday 21st

1 I might accept late projects provided the pupil had a convincing explanation. (**as**)
2 If you don't write clearly, you'll lose marks. (**unless**)
3 If you look online for information, you mustn't copy it word for word. (**don't**)
4 Your work won't get a mark unless your project is at least 1,000 words in length. (**if**)
5 All opinions will be accepted if they're backed up with evidence. (**that**)
6 If you copy your work, it's possible that you won't pass this subject. (**might**)

4 a Write the verbs in the first or second conditional form. Both may be possible. Then complete the sentences with your ideas.

1 Many animals .... (**not survive**) unless ...
2 If sea levels .... (**rise**) in the coming years, ...
3 Our school .... (**be**) greener if ...
4 We .... (**save**) our planet's environment as long as ...
5 If petrol .... (**get**) much more expensive ...
6 Unless we .... (**stop**) deforestation, ...

b Work in pairs. Compare your sentences.

5 a Write third or mixed conditional sentences.

1 the last ice age / not end / if the Earth's climate / not change.
2 if humans / be / less intelligent, they / not do / so much damage to the planet.
3 dinosaurs / survive / until today if a meteorite / not wipe them out.
4 if we / not invent / guns and bombs, the world / be / a safer place today.
5 if hamburgers / not become / so popular, deforestation / not become / a big problem.
6 we / not know / so much about the world if the internet / not be / invented.

b Work in pairs. Discuss the statements.

SPEAK

6 Work in pairs. Student A: look at page 141. Student B: look at page 142. Read out your situations and discuss their consequences.

»» Workbook, pages 42–43

LISTENING AND VOCABULARY No regrets

>>> Recognise imaginary situations

SPEAK AND LISTEN

1 **Work in pairs. Think of a famous politician, singer, writer and comedian. What question would you like to ask each one?**

2 1.39 **Listen to a discussion programme. What jobs do Sarah Law, David Brand, Harvey Fellows and Marina have?**

3 a **Read the tips in the HOW TO box.**

b 1.39 **Listen again. Decide if the following sentences are true (*T*) or false (*F*). If false, explain why.**

1. Sarah Law lost touch with her best friends. T/F
2. She spends a lot of time with other people. T/F
3. David Brand answers the presenter's question. T/F
4. He thinks the last government's responsible for today's problems. T/F
5. Harvey Fellows thinks politicians are honest and open. T/F
6. He would like to be a politician. T/F
7. Marina behaves badly in public. T/F
8. She can sing as well as Édith Piaf. T/F

HOW TO
recognise imaginary situations

Listen for:
- ☐ words like *if*, *unless*, *wish* and *if only*.
- ☐ sentences starting with *Supposing* or *Imagine*.
- ☐ past tenses to talk about the present or future: *If the world was going to end ...*
- ☐ the past perfect to talk about the past: *If I'd been in your position, ...*
- ☐ *would* to talk about the results of imaginary situations.

4 **Which tips in the HOW TO box did you use for help with Exercise 3b? Tick (✓) them.**

5 a 1.40 PRONOUNCE **Listen to the extract from the programme. Which word does the presenter emphasise most? Why?**

The question was, in case you've forgotten, 'Do you regret anything you've done?'

b 1.41 **Which word needs emphasis in each question to make its meaning clear? Listen and check. Then listen and repeat.**

1. I know what he regrets. What do you regret?
2. I know what you're proud of. What do you regret?
3. You said you regret something. What do you regret?

REACT

6 **Work in pairs. Do you agree with these statements? Why?/Why not?**

1. We make our best friends while we're at school.
2. Politicians should be more open and honest.
3. Artists need to be controversial to become famous.

WORK WITH WORDS

7 a **Work in pairs. Try and associate the abstract nouns below with a verb or adjective. Then compare with other students.**

disappointment failure fame fear freedom friendship honesty humour power regret sadness youth

'Disappointment' must be related to the adjective 'disappointed'. Is there a verb 'to disappoint'?

b 1.42 **Listen and match the nouns to the descriptions. Then listen and repeat the nouns.**

8 **Work in pairs. Answer the questions about the abstract nouns in Exercise 7.**

1. Which are seen as positive qualities in advertising?
2. Which would people value most in someone they're close to?
3. Which can be positive and negative? When?
4. Which would probably be considered positive in all cultures?

GO BEYOND
Do the Words & Beyond exercises on page 133.

Workbook, pages 44–45

GRAMMAR Wishes and regrets: *I wish/If only*

»» Talk about wishes and regrets

READ AND LISTEN

1 1.43 **Read and listen to the conversation. Why does Bea get frustrated with Gus?**

Gus: What's that?
Bea: It's just a doodle.
Gus: It's really good. If only I could do something well.
Bea: You can sing. I've heard you. I wish I had your voice.
Gus: But I can't sing *well*. I wish I hadn't given up those lessons.
Bea: Gus, I wish you'd stop being so negative.
Gus: Negative?
Bea: You could start having lessons again.
Gus: Yeah, you're right.

STUDY

2 Complete the explanations with examples from Exercise 1.

Wishes and regrets: *I wish/If only*

Use: To express unhappiness with a situation in the present or past, or with a future plan.

Form:
For present situations, use a verb in the past:
I ***can't do*** *anything well.*
If only ....
I ***don't have*** *your voice.*
I wish ....
For past situations, use the past perfect:
I ***gave up*** *those lessons.*
I wish ....

Complaints: *I wish/If only + would*

Use: To complain about annoying behaviour.

Form: *I wish/If only* + *would* + infinitive (without *to*)
You're being negative. It's annoying.
I wish ....

See GRAMMAR DATABASE, page 123.

PRACTISE

3 Complete the diary with the past simple or continuous form of the verbs. Use the correct form of *can* if necessary.

I think today might mark a turning point in my life. If only I (1) .... (**write**) that about every day! I had a chat with Bea at school. Sometimes I wish she (2) .... (**not be**) so honest, but if only I (3) .... (**have**) her positive attitude. She always sees the bright side. Anyway, I've been feeling envious of Brody for a while now. He's singing in the school play at the end of term, and I wish I (4) .... (**take**) part too. So I've decided to start singing lessons again. If only I (5) .... (**do**) them at lunchtime, though – I'm so busy after school. And I wish I (6) .... (**not have to**) wait till after the holidays to start. But I'm trying to be positive!

4 Write the regrets with *wish* and *If only*.

1 I regret arguing with Holly.
If only ....
2 We all have some things we regret doing.
We all have some things we wish ....
3 It's a real shame she believed what Joss said.
If only ....
4 I regret that she didn't listen to me.
If only ....
5 She's disappointed that you didn't invite her to your party.
She wishes ....
6 It's a pity we weren't able to make it up beforehand.
If only ....

5 Write what you would say or think in these situations. Use *I wish/If only* and *would*.

1 Your neighbours are making a lot of noise.
2 Your friend's got a cold and keeps coughing.
3 Your teacher talks so fast you can't take notes.
4 Your friend tells everyone your secrets.
5 Your teacher keeps giving you extra homework.

WRITE AND SPEAK

6 a Write four sentences about different people you know with *wish* or *if only*. Include:

- a regret about a future plan.
- a regret about the present.
- a regret about the past.
- a thing you find annoying.

b Compare your sentences with a partner and talk about the situations.

»» Workbook, page 46

LANGUAGE & BEYOND

Bram Stoker
'We learn from failure, not from success!'

Albert Einstein
'Anyone who has never made a mistake has never tried anything new.'

Mahatma Gandhi
'Freedom is not worth having if it does not include the freedom to make mistakes.'

Jimi Hendrix
'I've been imitated so well I've heard people copy my mistakes.'

»» Learn from your mistakes

SPEAK AND READ

1 a Work in pairs. Look at the photos. What do you know about the people?

b Read the quotes together and discuss what they say about mistakes. Compare your ideas with other students.

PHRASE BYTES

I think ... is saying that ...
The idea behind this quote is that ...
What do you think this one really means?

DO

2 a Work in groups. Read the situations. In which one(s) ...

1 did the person make a mistake? What did they do wrong? Why?
2 is the person avoiding mistakes? Is this good? Why?/Why not?

PHRASE BYTES

...'s situation shows us that ...
...'s real mistake is that he/she ...
...'s is an example of how ...

Luann plays the violin. When she practises at home, she plays well. One day her friends asked her to play. She got nervous about not doing her best and played a lot of wrong notes.

Luis made some biscuits for a family meal, but he didn't read the recipe carefully. The biscuits looked horrible so he left them in the kitchen. A family member saw them and tasted them. 'Who made these biscuits?' they asked. 'They're delicious. I've never tasted anything like them.'

Isa put information about her birthday party online. Hundreds of people turned up and things in her parents' house were stolen or damaged.

Wyatt never speaks in class. He says he's afraid to say things that aren't correct and has decided he won't speak till his English is really good.

b Match each conclusion to one of the situations. Then think of other typical or well-known examples.

1 A fear of mistakes can stop you learning.
2 A fear of mistakes can lead to more mistakes.
3 A mistake can teach you how to avoid a similar mistake in future.
4 A mistake can lead to something new and interesting.

REFLECT

3 Discuss these questions with your class. Do you agree with the REFLECTION POINT?

1 Why are we often afraid of making mistakes? Give different reasons.
2 Why does a fear of making mistakes stop you from learning new things?
3 How could losing your fear of mistakes help you at school?

REFLECTION POINT

Making mistakes is a vital part of the learning process and of the way that new ideas are created. If you're frightened of making mistakes, you'll learn slower and you won't make the best of your abilities.

EXTEND

4 For each of the statements in Exercise 2b, think of a situation that applies to you. Then decide what you can do to turn a mistake into a lesson that you can learn from.

KNOW YOURSELF

Workbook, page 49

SPEAKING What do you reckon?

4

Express and react to opinions

SPEAK

1 **Work in groups. Which city in the world do you think has the most famous buildings and monuments? What are they?**

WATCH OR LISTEN

2 1.44 **Watch or listen to the scenes. Kayla and George are on a school trip. What city are they in? How do you know?**

Kayla: There it is. The world's most famous tower. What do you think of it?
George: If you (1) ________ me, it's overrated.
Kayla: Do you really think so?
George: Yeah, I do. As far as I'm (2) ________ed, the Shard in London's much more impressive.

Kayla: What do you (3) ________ of this?
George: To (4) ________ quite honest, I don't really have an opinion. It's just an arch.
Kayla: I completely (5) ________. Look at the setting – the huge Champs-Elysées avenue leading up to it.
George: I see what you (6) ________, but the arch itself is pretty ordinary.

Kayla: This must be one of the world's best-known art galleries. What do you (7) ________?
George: It's ... big! But if you (8) ________ my opinion, it's too serious. Modern architecture's more fun.
Kayla: I'm not sure I (9) ________. The way I (10) ________ it, these old buildings will *always* be beautiful.
George: I think that's true up to a point, but if you've seen one palace, you've seen them all.
Kayla: Well, let's go in and see if we agree about the paintings!

3 1.44 **Complete the conversation with the words below. Then watch or listen again to check.**

agree ask be concern disagree
make mean reckon see want

4 a **Which phrase(s) in the conversations do the speakers use to ...**
ask for an opinion? express strong disagreement?
give an opinion? disagree but recognise the other opinion?

b 1.45 **Look at the PHRASEBOOK to check your answers. Then listen and repeat some of the phrases, paying attention to intonation.**

ACT

5 **Work in pairs. Do the tasks.**

- Choose another city with some famous sights that's not in your country.
- You're visiting the city. Prepare two or three conversations like the ones in Exercise 2. Don't mention the name of the sights you discuss.
- Present your conversations to other students. Can they guess where you are?

PHRASEBOOK 1.46

Ask for an opinion
What do you think/make of it?
What do you reckon?

Give an opinion
If you ask me, ...
As far as I'm concerned, ...
To be quite honest, ...
If you want my opinion, ...
The way I see it, ...

Express strong disagreement
I completely/totally agree/disagree.

Disagree but recognise the other opinion
Do you really think so?
I see what you mean, but ...
I'm not sure I agree.
I think that's true up to a point, but ...

Workbook, page 47

WRITING My trip advice

>>> Contrast ideas

SPEAK AND READ

1 **Work in pairs. What do you know about the monument in the photo below? Make notes.**

2 **Read the review. Check your notes from Exercise 1.**

TEENshare

HOME | TRAVEL | MONEY

Travel > Tips for great days out!

This summer I visited the prehistoric monument Stonehenge. It's located in the south of England and it's made up of two circles of stones, one inside the other. Some of them form giant arches. It's thought that the first stones were erected in about 2500 BC.

The visit was an unforgettable experience, in spite of the awful weather. I was surprised how close it is to a main road. You don't notice the traffic when you're near the stones, however. The guided tour was really informative. Despite being such a famous monument, experts are still not sure whether it was a temple, a calendar or something else. And while they know where the stones came from, they're unsure of exactly how they were transported there. The visit would have been better if we'd had the freedom to walk among the stones. Nevertheless, you could still feel their power despite the fact that there was a barrier around them.

I strongly recommend visiting Stonehenge. Even though you'll have seen it hundreds of times in photos, standing right by the stones is an awe-inspiring experience.

Get it right

despite, in spite of

~~*despite of*~~

STUDY

3 **Read the review again and do the tasks.**

1. Describe the main aim or aims of each paragraph.
2. Underline all the adjectives. Which ones express a personal opinion?

4 a **Read the tips in the HOW TO box.**

HOW TO

contrast ideas

- Linking word + **subject** + **verb**
  - *Although, though, even though* (strong contrast)
    Position: start or middle; *Though* can go at the end
  - *While/Whereas* (contrasts two things)
    Position: start or middle
  - *However/Nevertheless* (in a second sentence)
    Position: start, middle or end
- *In spite of/Despite* + **noun/pronoun/gerund**
  Position: start or middle
- *In spite of/Despite* + ***the fact that*** + **subject** + **verb**

b **Underline examples of different linking words in the review.**

PRACTISE

5 **Complete the sentences with words from the HOW TO box.**

1. The visitor centre was untidy and expensive, ________ the guided tour was really well organised.
2. ________ having to queue for over an hour, the wait was well worth it.
3. We spent hours walking around the monument ________ it was raining.
4. Most people took photos inside the building ________ of the ban on using cameras.
5. There were too many other tourists. ________, I still enjoyed the visit.
6. We'd definitely go there again despite ________ it's over three hours away by car.

PLAN, WRITE AND CHECK

6 **You're going to write a review of a place that you've visited. Use the review above to help you plan and organise your ideas.**

7 **Write your review. Use linking words from the HOW TO box to help you contrast ideas. Then check it.**

SHARE AND REVIEW

8 **Swap your review with a partner. Read your partner's review and review it.**

Workbook, pages 48–49

VOCABULARY Buildings and architecture

1 Match the words to the pictures.

Choose your building and features

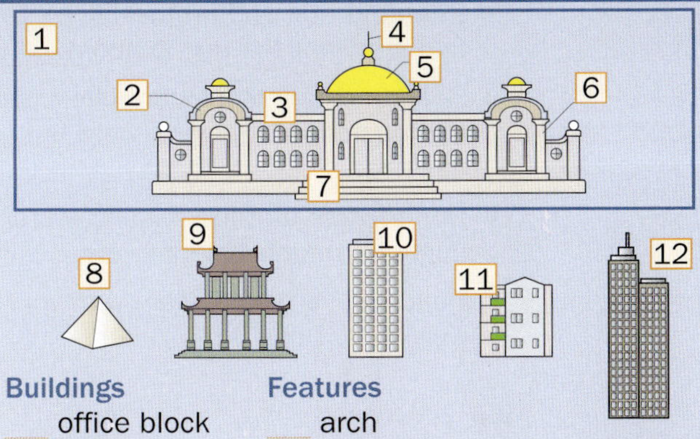

Buildings

___ office block
___ palace
___ pyramid
___ skyscraper
___ temple
___ tower block

Features

___ arch
___ column
___ dome
___ façade
___ spire
___ steps

___ /12

Abstract nouns

2 Complete the abstract nouns.

The Happy Architecture Company (HAC)

OUR MISSION STATEMENT

At HAC we believe architecture, if created with a sense of (1) hu___r, has the (2) p___r to make people happy. Architecture should never produce a feeling of (3) sa___s. That's why (4) ho___y and (5) fr___p are a vital part of all our contact with clients. They ensure our clients have no (6) f___r of making mistakes and avoid any feelings of (7) di___t or (8) r___t when a project's completed. For HAC, (9) f___e is not the aim. A famous building for an unhappy client would only be a result of our (10) fa___e to listen to their needs. At the same time, we're a young team, so we do ask for the creative (11) fr___m that (12) y___h requires to come up with original ideas.

HAC

___ /12

GRAMMAR Conditionals

3 Choose the correct options.

Ian: How's the school coming along?
Suki: Fine, but the principal was very busy when we met. If (1) *we* / *we'd* talked longer, I'd (2) *leave* / *have left* with a better idea of what he really wanted. But (3) *as long as* / *unless* there's plenty of light, the students will be happy.
Ian: (4) *I'd feel* / *I felt* happier if (5) *we knew* / *we'd known* more. I don't want him to be disappointed.
Suki: We sent the plans a month ago. I'm sure he'd (6) *call* / *have called* by now if he (7) *wasn't* / *hadn't been* satisfied with the building work.
Ian: Let's hope so. There'll be a lot more work in Littletown (8) *unless* / *providing* we do a good job.

___ /16

Wishes and regrets: *I wish/If only*

4 Write the verbs in the correct form – the past, past perfect or *would*.

Dear Sir or Madam,

As Principal of Littletown School, I'm writing to complain about the new building your company designed. To be quite honest, we wish we (1) ___ (can rebuild) it. If only you (2) ___ (tell) us it would be so expensive to heat in winter, with all that glass. What's more, your brochure spoke about how happy the building would make everybody. If only that (3) ___ (be) true. The school looks great, but all the technology keeps going wrong. In short, we wish we (4) ___ (not ask) your company to design it.

Yours faithfully,

Dan Martinez

PS I wish you (5) ___ (come) and fix the problems. The lights won't even come on in some of the classrooms.

___ /10

Your score: ___ /50

SKILLS CHECK

✓✓✓ Yes, I can. No problem!
✓✓ Yes, I can. But I need a bit of help.
✓ Yes, I can. But I need a lot of help.

I can understand opinions when I read. ___
I can recognise imaginary situations when I listen. ___
I can learn from my mistakes. ___
I can express and react to opinions. ___
I can contrast ideas when I write. ___

Workbook, pages 50–51

READ AND COMPLETE

1 Read the letter in a newspaper. Use the word in brackets to form a word that fits in each gap.

A Message to You

Dear teenage reader,

My name's Eduard, and I'm a politician. Yes, I know what you're thinking. 'Why should I read this?' After all, politicians rarely become famous for their (1) ______________ (HONEST), and all too often we're in the news for negative reasons. (2) ______________ (FORTUNE) power will always corrupt some people. Nevertheless, I believe that you'll regret it if you turn your back on politics. Politicians make decisions that affect all our lives and I'm (3) ______________ (PRIDE) of the work we do to try to create a better, fairer society. We might have been (4) ______________ (SUCCESS) in your eyes, but don't let our failure stop you from trying. If you join us, you'll have the chance to fix what we've done wrong. Politics desperately needs the new ideas that (5) ______________ (YOUNG) brings with it. Get involved and start shaping the future.

Eduard Bielsa

EXAM TIPS

do a word formation exercise

- Read the title and first few lines to find out what the text is about.
- Read each sentence carefully and decide what type of word is missing.
- Don't forget that the missing word might be negative, plural, etc.
- Read the sentence again with your word in it. Does it make sense?

understand opinions

See page 40.

2 Read the description of a talk below and think of the word which best fits each gap. Use only one word.

ACTIVE MINDS SEMINARS

In this week's talk, Dr Anya Polina will discuss Norwegian adventurer Thor Heyerdahl. Heyerdahl became a household name in 1970 when, (1) ______________ the challenges involved, he successfully led a 4,000 mile voyage across the Atlantic. He made the journey on a boat based on ancient Egyptian drawings.

Heyerdahl believed that people didn't (2) ______________ up with new ideas independently, but that travellers were responsible (3) ______________ taking new ideas round the world. So, the pyramids of Egypt are similar to those in South America because they were built by the same people. However, Heyerdahl (4) ______________ aware of a serious problem with this theory. How could one group of people build temples on opposite sides of the Atlantic when they had no way of crossing the ocean? Heyerdahl knew that as long (5) ______________ he could prove that crossing the ocean was possible, his beliefs would be taken seriously.
Come to the seminar to hear more about Heyerdahl.

EXAM TIPS

complete a gapped text

- Quickly read the text. What's it about? Where would you expect to see it?
- Read the text again and look at the words before and after each gap.
- Use only one word in each gap. Typical words include articles, prepositions, pronouns, verbs and linking words.
- Make sure you use the correct form for verbs and always check your spelling.

assess a text

See page 30.

LISTEN

3 2.01 **You will hear five short extracts in which teenagers talk about their future career plans. Choose what each person says from the list (A–H). There are three extra letters which you do not need to use.**

Speaker 1 ……
Speaker 2 ……
Speaker 3 ……
Speaker 4 ……
Speaker 5 ……

A thinks studying will open up a number of possible career options
B wants to be an entrepreneur
C doesn't want to do the same job for a long time
D wants to turn a life-long interest into a career
E is confident about fulfilling a dream
F has had several different plans for the future
G doesn't have any career plans at all
H deeply regrets making the wrong decision as a young child

Listening: ______ /10

WRITE

4 You responded to the advert below and have been chosen to take part providing your school gives you permission. Write an email to your school principal (140–190 words) asking for permission. Explain how you would benefit from the experience despite missing school for weeks.

A UNIQUE OPPORTUNITY

As part of a new TV series, we are looking for teenagers from different countries to build a wooden cabin in arctic Norway and live together there for two winter months. How would you cope with the cold dark days, living far from home and communicating only in English? Write and tell us why you want to be a participant.

Writing: ______ / 10

Progress check score ______ /30

EXAM TIPS

do a multiple-matching exercise

- Read the task and all the options carefully.
- Concentrate on the general message when you listen the first time.
- When matching options to speakers, remember that:
  - speakers rarely use exactly the same words as in the options.
  - there are options that don't match to any speaker.
  - you will listen again, so make notes the first time if you're unsure of any answers.
- Check or complete your answers when you listen again.

understand referring words
See page 32.

recognise imaginary situations
See page 42.

EXAM TIPS

write an email

- Read the task. Who are you writing to? Is it a formal or informal email?
- Read the task again. Underline any questions, requests or instructions.
- Decide how to react to any news or information in the task.
- Plan your email before you write:
  - Decide how many paragraphs to use.
  - Make sure your email covers all the points in the task.
  - Check your work. Is it the right length?

write a formal letter or email
See page 36.

contrast ideas
See page 46.

UNIT 5

CURIOUSER AND CURIOUSER

a

IN THE PICTURE Start a collection

>>> Talk about unusual collections

MarBLeKeypuppetstampTOyanimal
TicketautograPhComicbooKmUsiccDShEll

RECALL AND READ

1 Work in pairs. Name the types of collection in the photos. Use the 'word collection' above to help you. Then order the collections from the least unusual (1) to the most unusual (10).

a .... f ....
b .... g ....
c .... h ....
d .... i ....
e .... j ....

2 a Look at four things you should consider when starting a collection. What do you think they refer to?

affordability   origin   quirkiness   storage

b Read the magazine tips to check or find the answers.

HOW TO START A
COLLECTION

The more unusual and quirky your collection is, the more interesting it'll be. One option is to collect something out of the ordinary. How about a collection of paperclips, airsickness bags from different airlines or crisp packets?

If you'd rather collect something slightly more mundane, then find a theme for your collection. The more offbeat your idea is, the more remarkable the collection will be. If, for example, you want to collect toy animals, choose one type of animal. If stamps are your passion, choose a topic you're interested in and collect stamps connected to it.

Another thing to take into consideration is where you're going to store your collection. Don't collect large objects if you don't have the space. Try to keep your collection in a case that's easy to transport so that you'll be able to display your collection at school or a local fair.

If you eventually want to sell your collection, keep a written record of the items and where they came from. You may own a famous person's autograph, but how can you prove it's genuine and not a fake?

Finally, don't buy pieces for your collection if you can't afford them and don't try to complete it too quickly. An exceptional collection will take years to complete.

WORK WITH WORDS

3 2.02 Listen to six people talking about their collections. Match each person to one of the photos. Then listen again and check.

1 Josep ...... 4 Yolanda ......
2 Ayla ...... 5 Ahmed ......
3 Toni ...... 6 Lucy ......

4 2.03 Write the words in the correct column, *Unusual* or *Not unusual*. Then listen and check.

~~alternative~~ exceptional extraordinary mundane nondescript offbeat ordinary out of the ordinary predictable remarkable unpredictable weird

Unusual	Not unusual
alternative	

5 2.04 Replace each pair of words with one of the words from Exercise 4. Then listen and check.

1 Josep: Some of my friends think I'm a bit strange and unusual. To an outsider it must seem a really normal and unexciting thing to collect.
2 Ayla: Famous people can be surprising and changeable. This one's my favourite. It's a bit of an unconventional and non-traditional signature.
3 Toni: The more unusual and unconventional the story and characters the better.
4 Yolanda: I thought they were very unusual and surprising. I think the detail on the faces and clothes is surprising and impressive.
5 Ahmed: I know it's a bit normal and not special. There are some extremely good and unusually impressive examples from different countries. I think emails are boring and always the same.
6 Lucy: One day I thought the collection looked a bit ordinary and uninteresting so I bought the case to make it look a bit more unusual and different.

6 a ▶2.05 **PRONOUNCE** **Underline examples of two or more consonants together in the words in Exercise 4. Then listen and repeat the words. If the two consonants are hard to pronounce, try saying the word very slowly.**

b ▶2.06 **Listen and repeat other words with three consonants together. Again, say the words slowly at first if they're hard to pronounce.**

strange scream spring explain example expands arrests twelfth

7 THE MOVING PICTURE ▶ **Watch Christopher and Deb talking about their collections. Which adjectives from Exercise 4 would you use to describe them?**

EXTEND

8 a Replace the adjectives in purple with the words in the box. Use a dictionary to help you.

commonplace	odd	off-the-wall	run-of-the-mill

At first glance I thought the collection was very (1) **ordinary** but when I looked closer I found a couple of (2) **strange** items created by a(n) (3) **offbeat** graffiti glass artist. Suddenly the collection didn't seem so (4) **predictable**.

b Match the description to one of the collections in Exercise 1.

GO BEYOND

Do the Words & Beyond exercises on page 134.

SPEAK

9 Work in pairs. Discuss the different collections in the photos and agree on which one you would both like to own. Give reasons for your choice.

Workbook, page 52

READING Be a museum curator

>>> Understand the writer's purpose

SPEAK AND READ

1 Work in pairs. Explain the differences between the four types of printed material.

brochure catalogue leaflet manual

2 a Read the tips in the HOW TO box.

b 2.07 Read the text. Which type of printed material from Exercise 1 is it from? How much can you remember?

HOW TO

understand the writer's purpose

- ☐ Identify the text type. Think about its typical purpose: to inform, give instructions, sell something, etc.
- ☐ As you read, consider the purpose of individual sections/paragraphs. Ask yourself:
  - Do my circumstances (age, location, occupation ...) make me a target reader?
  - Is the writer presenting facts or opinions (see page 40)? Do I need to double-check facts?
  - Do I need to take action (follow advice, make a decision, get in contact ...)?
  - Is the writer persuading me to do something? If so, should I do it?

ARE YOU 14–18 YEARS OLD?

Are you interested in the natural world, world cultures, art and design, science and technology or history? Do you enjoy working in a team? Do you want to develop your organisational skills and gain hands-on experience of how a museum is run?

If your answer is 'yes', read about this exceptional opportunity to do something different. If your answer is 'no', read on anyway to find out what you'll be missing!

The City Museum is launching its third Young Curators Programme and we'd like *you* to be part of it. As a Young Curator, you'll come up with the concept for a new museum exhibition, help select the pieces to include in the exhibition and then turn your ideas into reality right here in the City Museum. Sounds exciting, doesn't it? But don't take our word for it; read what previous Young Curators have to say about the programme.

'I used to think that going to museums was the most boring thing ever but the YC programme was a real blast.' ***Marek Jaskulski* (14)**

'I didn't use to enjoy speaking in public before but now I feel much more confident.' ***Stephen Harper* (15)**

'Being teenagers means we have a different view of the world which allows us to create something offbeat and alternative.' ***Francesca Fenoy* (17)**

The theme of last year's exhibition was 'conflict'. The Young Curators selected exhibits related to ideological and personal conflicts. They also looked at how conflict can exist in art with the juxtaposition of images, colour, texture, shape and light. The 'conflict' exhibition, which included live music and a remarkable dance performance, was a great success. We want this year's exhibition to be even better. *You* can help us achieve it!

To take part in the Young Curators Programme, you'll need the consent of a parent or guardian. We suggest passing on this leaflet and making sure they read this message from the museum's director: 'A museum is a safe place where teenagers can push their artistic and intellectual boundaries. The Young Curators Programme is a unique opportunity for teenagers with varied interests to meet and create something out of the ordinary.' *Jill Maynard*

3 a Answer the questions without referring to the text.

1 Are you eligible to take part in the Young Curators Programme?
2 Would you like to take part? Why?/Why not?
3 How does the writer use last year's event to promote this year's programme?
4 What do you need to do next if you're interested in taking part?

b Read the text again. Do you want to change any of your answers?

4 Which tips in the HOW TO box did you use for help with Exercises 2b and 3a? Tick (✓) them.

REACT

5 Work in pairs. Make a list of museums you know in your country or abroad and choose the museum you would both like to curate. Give reasons for your choice.

There's the Science Museum in London.

And the Barça Museum in Barcelona.

GO BEYOND

Write a quirky title for the text that will catch the reader's attention.

Workbook, page 53

GRAMMAR Verbs followed by *-ing* and/or infinitive

Use gerunds and infinitives

READ

1 Read the news story. What does Ronaldo hope to do?

Children often dream about becoming a professional footballer but few of them manage to achieve their dream. Children also love to collect things but how many of them succeed in opening their own museum? Cristiano Ronaldo was eight when he started playing soccer for the amateur Andorinha team on the Portuguese island of Madeira. At the age of 28 he decided to open the CR7 Museum in his home town. At the museum visitors can see the individual and team awards he has won. They can also stop to admire a life-size wax figure of the player in a Portugal shirt. Ronaldo hopes to help the local economy by encouraging tourists to visit Madeira.

STUDY

2 a Look at the tables. Then <u>underline</u> 10 examples in Exercise 1.

Verbs followed by *-ing* or infinitive	
▪ *enjoy, keep, mind, practise* ▪ *admit, deny, suggest* ▪ *succeed in, dream about*	*doing*
▪ *choose, hope, manage* ▪ *ask (me), help (me), want (me)* ▪ *advise me, encourage me, invite me, teach me, tell me, warn me* ▪ *would like/love/hate/prefer (me)*	*to do*
▪ *can, could, should, will, would* ▪ *used to* ▪ *make me, let me*	*do*

Verbs followed by *-ing* and infinitive

verb + *doing*/*to do*: same/similar meaning
▪ *like, love, hate, prefer, begin, continue, start*

verb + *doing*/*to do*: different meaning
▪ *stop, forget, remember, try, mean*
I stopped thinking = I didn't think anymore
I stopped to think = I stopped doing something and started thinking

See GRAMMAR DATABASE, page 124.

b Which of the examples in Exercise 1 can be replaced by the *-ing* form or infinitive with *to* without changing the meaning?

PRACTISE

3 Choose the correct form.

UNUSUAL MUSEUMS

– We advise you not (1) **to wear** / **wearing** your best clothes when you visit the Trash Museum in Connecticut, USA. But if you'd like (2) **to see** / **seeing** the amount of garbage we create in a year, it's the place for you.
– If you travel to India, we suggest (3) **to visit** / **visiting** the Museum of Toilets in New Delhi. At the museum you can (4) **to learn** / **learn** about the history of the WC.
– Stop (5) **to think** / **thinking** that all art needs to be good. Enjoy (6) **to look** / **looking** at some terrible paintings at the Museum of Bad Art in Massachusetts, USA.

4 ▶2.08 Write the correct object pronoun. If you don't need a pronoun, leave the space blank. Then listen and check.

Pete: Dad? Can you help (1) .... with my homework?
Dad: I'll try. What would you like (2) .... to do?
Pete: Our English teacher asked (3) .... all to read about some unusual museums and choose the most unusual. I've chosen one but I'd like (4) .... to pick one too.
Dad: OK. Let (5) .... have a look. Which do you suggest (6) .... reading first?

5 Write questions.

1 in general, / you / enjoy / go / to museums?
2 normally, which type of museum / you / prefer / go / to?
3 if you could visit any museum in the world, which museum / you / like / visit / most?
4 in your opinion, should / your school / organise / more visits to museums?
5 can / you / remember / go / to an unusual museum in the past? If so, where and when?
6 if someone / ask / you / open / your own museum, / what / objects / you / show / there?

SPEAK AND WRITE

6 Work in pairs. Ask and answer the questions in Exercise 5. Then write a short description of your own museum for a tourist brochure. Use some of the verbs in Exercise 2.

Workbook, pages 54–55

>>> Deal with new vocabulary when you listen

SPEAK AND LISTEN

1 Work in pairs. Describe the pictures. What do they have in common?

a

b

c

d

2 a Read the tips in the HOW TO box.

b 2.09 Listen to a radio feature called 'Journey into blue'. Order the photos in Exercise 1.

1 ____ 2 ____ 3 ____ 4 ____

3 a Before you listen again, choose the best answer (A or B).

1 People today have a ____ positive attitude to blue than the ancient Greeks.
A less B more
2 There are no blues in prehistoric art because ...
A a blue pigment didn't exist.
B red, black and brown were more popular.
3 During the rise of the Roman Empire, blue was worn by ...
A dead people. B poor people.
4 Thanks to King Louis IX of France, ...
A we use the term 'blue moon'. B attitudes to blue changed.
5 'To have the blues' means ...
A to feel sad or depressed.
B to sing or play a certain type of music.
6 The speaker uses the term 'blue marble' to describe ...
A the meaning of the word 'cool'. B the Earth as seen from space.

b 2.09 Listen again to check or complete your answers.

4 Which tips in the HOW TO box did you use for help with Exercises 2b and 3? Tick (✓) them.

HOW TO

deal with new vocabulary when you listen

- ☐ Predict the topic and context. Read the task and questions carefully and look at any pictures.
- ☐ Use your general understanding of the topic to help you predict what might be said.
- ☐ Keep your attention on understanding the main ideas. They provide the context to help you guess what new words mean.
- ☐ Note *how* people speak. Are they angry? Excited? Predict what they might want to say.
- ☐ If listening twice, make a note of things to listen for the second time.

REACT

5 Work in pairs. What adjectives would you use to describe 'Journey into blue'? What information was new to you?

WORK WITH WORDS

6 a Add the verbs to the table.

decline grow lead to rise shrink transform

Go up ⬆	Go down ⬇	Change
increase	*decrease*	*result in*
____	*fall*	*turn into*
____	____	____
	____	____

b 2.10 Listen and check. Then listen and repeat.

GO BEYOND

Do the Words & Beyond exercise on page 134.

7 2.11 Complete the extracts from 'Journey into blue' using 10 of the verbs from Exercise 6. Then listen and check.

1 You can't ____ your cave with blue walls ...
2 Go back in time and your colour options ____ ...
3 While the Roman Empire was ____ ...
4 ... later blue started to ____ in popularity ...
5 This ____ the colour becoming increasingly ...
6 ... changing fashions would ____ us all wearing ...
7 Blue ____ popular with painters too.
8 ... we 'feel blue' when we ____ into sadness ...
9 I want you to ____ astronauts ...
10 Look back and watch the Earth ____ in size ...

8 Work in pairs. Write six sentences describing changes that have happened over the past 12 months in your town, your country or the rest of the world. Use the verbs in Exercise 6.

Workbook, pages 56–57

GRAMMAR Comparisons

»» Compare people, things and actions

READ AND LISTEN

1 2.12 Read and listen to the conversation. What colour did boys and girls wear before blue and pink?

Ben: Why's pink much more popular with girls and blue more closely associated with boys?
Zoe: Because pink's a more feminine colour?
Ben: Yes, but *why*? I heard that at the beginning of the 20th century, baby boys wore pink because people didn't think blue was as strong as pink. Blue was seen as a far prettier colour and worn by girls. It wasn't until the 1980s that companies started producing more and more pink products for girls.
Zoe: Why?
Ben: Well, if you keep making more things specifically for one sex, there's less chance that parents will use them again with younger brothers or sisters.
Zoe: And the more things that we see in 'our' colour, the stronger the association becomes. So what were the most popular colours before babies wore pink and blue?
Ben: They all wore white.

STUDY

2 Read the explanations. Then find examples of the types of comparison in Exercise 1.

Comparison
Comparatives, superlatives, (*not*) *as … as …*
Use: With adjectives and adverbs to compare things. *Blue was seen as a **prettier** colour than pink.* *What were **the most popular** colours for babies?* *People didn't think blue was **as strong as** pink.*
Comparing nouns
Use: To compare the quantity or number of things.
Form: *more/less/fewer* + noun *Toys are available in **fewer colours** these days.*
Intensifiers
Use: To make a contrast stronger (*a lot*, *far*, *much*) or weaker (*a bit*, *a little*, *slightly*). *It's a lot more difficult to find toys that aren't pink.*
Repeated comparatives
Use (1): For things that are changing.
Form: comparative + *and* + comparative *more and more difficult …*
Use (2): To show how one action affects another.
Form: *the* + comparative … *the* + comparative *The sooner attitudes change, the more options parents will have.*
See GRAMMAR DATABASE, page 124.

»» Workbook, page 58

PRACTISE

3 Write the comparative or superlative forms.

1 According to recent research, women see some colours such as blues, greens and yellows .... (vividly) than men.
2 For example, grass is usually .... (green) for a woman than a man.
3 However, ... (warm) colours such as red appear .... (strong) to men.
4 The colour red provokes .... (more) reactions in both sexes.
5 Women are .... (good) than men at describing colours.
6 However, women .... (not good) as men at seeing detail from a distance.
7 In our household, the pet dogs and cats have .... (bad) colour vision of all.

4 Choose the correct intensifier to make the colour facts true.

1 Red is *much more* / *a lot less* popular for company branding than most other colours.
2 Blue appears on *far fewer* / *many more* flags than purple.
3 There are said to be *a lot more* / *slightly fewer* shades of green than other colours.
4 Apparently, if you see the colour red on an exam paper, you'll do *a bit worse* / *a lot better* .
5 They say a silver-coloured car is *a bit safer* / *slightly more dangerous* than other cars.

5 Complete Sofia's talk with repeated comparatives. Do you agree with her?

It's getting (1) .... (difficult) to buy clothes. New fashions appear (2) .... (fast) each year. (3) .... (wide) the choice, ... (hard) it is to decide what to wear. I think (4) .... (long) a fashion lasts, the .... (good) it is because we spend (5) .... (little) money.

WRITE AND SPEAK

6 a Complete the sentences with words from both boxes. Then write two more sentences.

a little	a lot	far	slightly

fewer	less	more

1 Fashion today is .... exciting than in the past.
2 There are .... things for young people to do these days.
3 ....
4 ....

b Work in pairs. Read your sentences to your partner. Do they agree with you? Discuss your answers.

>>> Understand how adverts try to sell to you

SPEAK AND READ

1 a Work in pairs. Look at the ad and answer the questions.

1 Who's the ad for? What's it selling?
2 What makes it a typical ad for this type of product?
3 Why do ads like these target teens?

b Work in pairs. Student A: read the article on page 141. Tick (✓) the things you mentioned in Exercise 1a. Student B: read the article on page 142. Tick (✓) the things you mentioned in Exercise 1a. Tell your partner about what you read in the article.

DO

2 Work in pairs. Complete the tasks.

1 Look at the ad at the top of the page. Which of the methods in the articles does it use?
2 The ad claims you can personalise the product. Do you think the claim is true? Why?/Why not?

3 Answer the questions. Then compare your answers with your partner.

In the past 12 months, have you ...
1 bought a product because of the advertising campaign?
2 bought a product because a friend owns it?
3 'liked' or 'followed' a brand or product on social media?
4 worn or carried something that has a brand name or logo on it?

REFLECT

4 Discuss these questions with your class. Do you agree with the REFLECTION POINT?

1 How much influence do you think big brands and advertising companies have over what you buy?
2 What should you think about when you hear about a new product?
3 Why should you be careful of advertising you see on social networking sites?

EXTEND

5 Work in groups. Find a magazine and look at the ads. What techniques do the advertisers use in the different ads? Which of the ads do you think are most effective?

REFLECTION POINT

We are all influenced by advertising so it's important to identify the methods used to sell you a product. Be careful how much data you give to a brand or advertiser. The more a company knows about you, the more it will target you with advertising.

Workbook, page 61

SPEAKING Wait a second

>>> Interact with other people in a conversation

SPEAK

1 **Work in pairs. Look at the photos. What are Al, Eva and Liam doing? How do they feel?**

WATCH OR LISTEN

2 2.13 **Watch or listen to the scene. What do you think Al really wants to say to Eva? What does Liam want to tell Al?**

Al: Hi Eva.
Eva: Hello Al.
Al: Is this a good time?
Eva: Actually, I was just …
Al: (1) __________ I've got another call.
…
Al: Hello? Liam?
Liam: Hi Al. I need to talk to you about …
Al: Just a minute. I'm talking to Eva.
…
Al: Sorry, Eva. (2) __________
Eva: I was just saying that …
Al: Oh. (3) __________ , I've got a new phone. It's …
Eva: I'm sorry but I can't speak now, Al. I'm …
Al: Hold on. I'll be quick. (4) __________ I was wondering if you'd like to … see my new phone.
Eva: Oh. That reminds me, I have to call Liam. Bye, Al.
…
Al: Liam? Are you still there?
Liam: Yes. (5) __________ , I need to talk to you about Eva.
Al: Yes, but … Eva?
Liam: I know you like her, Al but … Wait a second. I've got another call.

Al

Eva

Liam

3 **Write the phrases in the conversation.**

a As I was saying
b By the way
c Hang on.
d So …
e What were you saying?

4 2.13 **Watch or listen again. Check your answers to Exercise 3. Are the phrases used for interrupting, changing the topic or returning to a topic?**

5 a **Find more examples of interrupting, changing the topic and returning to a topic. Add the missing examples to the PHRASEBOOK.**

b 2.14 **Listen and repeat the expressions in the PHRASEBOOK, paying attention to intonation.**

ACT

6 **Work in pairs. Write a short phone conversation between two friends. Use examples of interrupting, changing the topic and returning to a topic. Then act the conversations.**

PHRASEBOOK 2.15

Interrupt
Actually, …
Hang on.
Just a minute.
I'm sorry but …
Yes, but …
Wait a second.
____

Change topic
By the way, …
____

Return to a topic
What were you saying?
As I was saying, …
So …
____

>>> Workbook, page 59

WRITING Something different

Write an article

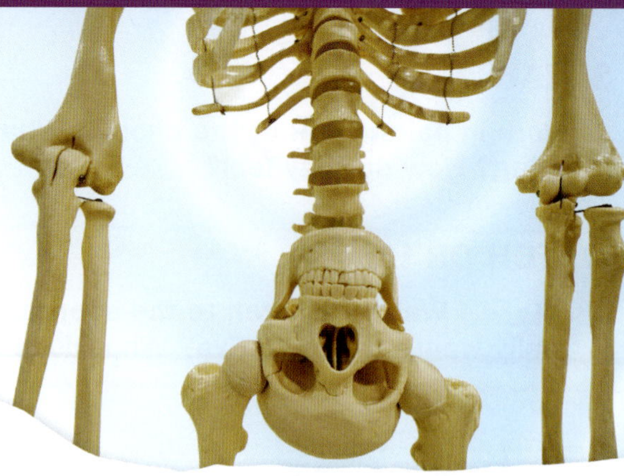

SPEAK AND READ

1 **Work in pairs. Make a list of a person, a place, an event and a thing that you consider to be unique in the world.**

2 **Read the article. Who or what is Wellcome?**

Do you enjoy being surprised?
Are you interested in things that are out of the ordinary?

Then come with me and explore the Wellcome Collection.
The Wellcome Collection is a 'destination for the incurably curious'. Located in London, it includes a collection of books, paintings and objects related to medicine, life and art in the past, present and future.
The man behind the collection was Sir Henry Solomon Wellcome, a pharmacist, entrepreneur, philanthropist and collector. Born in the American Wild West, he co-founded a multinational pharmaceutical company that used modern advertising techniques to promote its brands.
Wellcome was also a great traveller and had collected around 1.5 million items by the time he died in 1936. He was always fascinated by how our bodies work and his collection reflects this.
If you're interested in life and living, then I'd encourage you to visit the collection. But be warned – it can shock as well as entertain and educate. Above all, it's totally unique.

STUDY

3 **Read the article again and order the writer's aims.**

- ...... Give basic information about the topic.
- ...... Link the background information to the topic.
- ...... Give a personal opinion.
- ...... Invite the reader to read more.
- ...... Ask the reader some questions.
- ...... Provide related background information.

4 **a** **Read the tips in the HOW TO box.**

HOW TO
write an article

- Give your article an interesting title that will make people curious to read the article.
- Start with a short introduction.
  Include questions if appropriate. Encourage the reader to continue.
- Use two or three paragraphs to develop the topic.
  Include any background information the reader needs.
- Conclude with a personal opinion or comment.

b **Work in pairs. Discuss the possible titles for the article in Exercise 2. Choose the best title, giving reasons for your choice.**

1 See the world from a different perspective
2 Wellcome to your world
3 A unique collector

PRACTISE

5 **a** **Read the topics for three magazine articles. Write a title for each one.**

1 Teenagers today can't concentrate for long periods of time because they are constantly distracted by digital devices.
2 Young people don't always realise the dangers of clicking on banner ads and pop-up windows on internet sites.
3 Teens are encouraged to follow fashions and look the same as other teens instead of being encouraged to create their own look and be unique.

b **Choose one of the topics and write a short introduction for the article.**

PLAN, WRITE AND CHECK

6 **You're going to write an article for a teen magazine about a person, a place, an event or a thing that you consider to be different and unique in the world. Use your answers to Exercise 1 to help you choose the topic.**

7 **Write your article. Use the tips from the HOW TO box to help you plan the different sections. Then check it.**

SHARE AND REVIEW

8 **Swap your article with a partner. Read your partner's article and review it.**

Workbook, pages 60–61

VOCABULARY Usual and unusual adjectives

1 Write the first or last three letters.

AMAZING NEWS

For all the news that's

1 _ _ _ ernative
2 _ _ _ eptional
3 _ _ _ raordinary
4 _ _ _ beat
5 _ _ _ of the ordinary
6 _ _ _ arkable
7 _ _ _ redictable
8 _ _ _ rd

You won't find anything

9 mund _ _ _
10 nondescr _ _ _
11 ordin _ _ _
12 predicta _ _ _

___ /12

Verbs to describe change

2 Complete the amazing news headlines with the verbs in the box.

decrease	falls	grow	increases	leads
results	rise	shrinks	transform	turns

TODAY'S TOP STORIES

1 Head teacher .... to the size of a mouse.
2 Girl .... into deep sleep and follows yellow-brick road that .... to Australia.
3 Magician .... assistant into rabbit. Sales of carrots .... to new high.
4 Scotland .... in size and is now bigger than England.
5 Exclusive! Sales of ice creams .... in cold weather.
6 *Amazing News* continues to .... One new reader .... in one extra sale. The editor predicts that this will .... the newspaper world!

___ /10

GRAMMAR Verbs followed by *-ing* and/or infinitive

3 Write the verbs in the correct form.

BREAKING NEWS!

Earlier today we succeeded in (1) .... (talk) to our new reader and asked her what she'd like (2) .... (see) more of in *Amazing News*. She stopped (3) .... (think) for a moment and then suggested (4) .... (include) more international news stories. She encouraged us (5) .... (continue) producing the paper. She added that she wouldn't forget (6) .... (tell) her friends to buy it. Who knows? One day we might manage (7) .... (reach) double figures!

___ /14

Comparisons

4 Choose the correct options.

AMAZING NEWS WANTS TO HEAR FOM YOU!

1 Every day there are *more and more* / *much more* amazing news stories to report.
2 However, it's not *as easy as* / *easier than* it used to be to find original stories.
3 You can help make our lives *more* / *much* easier by sending us your stories.
4 *Stranger and stranger* / *The stranger* the story, the better as far as we're concerned.
5 The *more odd* / *oddest* story we've ever told was one about a talking goldfish.
6 Its use of English was only *a lot* / *slightly* worse than mine!
7 Can you do *better* / *the better* ? We think you can!

The Editor

___ /14

Your score: ___ /50

SKILLS CHECK

✓✓✓ Yes, I can. No problem!
✓✓ Yes, I can. But I need a bit of help.
✓ Yes, I can. But I need a lot of help.

I can understand the writer's purpose when I read. ....
I can deal with new vocabulary when I listen. ....
I can understand how adverts try to sell to me. ....
I can interact with other people in a conversation. ....
I can write an article. ....

Workbook, pages 62–63

6 UNIT THE WAY WE ARE

IN THE PICTURE Detailed descriptions

Use compounds to describe people and things

RECALL AND READ

1 a Work in pairs. Write a compound noun to describe each photo using a word from each box.

acoustic baseball basket bowling chess drawing golf maths tennis

alley ball board cap class course guitar racket teacher

b Discuss possible connections between the compound adjectives and the photos. Give reasons for your answers.

easygoing handmade hard-working long-haired old-fashioned self-confident

2 What do all the people in the photos have in common? Read Martha's message for a clue. Then decide who Martha's writing to.

WORK WITH WORDS

3 a The first word in a compound gives more information about the second one. Work in pairs. Discuss what the compounds in the box might mean.

A maths teacher's a teacher who teaches maths.

If something's awe-inspiring, it inspires awe.

Compound nouns
1 noun + noun: **maths teacher**, ...
2 adjective + noun: **acoustic guitar**, ...
3 verb + *-ing* + noun: **bowling alley**, ...
4 verb & preposition (from a phrasal verb): **play-off**, ..., ...

Compound adjectives
5 noun + verb + *-ing*/*-ed*: **awe-inspiring**, ...
6 adjective + verb + *-ing*: **easygoing**, ...
7 adjective + noun + *ed*: **bad-tempered**, ..., ...
8 adverb + verb + *-ing*/*-ed*: **hard-working**, **well-behaved**, ...

b Add the compounds in blue in the message to the table in Exercise 3a.

WHAT ARE THEY DOING NOW?

MARTHA DENIS, RESEARCH SCIENTIST

Hi! My name's Martha. I was 15 in the photo above. I'm 28 now and I'm a scientist in the field of genetics. I study human DNA to try and understand how our **genetic code** determines the way we are. It's really exciting to be at the **cutting edge** of scientific research. Genetics has been responsible for some of the greatest scientific **breakthroughs** of our time and **gene therapy** is starting to give us **groundbreaking** cures for common diseases.

I chose genetics because I've always been fascinated by what makes us all so different. I used to wonder why I was shy whereas my twin sister was easygoing, even though we had a similar **upbringing**. My job is to investigate questions like this. Right now I'm looking at what makes about 10% of us **left-handed**. Many animals show a preference for using one hand when they have to carry out complex tasks, but no other animal has such a strong bias towards right-handedness. So far, we haven't found a clear genetic cause and it's possible cultural pressures play a role too.

If you like science subjects and are curious and **open-minded**, genetics could be a good career choice. The challenges are **never-ending**, but the thought that your work will bring **far-reaching** benefits for society is really awe-inspiring.

6

4 a **Match the compounds in the message to the definitions.**

1 an important discoveries that come after hard work
2 willing to consider new ideas
3 the most advanced point of current knowledge
4 the arrangement of genes that makes someone develop in a particular way
5 continuing for a very long time
6 the way that parents look after their children and teach them to behave
7 a medical treatment in which genes are used to cure an illness
8 using new methods or achieving new results
9 with a natural tendency to use the left hand
10 affecting a lot of people in an important way

b 2.16 **Listen and check. Then listen and repeat the compounds.**

5 a 2.17 PRONOUNCE **Listen and repeat the words. Circle the voiced sounds.**

1 /t/ cut
/d/ ending
2 /b/ break
/p/ open
3 /k/ code
/g/ ground

b **Work in pairs. Say a word. Can your partner point to it?**

1 tip, dip
2 bad, bat
3 big, pig
4 cub, cup
5 cut, gut
6 dog, dock

6 THE MOVING PICTURE **Watch the video. What do Harrison and Edie say about being left-handed? Make notes.**

EXTEND

7 **Work in pairs. What do you think the adjectives mean? Check in a dictionary.**

absent-minded big-headed short-sighted thick-skinned

SPEAK

8 **Work in pairs. Answer the questions.**

1 What scientific breakthroughs have been in the news recently? What benefits do you think they'll have?
2 To what extent do you think we're born the way we are? How much influence do you think our upbringing has?
3 Would you like to be a research scientist? Why?/Why not?

GO BEYOND

Do the Words & Beyond exercises on page 135.

Workbook, page 64

READING Left and right

»» Recognise the main ideas and supporting details

SPEAK AND READ

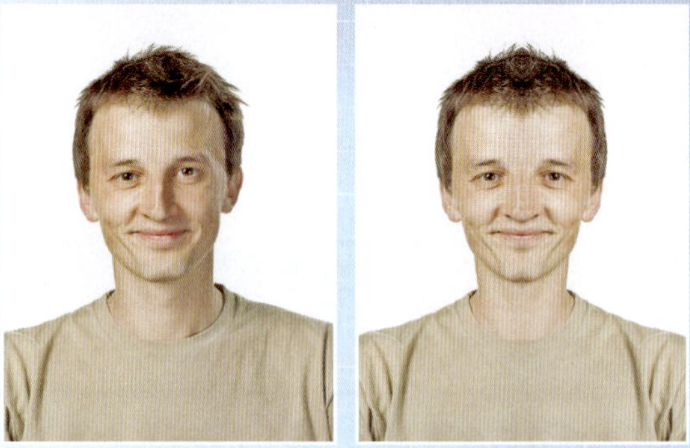

1 Work in pairs. Look at the photos. What's the difference between them?

2 2.18 Do the tasks. Then compare answers with a partner.

- Read the first two paragraphs of the article. Check your answer to Exercise 1.
- Write a short sentence summarising the topic of the article. *It's about the fact that ...*

THE ANIMAL BLUEPRINT

On the outside at least, we are very much symmetrical beings, which means that one side of our body is the mirror image of the other. It's a quality that we share with almost all other animals. Sponges are one of very few living organisms whose bodies are completely asymmetrical.

We are not perfectly symmetrical, however. Look at even the most symmetrical face, for example, and you will find small differences on each side. The photo on the right above, which was created using the mirror image of one half of the face on the left, shows just how strange perfect facial symmetry would look.

Nevertheless, studies across different cultures show that we find symmetrical faces attractive. There are two main theories for this. One suggests that symmetry is an external sign of genetic fitness, which sends us a subconscious message telling us that a person would make a good mother or father for our children. The other theory suggests that our brain simply finds symmetrical faces easier to process.

If we look inside our bodies, it's a different story. There's still a high degree of internal symmetry in our bones, muscles and so on, but we only have one heart, for instance, which needs to be on the left-hand side of the body, and our brain, while it has two very similar hemispheres, assigns different roles to each one. On the inside, we clearly have a left and right side.

It is perhaps surprising, then, that we start life symmetrically. It is only after six weeks of development that asymmetry becomes apparent, when our heart moves to the left and its inner structure begins to develop. What tells these early heart cells that they need to move left is something that scientists are just beginning to understand. In a minority of people (some scientists say 1 in 20,000), the process works in reverse, which means their heart is on the right. This does not pose a threat to their health providing all their other internal organs are on the opposite side too.

The blueprint for animal life, then, is external symmetry combined with a carefully controlled level of internal asymmetry. Both of which suggest that we all share a common ancestor.

3 a Read the tips in the HOW TO box.

b Work in pairs. Read the article and do the tasks.

1. Underline the main idea in each paragraph. This might be a whole sentence or part of one.
2. Match the other sentences in the first two paragraphs to a purpose (1–4) in the HOW TO box. Write the number after each sentence.
3. Find an example of an opinion and a conclusion in the other paragraphs.

4 Which tips in the HOW TO box did you use for help with Exercise 3b? Tick (✓) them.

HOW TO

recognise the main ideas and supporting details

- ☐ Read the title and first paragraph to establish the topic.
- ☐ Look for the main idea in each paragraph, usually in the first, second or last sentence.
- ☐ Other sentences support or develop the main idea. Look for:
  1. facts or images that show why the idea is (or isn't) correct.
  2. examples.
  3. explanations.
  4. more information or details.
  5. opinions.
  6. a conclusion.

REACT

5 Work in pairs. Answer the questions.

1. What do you think 'we' in the last sentence refers to? What's the implication of this sentence?
2. What information in the article was new to you?
3. What fact did you find most surprising? Why?

GO BEYOND

There are two words from six different word families in the article. Can you find them? Look for the noun, verb, adjective or adverb forms of the same word.

»» Workbook, page 65

GRAMMAR Relative clauses

Define and describe things

READ AND LISTEN

1 2.19 **Read and listen to a girl's presentation in class. What do the images show?**

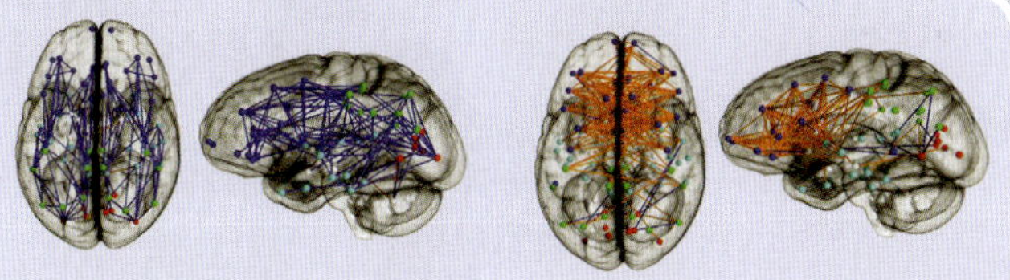

"The images you can see on the board show the connections inside our brain. If you're wondering whose brains they are, the ones on the left are a male brain. There are more connections between the front, where movement's coordinated, and the back, which deals with sight. That suggests a brain that's wired for action and doing one thing at a time. The female brain has more connections between the two sides, which might explain why girls are better at doing two things at the same time than boys, some of whom find multitasking really hard. So the images confirm what we already knew: girls are superior beings!"

STUDY

2 **Read the explanations. Then underline the relative clauses in Exercise 1. Which are non-defining? In which one has the pronoun been left out?**

Relative clauses

Defining relative clauses

Use: To identify people, things and places.

Form:

who/that	people
which/that	things
whose	possession
where	places
when	times
what	'the thing(s) that'
whom	the object of *who*

Note (1): The pronoun's optional if it's the object of the following verb.
Note (2): Use *which* or *whom* after a preposition.

Non-defining relative clauses

Use: To add extra information.

Form:

Don't use *that*.
Use a comma before the relative pronoun.
You can use *all/some*, etc + *of* + *which/whom*.

See GRAMMAR DATABASE, page 125.

Workbook, pages 66–67

PRACTISE

3 **Complete the article with relative pronouns. If the pronoun's optional, leave the space blank.**

Still learning about the brain

For a long time we completely misunderstood (1) _______ the brain does. The ancient Egyptians, for (2) _______ it had little importance, removed the brain from the bodies (3) _______ they mummified. One of the people (4) _______ first started to think seriously about its function was the Greek philosopher Aristotle. He thought the heart, (5) _______ beats faster when you get excited, was the organ in (6) _______ our thoughts and feelings formed and that the brain simply controlled our body temperature.
We live at a time (7) _______ the brain is much less of a mystery. We know the brain is divided into parts, all of (8) _______ have a specific function, and that a quarter of it deals with just one sense: vision. We know it's the organ in our body (9) _______ uses up the most energy, (10) _______ makes our head the hottest part. Around a fifth of all the food (11) _______ we eat is needed to feed the brain. But it's also the organ about (12) _______ we have the most to learn.

4 **a** **Work in pairs. Combine the sentences using relatives clauses. Student A: do the exercise below. Student B: go to page 142.**

THE ALL-BODY QUIZ

1 Christiaan Barnard carried out the first successful transplant of this organ.
He was born in South Africa.
Christiaan Barnard, who was born in ...
Q: WHICH ORGAN?

2 James Watson and Francis Crick discovered the helix structure of this molecule.
Their work won them a Nobel Prize in 1962.
Q: WHICH MOLECULE?

3 These organs filter the blood and remove things.
They are each about the size of your fist.
Your body doesn't need these things.
Q: WHICH ORGANS?

4 REM sleep is a time in your sleep.
During REM sleep your eyes move rapidly.
An important activity happens in REM sleep.
Q: WHAT ACTIVITY?

b **Read your partner your sentences and ask the questions.**

WRITE AND SPEAK

5 **Work in pairs. Write three more sentences and questions for a quiz. Then test another pair.**

>>> Follow a conversation

SPEAK AND LISTEN

1 Work in pairs. To what extent do you think the statements are true? Give reasons for your answers.

1 It's difficult being a teenager.
2 In general, adults don't understand teenagers.

2 2.20 Listen to a radio interview. Who are Talia and Zach? What two things have they done?

3 a Read the tips in the HOW TO box.

b 2.20 Listen to the interview again and answer the questions.

1 What does Talia say about her parents?
2 What does Zach interrupt her to say?
3 How did Talia and Zach start writing together?
4 In what ways has the blog helped parents?
5 What two reasons does Talia give for communication breakdown between teens and parents?
6 What makes the book practical as well as informative?

4 Which tips in the HOW TO box did you use for help with Exercise 3b? Tick (✓) them.

REACT

5 Work in pairs. Discuss your answers to the questions.

1 Would you like to read the blog?
2 Would you like your parents to read the book?

WORK WITH WORDS

6 a Work in pairs. Complete the second sentences with the three-word phrasal verbs in the box.

be up to	check up on	get away with	get through to
get up to	grow out of	live up to	look down on
look up to	stand up for		

1 It's really hard to make them understand you.
It's really hard to ________ them.
2 They'll stop doing it when they get older.
They'll ________ it.
3 They have a very low opinion of the people we admire and respect.
They ________ the people we ________ .
4 They never try to find out what we might be doing.
They never ________ what we might ________ .
5 We often do things we shouldn't and don't get punished.
We often ________ things we shouldn't and ________ it.
6 It's impossible to be as good as their expectations.
It's impossible to ________ their expectations.
7 I wish they'd defend us against criticism.
I wish they'd ________ us.

b 2.21 Listen and check. Then listen and repeat the sentences.

7 Work in pairs. Discuss who would say the sentences in Exercise 6a – a teenager, a parent or both.

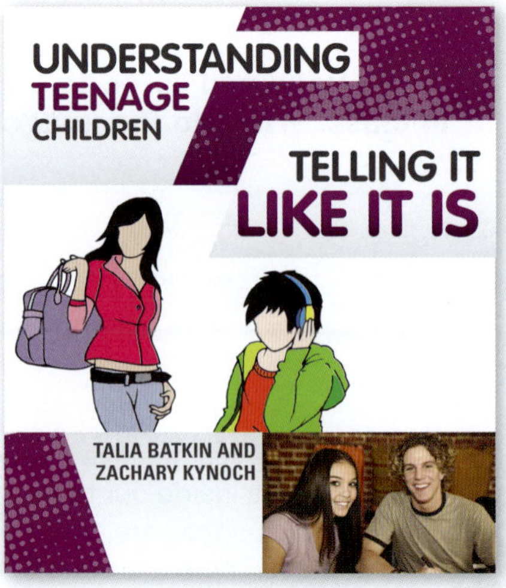

HOW TO
follow a conversation

- ☐ Recognise phrases that give speakers time to think: *well*, *you know*, *kind of*, *um*, etc.
- ☐ Notice turn taking:
  - – Inviting someone to speak with questions and statements you want them to confirm: *So you ...* , *And then you ...*
  - – Interrupting: *Can I just say that ...* , etc.
  - – Returning to a topic: *I was going to say ...* , etc.
- ☐ Listen for why the speaker's saying something:
  - – *Anyway* changes the subject.
  - – *Basically* introduces a summary.
  - – *I mean* introduces a reason or explanation.

GO BEYOND
Do the Words & Beyond exercises on page 135.

Workbook, pages 68–69

GRAMMAR *-ing* and *-ed* clauses

Use clauses that start with *-ing* or *-ed*

READ

1 Read the message. Who wrote it? For whom? What warning and hope does it contain?

blog about contact me

A MESSAGE FOR MUMS AND DADS
If you're reading this blog, you're probably parents having problems with your teenage son or daughter. We think it's good that you've come here. After all, you can only solve a problem by recognising that there is one. But before reading on, remember that this is a blog written by teenagers for teenagers. Being at least 30, you probably have little idea of what we get up to! You might get the odd shock reading this blog, but we hope it helps you understand how we see the world.

STUDY

2 Read the explanations. Then find an example of each use of *-ing* clauses in Exercise 1. Also find two reduced relative clauses.

***-ing* and *-ed* clauses**

***-ing* clauses**

Use: To replace the subject + verb in one clause if a second clause has the same subject.
1 Two actions at the same time:
*I was online **looking** for information.*
*I'd forgotten how I felt **growing** up.*
2 To explain something:
***Not knowing** who to ask for advice, I went online.*
3 After *when*, *while*, *before* and *after*:
***After reading** the blog, I felt really positive.*
4 After *by* to say how to do something:
*You can only solve problems **by talking**.*

***-ing* and *-ed* as relative clauses**

Use: As a reduced form of a relative clause.
-ing clauses have an active meaning:
*The people **writing** the blog are ...* (= who write)
-ed clauses have a passive meaning:
*The advice **given** is really practical.* (= that is given)

See GRAMMAR DATABASE, page 125.

PRACTISE

3 a Make the underlined phrases in the post shorter with *-ing* clauses.

Posted August 12th
Hi! I'm in my room (1) and I'm doing homework. Or rather, I'm staring at the screen (2) and I'm trying to concentrate, but I keep thinking about my online friend. We met (3) when we were chatting online, and (4) because we had a lot in common, we got on really well. Now she wants to meet me. But I'm sitting here (5) and I'm wondering if that's wise. Share

b Make the underlined phrases shorter with *-ing* and *-ed* relative clauses.

It all started with a message (1) that was sent to my page by someone (2) who claimed that we'd met before. It was from the girl (3) who was living in my house before us and she sent me a photo of her (4) that was taken in our garden to prove it. I'm really shy, (5) which means I find it easier to talk online. Will we get on face to face?
comments (2)

4 a Complete the responses to the post in Exercise 3 with *while*, *before*, *after* and *by*.

A Have you talked to your parents? I'd only make a decision (1) ______ talking to them.
B Has anything come up (2) ______ chatting to her that's made you feel suspicious?
C You can check up on her story (3) ______ asking your neighbours. Do they remember her?
D Why don't you suggest talking on the phone (4) ______ meeting? And you can avoid problems (5) ______ speaking to her when you're with your parents or a friend.

b Work in pairs. Which response do you think gives the best advice?

5 Complete the posts with the *-ing* or *-ed* form of the verbs in the box.

argue be call do look make mean post read save

1 I always chat online while ______ my homework, ______ my parents really angry. I tell them I can do both, but just can't get though to them!

2 I didn't get up to much this weekend. I was at home ______ with my brother. He can annoy me just by ______ at me! Is that normal?

3 A friend lent me a presentation ______ on a pen drive. ______ her only copy, she told me to be really careful, but I accidentally reformatted the pen drive, ______ the presentation's gone. Any advice?

4 There's a group of students at school ______ me names. And when I got home today there were some really horrible comments ______ on my page. I felt really upset after ______ them. What's the best way to stand up for yourself in these situations?

SPEAK

6 Work in pairs. Discuss the posts in Exercise 5. What's the best advice for each person?

Workbook, page 70

LANGUAGE & BEYOND

See things from another person's perspective

SPEAK AND READ

1 **Work in pairs. Describe what you can see in the picture.**

2 **Work in pairs. For each thing that Mark and Maria say, make notes on how other people will react. Then compare notes with other students and discuss any differences.**

PUT YOURSELF IN THEIR SHOES

Before you argue with someone, always try and see things from their perspective.

1 ....

Let the other person speak. Then think. What are they really saying? Always question your first reaction.

2 ....

Listen. Look. How does the other person feel? Those feelings are real, so try to understand them.

3 ....

Try and really *see* how the other person sees things. What would *you* do in their position?

4 ....

When people disagree, both ways of seeing things are usually valid. Try to reach agreements that reflect this.

DO

3 **Match the headings to the tips for seeing things from another person's perspective.**

Be ready to compromise | Use your imagination | Don't speak too soon | Respect emotions

4 **Work in groups.**

- For each comment in the picture, try and see things from the perspective of the other people. Use the tips in Exercise 3 to help you.
- Decide what the best possible reaction to each comment should be.

REFLECT

5 **Discuss these questions with your class. Do you agree with the REFLECTION POINT?**

1 Did you make similar predictions about people's reactions in Exercise 2? Why?/Why not?
2 Did you see things differently in Exercise 4 after reading the four tips? Discuss how your perceptions changed.
3 Why is it so important to always try and see things from another person's perspective?

REFLECTION POINT

No two people see things in the same way. Their needs, priorities, beliefs, knowledge and experiences all influence how they think and feel. That's why you should always try and see things from the other person's perspective, especially when you talk about important things.

EXTEND

6 **Work in pairs. Think about a recent situation in which you disagreed with a friend or family member. What happened? Would you have behaved differently if you'd tried harder to put yourself in their shoes?**

PHRASE BYTES

If I'd put myself in ...'s shoes I might have ...

I definitely wouldn't have ...

RESPECT OTHERS

Workbook, page 73

SPEAKING I was wondering …

Ask polite questions

SPEAK

1 **Work in pairs. Look at the photos. Who do you think the people are? What do you think they're talking about?**

WATCH OR LISTEN

2 2.22 **Watch or listen to two scenes. What's the difference between them? How does this affect what happens?**

Sophie: Excuse me, Sir.
Kalu: Sophie. What can I do for you?
Sophie: It's about the presentation. (1) ______________ do it another day?
Kalu: (2) ______________ what day it is?
Sophie: This Thursday, Sir.
Kalu: That's very short notice! (3) ______________ telling me why you can't do it on Thursday?
Sophie: I just haven't had time to prepare.
Kalu: You've had three weeks.
Sophie: I know, I'm sorry. (4) ______________ I could change with Naomi. (5) ______________ when she's doing hers?
Kalu: I've got a list. In two weeks' time.
Sophie: (6) ______________ I changed with her?
Kalu: I don't mind. (7) ______________ Naomi would be happy with the change, though?
Sophie: (8) ______________ I ask her? We're good friends.
Kalu: No, go ahead. But if she says no, we'll be expecting your presentation on Thursday.
Sophie: OK, thanks Sir.

3 2.22 **Complete the conversation with the phrases in the box. Watch or listen again to check.**

Could I possibly	Do you mind if
Could you remind me	I was wondering if
Do you know	Would you mind
Do you know if	Would you mind if

4 2.23 **Listen and repeat the questions, paying attention to intonation.**

5 **Write polite questions. Use a different question each time.**

1 Lend me a pen.
2 What's the homework?
3 Say that again.
4 Where can I find the information?
5 OK if I give it in on Monday?

ACT

6 **Work in pairs. Do the tasks.**

- Choose one of the scenarios below, or think of another one:
  You need to go home early.
  You haven't done your homework.
- Prepare a conversation with a teacher. Use polite questions.
- Present your conversation to another pair.

PHRASEBOOK 2.24

Polite direct questions

Could I possibly do/go … ?

Indirect questions

Could you tell me why/where you … ?
Do you know if she'd be/want … ?
Do you know when/why she's … ?
Do you mind if I ask/talk … ?
Would you mind if I changed/spoke … ?
Would you mind telling me when/what you … ?
I was wondering if I could … ?

Workbook, page 71

WRITING Seen from the outside

»» Give impressions in a description

SPEAK AND READ

1 Write three sentences about your personality. Then show your sentences to your partner. Do they agree with you?

2 Read the description. Who do you think Sonia is?

If you're wondering who the boy in the photo is, his name's Dani. He's medium-height, fair-haired and according to him, blue-eyed, but the truth is his eyes look grey. He looks like me, giving the impression we're alike, but we aren't.

What's he like? Well, he's quite popular and he comes across as friendly and easygoing when you meet him. It looks as if nothing bothers him, but he's actually self-conscious, which he hides by avoiding being the centre of attention. He behaves as if he could do no wrong at school, but despite appearing to be a little angel, he transforms into a bad-tempered monster at home. He also has a really annoying habit. He tries to speak like a rapper to sound cool, but just sounds silly.

In class, he doesn't say much, so he seems disinterested at times, but in reality he's quite curious and open-minded – just as long as the subject's computers. He's computer-mad, in fact, and his secret ambition is to come up with a groundbreaking new gadget. A remote control for his bad moods would be good!

Sonia

Get it right

He speaks ~~as~~ like a rapper (= in a similar way)

He works ~~like~~ as a rapper (= it's his job)

STUDY

3 Read the description again. Is each one a fact (*F*), or does it depend who you ask (*D*)?

1 Dani's got blue eyes. F/D
2 He looks like Sonia. F/D
3 He's easygoing. F/D
4 He always behaves well. F/D
5 It's cool when he speaks like a rapper. F/D
6 He loves computers. F/D

4 a Read the tips in the HOW TO box.

HOW TO

give impressions in a description

- For things you can see:
  - *look* + adjective
  - *look like* + noun
  - *look like/as if* + subject + verb
  - *appear* + infinitive (with *to*)
- For things you can hear: *sound* (+ *like/as if*)
- For a more general impression:
  - *behave/act like/as if*
  - *seem* (+ *like/as if*)
  - *give the impression* (*that*)
  - *come across as*

b Underline examples of the expressions in the description.

c Which four words and phrases are used to contrast impressions with reality?

the truth is, …

PRACTISE

5 Write one word in each gap to complete a friend's description of Sonia.

What's Sonia like? She (1) .... very short-tempered and she can come (2) .... as bossy, but that's because she's got such an annoying brother. If she didn't give the (3) .... she was in charge, Dani would behave even worse. They (4) .... similar when you see them, but that's where the similarity ends. She (5) .... to be very self-confident and she is! Except when she has to talk in public. Then, she looks and sounds (6) .... if she wasn't at all nervous, but inside she's terrified. But that's something she keeps secret.

PLAN, WRITE AND CHECK

6 You're going to write a description of yourself from the point of view of a brother or sister, friend, classmate, parent or teacher. Use the description in Exercise 2 for ideas on how to organise it and what type of information to include.

7 Write your description. Use expressions from the HOW TO box to help you express how other people see you. Then check it.

SHARE AND REVIEW

8 Swap your description with a partner. Read your partner's description and review it.

»» Workbook, pages 72–73

VOCABULARY Compounds

1 Complete the ad with the words in the box.

breaking bringing code edge ending handed minded reaching therapy through

FOR (1) OPEN-__________ PARENTS WITH DIFFICULT TEENS!

Fed up with (2) never-__________ arguments with your kids? It's wired into their (3) genetic __________. But until (4) gene __________ gives a permanent solution, try the Mood Reducer. The result of (5) ground__________ research, this gadget is at the (6) cutting __________ of remote control technology – a (7) break__________ with (8) far-__________ consequences for households worldwide. No (9) up__________ is too difficult to overcome. Order your right- or (10) left-__________ version now!

___ /10

Three-word phrasal verbs

2 Complete the ad using *away*, *down*, *out*, *through* or *up* in each gap.

FOR TEENS WITH DIFFICULT PARENTS!

Find it hard to (1) get __________ to your parents and (2) live __________ to their expectations? Tired of hearing that you'll (3) grow __________ of it when you (4) get __________ to something wrong? Fed up with them (5) checking __________ on you and (6) looking __________ on your friends? The Tolerance Transmitter allows you to (7) get __________ with anything, no matter what you (8) are __________ to. Turn it on and your parent will instantly (9) look __________ to you. (10) Stand __________ for your rights with the Tolerance Transmitter!

___ /10

GRAMMAR Relative clauses

3 Complete the ad with relative pronouns. Use one of the pronouns in the box twice and leave one space blank.

that where which who whom whose

OUT OF SIGHT, OUT OF MIND!

The Out-of-sight hoodie, (1) __________ is available at our website, is a garment (2) __________ allows you to go (3) __________ your friends go without being seen! The garment, (4) __________ qualities are obvious, is a must for teenagers for (5) __________ privacy is important. It works at home and school and is cheap, all of (6) __________ make it a garment (7) __________ you'll never want to be without. The Out-of-sight hoodie: for the teen (8) __________ doesn't want to be seen.

___ /16

-ing and *-ed* clauses

4 Complete the ad with the *-ing* or *-ed* form of an appropriate verb.

NEVER LATE AGAIN!

You promise your parents you'll be home by 10 before (1) __________ out. You check your clock after (2) __________ home. But (3) __________ a busy teenager, you lose track of time. You miss the message (4) __________ to your phone and you're now late, (5) __________ your parents worry. They're up (6) __________ for you when you get back ... and they're cross. Sound familiar? By (7) __________ our Back-track App, you can turn back the clocks in your home. Problem solved!

___ /14

Your score: ___ /50

SKILLS CHECK

✓✓✓ Yes, I can. No problem!
✓✓ Yes, I can. But I need a bit of help.
✓ Yes, I can. But I need a lot of help.

I can recognise the main ideas and supporting details when I read. __________
I can follow a conversation. __________
I can see things from another person's perspective. __________
I can ask polite questions. __________
I can give impressions in a description. __________

Workbook, pages 74–75

READ

1 Read the website comments and choose the correct people (A–D). You can choose the people more than once.

Which person ...

was impressed by the design of the website?	1 ......
suggests buying clothes somewhere different?	2 ......
relies on the online store to purchase clothes?	3 ......
has a preference for visiting the real shop?	4 ......
was ultimately disappointed by the site?	5 ......
thinks that there are many more products available online?	6 ......
thinks the online store encourages people to buy too much?	7 ......
believes that the majority of comments are too negative?	8 ......
claims the brand doesn't live up to its 'alternative' image?	9 ......
uses the online store to decide what to buy at the nearest shop?	10 ......

Reading: ______ /10

EXAM TIPS

do a multiple-matching exercise

- Quickly read the texts. What's the general message of each one?
- Read each question. Use key words in the question to help you find the answer.
- Don't just look for similar vocabulary. Make sure the answer matches the question exactly.
- Check that other texts don't contain a better answer.

understand the writer's purpose
See page 52.

recognise the main ideas and supporting details
See page 62.

The OOTO Collection

What do you think of The OOTO Collection online clothing store? Leave your comments here.

A Ryan

I enjoy shopping for clothes and The OOTO Collection is my favourite 'alternative' shopping destination. I like to browse the online store when my parents don't know what I'm up to (lol), so that I can check out the latest trends. There seems to be a lot more choice online but I much prefer buying from the actual store. It's a 30-minute walk into town but I think it's worth it. For a start it's slightly cheaper because you don't have to pay extras and it's way quicker because you don't have to wait to receive the clothes. I reckon if you live nearby then you should make the effort to go to the store. The exercise will make you feel much better too.

B Ada

Not having a bank account until recently, I'd never considered ordering anything online until a friend suggested trying The OOTO Collection. She'd been very happy with it, so it seemed like a good idea at the time. My friend helped me use the website which I must say looks amazing. There's a seemingly never-ending selection of clothes and there are lots of special offers which succeed in making you feel like you're getting a really good deal. But by the time you reach the checkout, you've bought more things than you originally wanted and you realise you have to pay for your order to be sent, so it wasn't such a great deal after all. And then when the order finally arrives, the clothes don't fit you and you have to pay extra to return them!

C Marga

After reading some of the reviews here I wanted to stand up for OOTO's online store. I think the people writing here have probably had a problem with an order and want to get back at the store. I'm sure there are lots of really happy customers out there who haven't felt the need to express their views here. Also, I think some of you should be a bit more open-minded and see things from another perspective. I don't live anywhere near an OOTO store. In fact, each day there are fewer places to buy any clothes locally. I have ordered from several online stores and none of them has come close to having the wide selection and excellent customer service of the OOTO online store. It's been a real lifesaver for me and my friends.

D Harrison

The more comments I read, the more amazed I am! There's nothing 'Out-Of-The-Ordinary' about OOTO. It's another predictable run-of-the-mill clothes shop that wants to give the impression of being cutting edge so that it will encourage young people like you and me to shop there. Supporting the dominance of The OOTO Collection will have far-reaching consequences – wait and see. Our high streets are already being transformed into ghost towns as local shops close to make way for big chains such as OOTO. If you really want to be offbeat, try something really groundbreaking and buy your clothes somewhere small and unique. If I could get through to just one of you then I'd be happy.

LISTEN

2 2.25 **You will hear a conversation between two friends about the runner Usain Bolt. For each question, choose A, B or C.**

1 What's Sharon's opinion of Bolt's autograph?
A It's very original.
B It's very hard to read.
C It's quite ordinary.

2 Sharon's concerned that the autograph ...
A might not be authentic.
B is a good investment.
C doesn't have a certificate.

3 Why does Sharon think it was expensive?
A Because Usain Bolt is famous.
B Because Trey's father asked him not to reveal the price.
C Because a pair of his shoes sold at auction for £25,000.

4 According to Trey, what's the main reason for Bolt's speed?
A His knees are both exactly the same.
B His legs are longer than other runners.
C He's always trained harder than his competitors.

5 Why did Sharon go to see Trey?
A To find out something she didn't know about him.
B To ask him about something she didn't know.
C To tell him something he didn't know.

Listening: _______ /10

WRITE

3 You've seen this announcement on the school noticeboard. Follow the instructions.

Do you want to see your work published in an English magazine? All you have to do is write a short story (140–190 words). Your story must begin or end with this sentence.

Sometimes you have to stand up for what you believe in.

Your story must include:
- a description of a person
- a change in the way someone feels.

Writing: _______ / 10

Progress check score _______ /30

EXAM TIPS

do a multiple-choice listening exercise (one long audio track)

- Find out what the audio's about. Read the instructions, questions and options carefully.
- Listen for the main message and the speaker's attitude or feelings.
- Think about your answer to each question. Then look at the options. Is your answer there?
- Choose an option because of its meaning, not just because it has similar words to the audio.
- When you listen again, check your choices.

deal with new vocabulary when you listen
See page 54.

follow a conversation
See page 64.

EXAM TIPS

write a story

- Read the task carefully. What do you need to include in your story?
- Make a plan with a clear storyline. Use your imagination!
- Use different past tenses, linking words and time expressions to connect events.
- Use adjectives, adverbs and descriptive expressions to add interest.
- Make sure your story is the right length and includes everything in the task.

give impressions in a description
See page 68.

UNIT 7

ON SCREEN

IN THE PICTURE At the cinema

>>> Talk about going to the cinema

a

d

RECALL AND READ

1 Work in pairs. Write a film title for each of the genres. Tick (✓) your three favourite film genres.

action/adventure	cartoon	comedy	documentary
horror	musical	science fiction	thriller	western

2 Work in pairs. Look at the photos. Each photo is related to a question from a survey about going to the cinema. Write the questions you think the survey might ask.

3 a Read Montse's answers (1–6) to the survey questions. How many of them answer your questions?

b ▶2.26 Listen to the questions. Compare them to your questions from Exercise 2.

WORK WITH WORDS

4 a Complete the descriptions with the film words in the boxes.

Parts of a cinema: aisle auditorium foyer rows

The box office is usually located just outside the cinema or in the (1) ____________ . The (2) ____________ is the main part of the cinema where the audience sits. The seats are placed in (3) ____________ facing the screen. A central (4) ____________ often divides the two halves of seating.

Types or parts of a film: credits dubbed remake subtitled

Films have opening and closing (5) ____________ to list the people involved. A (6) ____________ film allows the audience to hear the original soundtrack. Blockbuster films are usually (7) ____________ into more than 30 languages. A (8) ____________ is a film that uses the same story as one made before.

Other film words: cinemagoer session spoiler trailers

Someone who goes to watch films is called a (9) ____________ . They can usually go to an afternoon or evening (10) ____________ or screening. Before the film there are often (11) ____________ for films coming soon. If someone tells you what happens in a film before you've seen it, it's called a (12) ____________ .

b ▶2.27 Listen and check. Then listen and repeat.

5 ▶2.28 Listen to Pablo answering the same survey questions. Make notes and compare Montse and Pablo's answers.

The Screen One CINEMAGOER SURVEY

1 I always sit in the middle of the auditorium. I don't like being too near the front or the back. And I like to be in the middle of the row so that I'm right in the centre.

2 I always wait until the end of the closing credits before I leave. I don't understand why people want to go as soon as the credits appear. It's rude.

3 Not very often. I wear glasses, so it's annoying having to wear another pair on top. And it's usually not worth the extra you have to pay.

4 Yes, I do. I'm from Spain where they dub most foreign-language films. In bigger cities you can usually find cinemas that show subtitled rather than dubbed films. I prefer those because I can practise my English.

5 People using phones during the film. I really hate that. Or when I sit down to watch a film and realise it's a remake of a foreign-language film. When they remake films, they're never as good as the original.

6 I prefer to go to small independent cinemas rather than large multiplex cinemas. I like old buildings with an old-fashioned box office and ... how do you say it ... a foyer where you can buy something to eat or drink?

6 a 2.29 **PRONOUNCE** **A diphthong is two vowel sounds pronounced as one syllable. Listen and write the words next to the correct diphthong in the tables.**

allow aisle annoy close escape row sound spoiler subtitled trailer white

b 2.30 **Listen and repeat the words in each table.**

1

/eɪ/	
/aɪ/	
/ɔɪ/	

2

/əʊ/	
/aʊ/	

EXTEND

7 Some of the words from Exercise 4 have more than one meaning. Write the correct form of the words in the box in the sentences. Use a dictionary to help you.

dub row trailer

While on location, the film's star had her own (1) .... to relax in. On the third day, she fell out with the director and they had a blazing (2) .... She's an amazing screen actor. She's been (3) .... the new Queen of Hollywood.

GO BEYOND

Do the Words & Beyond exercises on page 136.

8 **THE MOVING PICTURE** **Watch the silent video. What are the people saying? Write the dialogue and dub the video. Then compare your version with the original.**

SPEAK

9 Work in pairs. Write two more questions for the survey in Exercise 3. Ask other students your questions and make a note of their answers.

Workbook, page 76

READING Code of conduct

>>> Identify the tone of a text

SPEAK AND READ

1 **Work in pairs. Make a list of things you should and shouldn't do in these public places to respect other people – *in a library, on a train, at a cinema*.**

2 2.31 **Read the text. What type of text is it? Where would you see it? What's its purpose?**

A NOTICE TO OUR PATRONS

Welcome to the Screen One Multiplex. Please make yourself at home. But please remember that you are not *at home*. In order to make your visit a positive and magical experience for everyone, please take a moment to read this notice.

5 THINGS YOU MUST REMEMBER TO DO WHEN YOU GO TO THE CINEMA

Arrive unfashionably early

We all know that arriving fashionably late to social events gives people the impression that you're an extremely busy person. But arriving late for a film means you have to find a seat in the dark, making other people stand to let you pass, ruining the start of the film for you and other cinemagoers. Make *early* the new fashion.

Keep the talking down

In our recent survey, over half of you chose 'talking during the film' as the most annoying habit of other cinemagoers. We strongly believe that people who talk during a film should be banned for life! So if you're one of those irritating people who exchange comments, ask what's going on, or predict what's going to happen next, please keep talking to a minimum.

Switch to silent

In the real world, the average person looks at his or her phone 150 times a day. That's once every 6.5 minutes of every waking hour. But *this* is not the real world – this is a fantasy world where you can forget about your digital life. Using a device is annoying to the people sitting behind you. And don't even think of answering or making a call.

Watch your table manners

People often ask us why we sell popcorn and sweets with noisy wrappers. The answer is simple – there aren't any quiet snacks! So we need your help. Avoid situations in which you think 'I shouldn't have unwrapped a sweet in that quiet scene'. And please – you *mustn't* slurp your drink or rattle your ice!

Don't make your feet the main feature

Finally, remember! Putting your feet on the seats; kicking the seat in front of you; taking off your shoes; throwing your litter on the floor … Do we need to state the obvious?

3 a **Read the tips in the HOW TO box.**

b **What's the tone of the notice? Give reasons for your answer.**

4 **Read the poster again. Tick (✓) the statements that are true.**

1 The cinema encourages people to behave in the same way as at home.
2 Cinemagoers who arrive late are not allowed into the auditorium.
3 People who talk during the film will be banned from the cinema.
4 Digital devices should not be used during the screening.
5 People are requested to eat and drink quietly.
6 Patrons are encouraged to take off their shoes and relax.

5 **Which tips in the HOW TO box did you use for help with Exercises 3b and 4? Tick (✓) them.**

REACT

6 **Work in pairs. Answer the questions.**

1 Do you think the cinema notice is a good idea? Why?/Why not?
2 Which of the five things do you do when you go to the cinema?

HOW TO

identify the tone of a text

- ☐ Identify the text type. Is its tone usually serious or humorous?
- ☐ Look at images, symbols, style of letters. Do they reveal the tone?
- ☐ Start reading. Be aware of signs that the tone isn't serious:
  - jokes or funny comments/ situations.
  - the humorous use of exaggeration.
  - playing with words with two meanings or the same sound.
  - irony: saying the opposite of what you really mean.

GO BEYOND

Look at the notice again. What do you think these words mean? Check in a dictionary.

ruin, irritate, unwrap, slurp, rattle

Workbook, page 77

GRAMMAR Modals of obligation, prohibition and advice

>>> Use modal verbs to say what is and isn't necessary or recommended

READ AND LISTEN

1 2.32 Read and listen to Jan's description of Secret Cinema. What type of film did she see?

Brett: What's 'Secret Cinema'?
Jan: I can't tell you much about it because it's secret! You have to register at their website to receive information about each event but you mustn't tell anyone else about it.
Brett: But basically you go to see a mystery film in an unusual location, right?
Jan: It doesn't have to be a film. It can be a concert too. And it's more than just a film – it's an event. You ought to try it.
Brett: Do you have to do anything strange?
Jan: The first time I went I was a bit nervous but I needn't have worried.
Brett: Why? What happened?
Jan: We all had to wear special clothes and meet at the station. We weren't allowed to use our real names. Then we were taken to a huge warehouse that had been converted into a spaceship.
Brett: You should've taken me with you.
Jan: I couldn't! But you really must try it.

STUDY

2 Underline the modals in Exercise 1. Then look at the table and match them to their meaning.

Modals of obligation, prohibition and advice	
Obligation	
Present	**Past**
must, have to	*had to*
Formal contexts: *must* and *have to* mean the same. **Less formal contexts:** use *must* for personal decisions and *have to* when there's no choice.	
No obligation	
don't have to *needn't*	*didn't have to* *needn't have done*
Prohibition/no permission	
mustn't *can't*	*wasn't allowed to* *couldn't*
Advice	
should(n't) *ought (not) to* *had better (not)*	*should(n't) have done* *ought (not) to have done*
Only use *had better (not)* for advice in a particular situation.	
Form: modal + infinitive (without *to*) except where indicated	
See GRAMMAR DATABASE, page 126.	

PRACTISE

3 Choose the correct option. If both options are possible, choose both.

HIGH SCHOOL
VIDEO CHALLENGE

To enter the competition you (1) ***must / have to*** be aged 14 or over. Younger students (2) ***don't have to / can't*** take part without the consent of a parent or guardian. Although it is not compulsory, students (3) ***have to / should*** work in teams.
To take part, each team (4) ***ought to / has to*** record a video of themselves lip-syncing a song. Although you (5) ***don't have to / mustn't*** ask for permission to use the song, you (6) ***can't / mustn't*** enter without including the name of the song's composer. To increase your chances of winning, you (7) ***must / ought to*** choose a song that is well-known.

4 2.33 Complete the conversation with the expressions in the box. Then listen and check.

couldn't	did you have to	didn't have to		
had to	has to	have to	must	needn't have

Kay: Have you seen the ad for the lip-dub competition? We (1) .... enter.
Al: What's a lip-dub?
Kay: It's a music video. I made one with some friends once.
Al: What (2) .... do?
Kay: We (3) .... sing along to a song. When we started filming, we (4) .... stop because one of the rules of a lip-dub is that it (5) .... be filmed in one continuous take.
Al: Did you (6) .... learn the lyrics?
Kay: I did but I (7) .... learned them. We only sang three lines each.
Al: I don't like performing in public.
Kay: We (8) .... appear in the video if we didn't want to. Some people helped with the camera.

SPEAK

5 Work in pairs. Al and Kay didn't win the competition. What could you say to them afterwards? Use *should(n't) have, ought (not) to have, had better (not)* ...

1 They didn't choose a well-known song. *You ...*
2 They forgot to ask their friends to take part.
3 They didn't include the composer's details.
4 They want to enter another similar competition.
5 They haven't got an idea for the video yet.

Workbook, pages 78–79

LISTENING AND VOCABULARY The greatest films never made

››› Understand purpose and intention

SPEAK AND LISTEN

1 Work in pairs. Describe the pictures. What do you think they all have in common?

2 a Read the tips in the HOW TO box.

b 2.34 Listen. Identify the type of audio and its purpose. What are the speakers trying to do? Check your answers to Exercise 1.

3 a 2.35 Complete the phrases with the words in the box. Listen and check. Then listen and repeat.

agree	believe	guess	know	surprise	think

1 **Peter:** 'I think you'll .... with me when I say ...'
2 **Peter:** 'It might .... you to know ...'
3 **Peter:** 'You might .... who I'm referring to ...'
4 **Jenny:** 'As you can probably ....'
5 **Mo:** 'When you .... about it ...'
6 **Mo:** '.................. me when I say ...'

b 2.34 Listen to the TV show again. What do the phrases in Exercise 3a refer to? Make notes of your answers.

4 Which tips in the HOW TO box did you use for help with Exercises 2b and 3b? Tick (✓) them.

HOW TO

understand purpose and intention

- ☐ To understand its purpose:
  - identify the type of audio: interview, talk, etc.
  - identify the topic.
  - listen to the general tone – is it serious or humorous?
  - think why it was recorded: to inform, entertain ...
- ☐ To understand a speaker's intention:
  - think how they want you to react: to agree, laugh, take action ...
  - listen for phrases like *I think you'll agree* that ask for a particular reaction.

REACT

5 Work in pairs. Which one of the stories do you think is a lie – *The Lord of the Rings*, *The Man Who Killed Don Quixote* or *Skywatch*? Why?

WORK WITH WORDS

6 a Choose the correct words from the box to form the common adjective + noun collocations, some of which are used in the TV show.

complete	heavy	strong

circumstances	decision	illness

1 .... + cold, rain, traffic
2 .... + accent, contender, smell
3 .... + disaster, surprise, waste of time
4 final, unanimous, wrong + ...
5 mysterious, normal, special + ...
6 fatal, serious, long + ...

b 2.36 Listen and check. Then listen and repeat.

7 a Choose the correct collocations from Exercise 6a to complete the sentences.

1 There are some .... for the title of Best Film Trilogy of all time.
2 Tolkien thought the film would be a .... and refused to let them go ahead.
3 On the second day .... caused a flood that destroyed the equipment.
4 The director discovered that the French actor playing Don Quixote had a .... and needed to be flown to France.
5 For every thousand scripts that reach someone with the power to make the ...., only one is actually made.
6 The production was abandoned quite suddenly under '..................'.

b 2.37 Listen and check your answers.

8 Work in pairs. Write six sentences using other collocations from Exercise 6a.

GO BEYOND

Do the Words & Beyond exercise on page 136.

Workbook, pages 80–81

GRAMMAR Future in the past

Talk about future events seen from the past

READ

1 Read the article. What does the film industry think will be the next big thing?

People are always trying to predict what the next big thing will be. Every day there seems to be a new gadget that's going to change our lives or a pop singer who's going to become a massive star.
In October 2009, when the film *Avatar* was about to be released, everyone thought 3-D would be the next big thing in the world of entertainment. According to the experts, people were going to stop watching films at home and go back to the cinema. 3-D was supposed to save the film industry. However, 3-D televisions would soon be selling in shops and the film industry would have to think of something new. Now they're talking about 4-D. Will *that* be the next big thing?

STUDY

2 Complete the explanations with examples from Exercise 1.

Future in the past

Use: To talk about future events seen from the past.

Form: The past form of different future forms.
'3-D will be the next big thing.'
Everyone thought 3-D ________ the next big thing.
'People are going to stop watching films at home.'
People ________ stop watching films at home.

Other forms:
Avatar ***was about to be*** *released.*
3-D ***was supposed/meant/expected to save*** *the film industry.*
3-D televisions ________ in shops.

See GRAMMAR DATABASE, page 126.

PRACTISE

3 a Look at the quotes. Then use them to complete the descriptions.

It's going to change the world!

It will be as important as the personal computer!

It will soon be changing how we travel short distances.

We expect it to be something totally new and revolutionary.

a In 2001 everyone was talking about a new invention that (1) ________ the world. Famous entrepreneurs said the mystery device (2) ________ as important as the personal computer or the internet. It (3) ________ how we ________ short distances. It (4) ________ something totally new and revolutionary. However, people were disappointed when they finally saw the 'human transporter' called …

We're going to launch two consoles.

It's unlikely to sell.

We're about to prove people wrong.

Gamers will love it!

b Towards the end of 2006, two of the world's biggest gaming giants (5) ________ two new consoles. Everyone thought that one of them (6) ________ because the company hadn't had much success recently. However, they (7) ________ people wrong. No-one had predicted that gamers (8) ________ it so much. The console was called …

b Can you guess the names of the two products? Check your answers on page 142.

4 2.38 Write the verbs in the future in the past. Then listen and check.

Al: Katy! What a surprise. I (1) ________ (**about to** / **phone**) you.
Katy: Really? What happened to you on Saturday? We (2) ________ (**go**) to the cinema, remember?
Al: I know. I'm sorry. I (3) ________ (**call**) you but …
Katy: Why didn't you call?
Al: Because I knew you (4) ________ (**not understand**).
Katy: Why did you think that?
Al: Lidia phoned and told me that she (5) ________ (**see**) the same movie.
Katy: And?
Al: I couldn't tell her that I (6) ________ (**meet**) you.
Katy: Why not? It (7) ________ (**not meant** / **be**) a date.
Al: I know but …
Katy: I thought you (8) ________ (**like**) Lidia to come. That's why I told her to phone you.

WRITE AND SPEAK

5 Work in pairs. Do the task on page 141.

Workbook, page 82

LANGUAGE & BEYOND

>>> Respect rules and social boundaries

RESPECT OTHERS

SPEAK AND READ

1 Work in pairs. Describe the photo. Where are the people? What are they doing?

2 Read the situations and choose the option (a, b or c) that reflects what you would do. Compare your answers with your partner and check your results.

ARE YOU OUT OF LINE?

Mostly as: You're out of line!
Mostly bs: You're not out of line.
Mostly cs: You're helping to stop someone being out of line.

DO

3 a The next day you talk to your friend. Look at what your friend says when you meet. What can you say to persuade them to change their behaviour?

1 'I don't like standing in queues. People can do what they want.'
2 'It's not against the law to talk in the cinema.'
3 'I paid for my train ticket. I can do what I want.'

b Work in pairs and role-play the scene. Can the friend be convinced to keep in line?

REFLECT

4 Discuss these questions with your class. Do you agree with the REFLECTION POINT?

1 How much are you influenced by other people's behaviour?
2 Does your behaviour influence other people? Explain why or why not.
3 Why should we respect social boundaries?

EXTEND

5 The way we behave and perceive social boundaries changes from country to country. What three pieces of advice would you give someone visiting your country about what is acceptable and unacceptable behaviour in social or public situations?

QUESTIONNAIRE

1 You go to the cinema with a friend. When you arrive there are a lot of people queuing to buy tickets. Your friend jumps the queue and goes to the front. What do you do?

a Go with your friend to the front.
b Stay at the back and wait your turn.
c Tell your friend to come to the back of the queue.

2 During the film, your friend starts talking to you quite loudly. What do you do?

a Answer your friend.
b Say nothing.
c Politely ask your friend to be quiet.

3 On the train home, your friend puts their feet up on the seat opposite even though there are people standing. What do you do?

a Put your feet up too.
b Do nothing.
c Suggest your friend takes their feet off the seat.

REFLECTION POINT

There are situations in which we have to respect social boundaries that aren't always covered by official rules or regulations. Respecting social boundaries helps us to live and work together. The way we behave in these situations has a direct influence on other people, especially our friends.

>>> Workbook, page 85

SPEAKING It was awesome!

Express likes and dislikes

SPEAK

1 **Look at the cinema photos. How do you think the people feel about the film they've just seen?**

WATCH OR LISTEN

2 2.39 **Watch or listen to the scenes to check your answers to Exercise 1.**

1

Connor: (1) ____________ . I'm a huge fan of the director's, so I was expecting something offbeat and I wasn't disappointed. (2) ____________ the ending. If I had to criticise something, it would be the script. Personally, I wasn't crazy about it.

2

Naomi: (3) ____________ . I was looking forward to this movie so much.
Megan: We both had such high hopes, didn't we? But for me, (4) ____________ .
Naomi: Yes. (5) ____________ . The opening credits were good though.

3

George: Do you want to know what I really think? (6) ____________ . It was a complete waste of time. (7) ____________ .
Kayla: To be honest, (8) ____________ . It wasn't *that* bad but it wasn't great either. Remakes aren't really my cup of tea anyway.

3 **a** **Decide if the phrases are positive (+), negative (–) or uncertain (?).**

a I couldn't stand it.
b It didn't live up to my expectations.
c It was awesome.
d I don't really know how I feel.
e It didn't do anything for me.
f I particularly liked ...
g I can't make up my mind about it.
h It was a bit of a disappointment.

b 2.40 **Listen and check your answers. Then listen and repeat.**

4 **Complete the conversations with the phrases from Exercise 3a.**

5 2.39 **Watch or listen again to check your answers to Exercise 4. Then underline other phrases in the conversations that express likes and dislikes. Which phrases are the strongest?**

ACT

6 **Work in pairs.**

- Choose a well-known film or TV show that you've seen recently.
- Prepare a conversation, saying what you liked and disliked about it. Include information about the show but don't say the title.
- Can other students identify the film or TV show?

PHRASEBOOK 2.41

Express likes

It was awesome/brilliant/amazing/impressive ...
I particularly liked ...
It lived up to my expectations.
I'm a huge fan of ...
I wasn't disappointed.

Express dislikes

It didn't live up to my expectations.
I couldn't stand ...
It didn't do anything for me.
It was a bit of a disappointment.
It was a complete waste of time.
It's not my cup of tea.
I'm not a huge fan of ...
I was disappointed.
I wasn't crazy about ...
If I had to criticise something ...

Express uncertainty

I can't make up my mind about it.
I don't really know how I feel.

Workbook, page 83

WRITING The perfect choice

Make suggestions and express preferences

SPEAK AND READ

1 Work in pairs. Match the classic film titles to the sports.

1 *Bend It Like Beckham* — a basketball
2 *Hoop Dreams* — b baseball
3 *Field of Dreams* — c football

2 Read the postings at a film forum website and check your answers to Exercise 1. Which sport would Jonathan like to find a film about? Does he find a suitable film?

MOVIE FORUMS — NEW POSTS REGISTER LOGIN

Hi. Can anyone suggest a good sports movie to show at our school film club? – *Jonathan*

What about showing *Hoop Dreams*? It's a documentary about two African-American teenagers trying to become basketball stars. It's awesome, in my humble opinion. – *Vince*

Hoop Dreams is good but I prefer *Field of Dreams*. It's a drama about a farmer who builds a baseball field on his farm in Iowa, USA, which is where I live. I suggest you check it out. It's ace (imho)! – *Gene*

Thanks for the suggestions but I think I'd rather find a film about football instead (I mean soccer, not American football). Any ideas? – *Jonathan*

Have you considered showing *Bend It Like Beckham*? It's about two teenage girls who want to become footballers. Wouldn't you rather show a film that girls can identify with too? And it's a comedy rather than a drama. – *Keira*

Thanks, Keira. *Bend It Like Beckham* sounds like it would be perfect. And I see it's got a 12 Certificate, so all the students can see it. Brilliant! – *Jonathan*

Get it right

Why don't we see a comedy?
I'd rather see an action film **than a comedy.**
I'd rather see an action film **instead.**

STUDY

3 Read the posts again and answer the questions.

1 Which genres are the three films?
2 Why do you think Gene prefers *Field of Dreams*?
3 What do you think 'imho' stands for?
4 Give three reasons why *Bend It Like Beckham* would be a perfect choice for the film club.

4 a Read the tips in the HOW TO box.

b Underline examples of making suggestions and expressing preferences in the posts.

HOW TO
make suggestions and express preferences

- To make suggestions:
  What about + verb + *-ing*
  Have you considered/thought about + verb + *-ing*
  I suggest you ... ; *You could ...* ; *Why don't you ...* ?
- To express preferences in general:
  I prefer + noun
  I prefer + infinitive (with *to*) / verb + *-ing*
- To express preferences in a specific situation:
  I'd prefer + noun
  I'd prefer + infinitive (with *to*)
  I'd rather ... (*than*)

PRACTISE

5 Write one word in each space to express a preference or make a suggestion.

Meg: Do you want to watch a film on TV?
Tariq: In general I (1) ________ watching films at the cinema to watching them at home.
Meg: OK. (2) ________ don't we go to the cinema? Which type of film (3) ________ you prefer to see – an action film or a drama?
Tariq: I'd (4) ________ see an action film (5) ________ a drama. But could we see a foreign film (6) ________ ?
Meg: We (7) ________ go to a subtitled Russian film or a dubbed Italian film.
Tariq: (8) ________ always prefer subtitled films.

PLAN, WRITE AND CHECK

6 You're going to write a response to this post on a film website.

Hi. I'm from the US and want to start watching movies from other countries. Can anyone suggest which movies I should watch from their country? Thanks.

7 Write your response. Use phrases from the HOW TO box to help you give suggestions and express your own preferences. Then check it.

SHARE AND REVIEW

8 Swap your reply with a partner. Read your partner's post and review it. Then write a response to your partner's post.

Workbook, pages 84–85

VOCABULARY Film words

1 Complete the message with film words.

WELCOME TO TOFF,
THE ONLINE FILM FESTIVAL WHERE ...

- the cinema's (1) a __________ is your living room.
- the central (2) a __________ between the (3) r __________ of seats is the space between your armchair and sofa.
- you can get snacks from the kitchen, not the bar in the (4) f __________ .
- every film's a new idea – no (5) r __________ allowed!

AT TOFF, *YOU* DECIDE HOW TO WATCH THE FILMS.

- Attend an afternoon or evening (6) s __________ .
- Watch (7) t __________ of all the films to help you decide what to watch.
- Choose between (8) d __________ or (9) s __________ versions of foreign films.
- Sit through the closing (10) c __________ or make a cup of tea instead.

At TOFF, you, the (11) c __________ , come first.

Here's a (12) s __________ , so turn away now if you don't want to know – you're going to love it!

___ /12

Adjective + noun collocations

2 Complete the collocations with the words in the box. Then write them in the sentences.

circumstances cold decision illness smell surprise

1 complete __________
2 fatal __________
3 heavy __________
4 normal __________
5 strong __________
6 unanimous __________

Follow us on TOFFer

7 I didn't expect to like it. It was a __________ .

8 This film's about a scientist who thinks she has a __________ but then doesn't die.

9 We've all agreed which film should win the *Palme T'off* award. It was a __________ .

10 Loving this Indian film. There's a __________ of curry coming from the kitchen!

11 I've got a __________ , so I can't go out this weekend. TOFF has saved my life!

12 Under __________ I wouldn't go to a film festival. Thank you, TOFF.

___ /12

GRAMMAR Modals of obligation, prohibition and advice

3 Complete the description with *couldn't, had to, must, needn't have, ought to have, wasn't allowed*.

If there's one film you (1) __________ see at this year's festival, it's *Modal Mundo*. Hannah Modal was a girl with very strict parents who (2) __________ to fulfil her dream of becoming an ice-skater. For years she (3) __________ practise in secret and (4) __________ tell anyone what she was doing. One day a friend found out. Hannah thought her friend would tell her parents but she (5) __________ worried. The friend told Hannah that she (6) __________ shared her secret sooner. That's what friends are for.

___ /12

Future in the past

4 Write one word in each gap.

FESTIVAL NEWS

Last year when Scott Thomas was about (1) __________ finish filming his first movie, he didn't know it (2) __________ become a huge hit or that his face would soon (3) __________ appearing on the covers of magazines around the world. Critics thought that *Future in the Past* (4) __________ going to be just another science fiction teen movie. It was widely (5) __________ to be a financial disaster. How wrong everyone would (6) __________ . After the film had its premiere at last year's TOFF, the world of cinema (7) __________ never be the same again.

___ /14

Your score: ___ /50

SKILLS CHECK

✓✓✓ Yes, I can. No problem!
✓✓ Yes, I can. But I need a bit of help.
✓ Yes, I can. But I need a lot of help.

I can identify the tone of a text when I read. __________
I can understand purpose and intention when I listen. __________
I can respect rules and social boundaries. __________
I can express likes and dislikes. __________
I can make suggestions and express preferences. __________

Workbook, pages 86–87

UNIT 8

BUY, SELL, TRADE

IN THE PICTURE World trade

>>> Talk about how things are made, sold and transported

RECALL AND READ

1 **Look at the image and list things you can see. Then compare with a partner. How many things are the same?**

2 a **Work in pairs. What do you think an aerotropolis is?**

b 2.42 **Listen to the first part of a presentation and check your answers. In what ways is an aerotropolis 'green'?**

3 2.43 **Match the descriptions of the areas (1–8) on the image to the headings. Then listen and check your answers.**

Business park ~~E-commerce zone~~ ~~Free-trade zone~~
Freight hub Hotels and entertainment Industrial park
Residential and shopping World trade

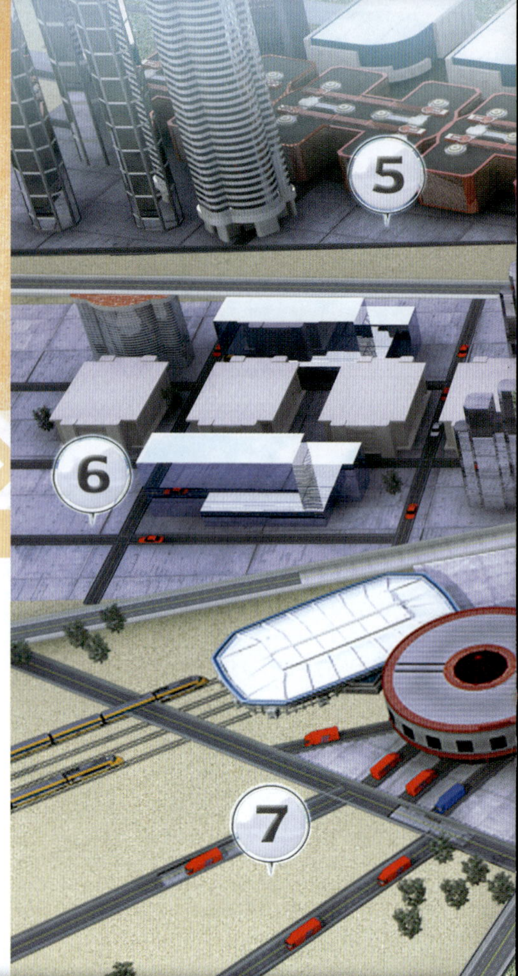

Explore Aerotropolis and discover what makes it unique.

1 *E-commerce zone*
Companies that store and ship goods for online stores are located here, where storage space is provided in warehouses.

2 *Free-trade zone*
This is where goods that are on their way to another destination can be changed, manufactured or stored without passing through customs.

3 ....
This area provides overnight accommodation for travellers, and leisure activities for travellers and residents.

4 ....
Located on the edge of the city is an area for houses, retailers, schools and other facilities for residents of the city.

5 ....
This area has a conference centre for conventions, exhibition halls for trade fairs, and large office blocks for international trade organisations.

WORK WITH WORDS

4 a **Find the words below in the descriptions (1–8). Match six of them to the definitions.**

cargo/freight (n) commerce (n) goods (n) industry (n)
manufacture (v) motorway (n) railway (n) retailer (n)
ship (v) store (v) transport (v) warehouse (n)

1 .... : objects produced for sale
2 .... : keep something in a particular place
3 .... : the production of products in factories, or a particular company that does this
4 .... : make products in large quantities in a factory
5 .... : send products to customers
6 .... : the activity of buying and selling products and services to make a profit

b 2.44 **Work in pairs. Write definitions for the other six words. Then listen and compare your definitions.**

c 2.45 **Listen and repeat all the words.**

5 a 2.46 PRONOUNCE **The stress in some words moves when their form changes. Listen and underline the stressed syllable in each word.**

1 commerce (n) commercial (adj)
2 industry (n) industrial (adj)
3 exhibit (v) exhibition (n)
4 organise (v) organisation (n)
5 active (adj) activity (n)
6 transport (n) transport (v)

b 2.46 **Listen and repeat the words.**

Aerotropolis: The city of the future

6 **THE MOVING PICTURE** **Work in pairs. Student A: watch part one of the video and describe what you see. Student B: listen and take notes. Change roles for part two. Then watch the whole video and compare your notes with what you see.**

EXTEND

7 a **Work in pairs. Complete the definitions with the correct form of the word in capitals. Then find the correct forms in the aerotropolis descriptions. What do the sentences define?**

1 This digital device lets you know your exact ________ . **LOCATE**
2 The ________ of the White House. **RESIDE**
3 They provide ________ space in kitchens. **STORE**
4 A form of cheap ________ for young travellers. **ACCOMMODATE**

b **In which word does the stress change when its form changes? Use a dictionary to check.**

SPEAK

8 **Work in pairs. Do one or both of the tasks.**

- Compare and contrast your city or a city you know well with the one in the image. What similarities and differences are there?
- Discuss the aerotropolis as a plan for a city. What are its advantages and disadvantages? Would you like to live in one? Why?/Why not?

6 ________

This area is where office buildings for commercial companies are grouped together.

7 ________

With its connection to the motorway and railway network, freight transported by trains or trucks can be unloaded here and shipped around the world as air cargo.

8 ________

A location where factories and office space for a range of industries can be found.

GO BEYOND

Do the Words & Beyond exercises on page 137.

Workbook, page 88

READING The world in a box

>>> Understand references

SPEAK AND READ

1 2.47 **Work in pairs. Look at the title of the article and the photos. Discuss what you think the article's about. Then read it to check your ideas.**

Inventions that changed the world

At 399 metres long (the length of four football pitches), Maersk Triple-E class container ships are the world's largest man-made moving objects. They can transport up to 18,000 containers – enough space for 36,000 cars. But despite their breathtaking size, it isn't the ships that have changed our world, it's the **20-foot long steel boxes** they transport.

To appreciate **their** impact on our lives, it's necessary to look back at how **things** were done before they were invented. Until the 1960s, ships had to be unloaded by hand. It would take a hundred men two weeks to do **that** on big ships. It was a slow, labour-intensive process that made **it** expensive to import goods.

The idea of using containers occurred to American trucking company owner Malcolm McLean one day in 1937. Frustrated by how long **it** took for his cargo to be unloaded at the docks, he realised that if larger quantities of **freight** could be moved off the ship at the same time, he would get his cargo faster.

McLean, **on the right** in the photo above, developed his idea and almost 20 years later he was ready to put it into action. On April 26, 1956, 58 shipping containers were loaded onto two converted oil tankers in Port Newark, New Jersey and transported to Houston, Texas. The revolution had started.

Containers could be moved quickly by crane and transferred unopened onto trucks and trains. Large ships could now be unloaded in less than 24 hours by just a handful of workers. The cost of importing goods, **which** had once accounted for around 30% of their price, eventually fell to less than 1% according to some estimates.

The result was that goods manufactured more cheaply in one place could be sold for the same price on the other side of the world. Electronic goods **that** had been imported from Japan, for example, could now be sold at a competitive price in shops across Europe and the USA. The age of globalised consumerism had begun.

Despite **his** hugely successful business career, McLean was relatively unknown when he died in 2001. But on the day of his funeral, ships' horns around the world rang out as a tribute to **the man** whose invention changed the world.

2 a Read the tips in the HOW TO box.

b Decide what the words in green in the article refer to.

3 Choose the correct answer (A, B or C).

1 McLean's idea …
- **A** was quick to put into action.
- **B** frustrated him.
- **C** saved a lot of time at the docks.

2 The main reason containers were revolutionary was that …
- **A** they made it cheap to transport goods by sea.
- **B** they could also go on trains and trucks.
- **C** they allowed Japan to export electronic goods.

3 The article's main purpose is to …
- **A** show how big container ships are.
- **B** show how important the container is.
- **C** tell us about Malcolm McLean.

4 Which tips in the HOW TO box did you use for help with Exercises 2b and 3? Tick (✓) them.

HOW TO
understand references

- ☐ Identify what these words refer to. The reference may come later.
  - Pronouns, possessives and determiners. (See page 11.)
  - Adverbs: *here*, *there*, *now*, etc.
  - Synonyms, the general word *thing*.
- ☐ Note that *it* can also:
  - refer to a later clause: *It took weeks to unload big ships.*
  - add emphasis: *It isn't the ships that have changed our world, it's …*
- ☐ Identify phrases that tell you where to look: *above*, *below*, *on the right*, etc.

REACT

5 Work in pairs. Discuss the article. Do you think Malcolm McLean deserves to be more famous?

GO BEYOND

Write another multiple-choice question about the article. Give it to another student to answer.

Workbook, page 89

GRAMMAR Passive forms

»» Talk about things that are done by other people

READ AND LISTEN

1 2.48 **Read and listen to Tom. What's his hobby? Why does he do it?**

'My hobby's spotting container ships. They're amazing! Roughly 90% of all we buy is sent to us by ship. Some food companies even send fish to China to have the bones taken out. Right now, more than 5 million individual containers are being shipped around the world. To stop them being lost, each will have been given a number so it can be tracked, but it's thought that about 10,000 are thrown off ships in storms every year. One was washed up on our beach recently!'

STUDY

2 Read the explanations. Then find examples of each passive form in Exercise 1.

Passive forms

Use: To focus on the action, not who/what does it.

Different tenses

Form: *be* + past participle (+ *by* + agent)
Note: Verbs with two objects have two passive forms:
Goods are sent to us by ship.
We are sent goods by ship.

Passive infinitives and gerunds

Forms: modal + *be done* / *have been done*
want/choose, etc + *to be done*
enjoy/keep, etc + *being done*

***have/get* something done**

Use: For things you pay or ask someone to do.

Form: *have/get* + thing + past participle

believe, know, say, think

Use: For general opinions.

Form: *It* + passive:
It is believed that ...

See GRAMMAR DATABASE, page 127.

PRACTISE

3 Write the verbs in the correct passive tense.

THE FOOD DEBATE: THE LOCAL VIEW

I'm a 'locavore'. Too much of our food (1) ______ (**bring**) from far away and our planet (2) ______ (**harm**) by the planes that (3) ______ (**use**) to transport it. Also, if that food (4) ______ (**produce**) locally, the profits would have gone to local farmers. Farms (5) ______ (**drive**) out of business sooner or later without our support. They (6) ______ (**help**) a lot by the locavore movement. Until recently, their produce (7) ______ (**not sell**) locally. Now it is, so I always check where the food that I buy (8) ______ (**grow**).

4 Complete the text with the correct passive infinitive or gerund form.

THE FOOD DEBATE: THE GLOBAL VIEW

I've got nothing against imported food. After all, bananas can't (1) ______ (**grow**) here, so they have to (2) ______ (**fly**) in from somewhere else. It's the same for chocolate. I know that the chocolate in our shops must (3) ______ (**made**) somewhere far away. So we can't stop some food from (4) ______ (**import**). As for the environment, I think the issues need (5) ______ (**put**) in context. A food's carbon footprint shouldn't just (6) ______ (**measure**) by the distance it travels. How it was produced should also (7) ______ (**take**) into account. No-one likes (8) ______ (**tell**) that they're harming the environment, but sometimes food from far away damages the environment less than food grown locally.

5 Complete the second sentence so that it means the same as the first one. Use passive forms from the study box.

1 The government should give land to everybody so we can grow our own food.
Land ______ so we can grow our own food.
2 If they know that air travel increases global warming, they ought to abolish cheap air travel.
If it ______ that air travel increases global warming, cheap air travel ______.
3 They should force all homeowners to pay someone to install solar panels on their roofs.
All homeowners ______ to ______ on their roofs.
4 The government could send everybody a card allowing them to use public transport free.
Everybody ______ allowing public transport ______ free.
5 We ought to pay someone to mend our old things rather than throw them away.
We ought to ______ rather than throw them away.

WRITE AND SPEAK

6 a Work in pairs. Discuss the statements in Exercise 5. Which do you agree with? Why?

b Choose one statement. Prepare a one-minute speech to defend it. Then make your speech to other students. Are they convinced by your arguments?

»» Workbook, pages 90–91

LISTENING AND VOCABULARY Customer service

»» Recognise a speaker's attitude and feelings

SPEAK AND LISTEN

a

b

c

d

1 **Work in pairs. Describe what you can see in each picture.**

2 3.01 **Listen and match the conversations to the pictures. Then compare your answers with a partner and discuss any differences.**

3 a **Read the tips in the HOW TO box.**

b 3.01 **Listen again. Match each conversation to one of the statements (A–F). There are two statements which you don't need to use.**

1 ____ 2 ____ 3 ____ 4 ____

A The customer's satisfied with the service received.
B The customer gets unfriendly service from the start.
C The customer's feelings change from good to bad.
D The customer's angry because things cost more than expected.
E The customer's attitude gets worse as the conversation goes on.
F The customer's anxious throughout the conversation.

4 **Which tips in the HOW TO box did you use for help with Exercise 3b? Tick (✓) them.**

HOW TO

recognise a speaker's attitude and feelings

- ☐ Listen to how people speak. Do they sound polite, happy, upset ... ? If they shout, are they angry or excited?
- ☐ If the speaker doesn't directly say how they feel, try and guess. Ask yourself: 'Why did they say that?'
- ☐ Listen for signs of a positive attitude: respecting turn-taking, use of polite language, showing interest, respecting feelings, etc. Someone with a negative attitude won't do these things.

REACT

5 **Work in pairs. Have you or has someone you know been in one of the situations in the conversations? Say what happened.**

WORK WITH WORDS

6 a 3.02 **Complete the conversation extracts with the right form of the buying and selling words. Then listen and check.**

bill (n) charge (n, v) cost (n, v) currency (n)
delivery (n) exchange rate (n) export (n, v)
import (n, v) purchase (n, v) tax (n, v)

1 It's about my phone ____________. It's 635 euros!
If you go abroad, you're ____________ for all your internet use.
2 I'm phoning about a tablet I ____________.
I paid extra for speedy ____________.
3 Which ____________ would you like to change?
How much does it ____________?
We just apply our ____________ for the day.
4 It's been ____________ from the US, so you have to pay ____________ ____________ on it here.

b 3.03 **Listen and repeat the words.**

7 **Work in pairs. Student A: look at the questions on page 141. Student B: look at the questions on page 142. Think about your answers. Then ask your partner your questions and discuss your answers.**

Get it right

They **charge** for delivery.
Delivery **costs** 20€.

GO BEYOND

Do the Words & Beyond exercises on page 137.

Workbook, pages 92–93

GRAMMAR Modal verbs of speculation and expectation

Give possible explanations for things

READ AND LISTEN

1 3.04 **Read and listen to the conversation. Marga's a mystery shopper. What do you think a mystery shopper does?**

Jean: What did you think of Angie? She's been trained, so she should be ready to serve customers.
Marga: She seemed to be looking at something under the counter when I approached her. She may have been checking messages.
Jean: She couldn't have been. We don't allow phones at work. She must have been looking for something.
Marga: She also looked like she might be upset about something.
Jean: It's her lunch break but Bill, the other assistant in the department, is ill today.
Marga: That'll be why. But she shouldn't have let it show. She might have lost you a customer.
Jean: She could have told me she was unhappy about covering for Bill!
Marga: She kept looking at the entrance too. I think she might have had plans to meet someone.

STUDY

2 **Read the explanations. Then underline the modal verbs in Exercise 1. Which give possible explanations? Which express a criticism?**

Modals of speculation and expectation

Use: To give possible explanations for things based on evidence, or say what you expect to happen.

will/won't, must	I'm sure
should(n't)	I expect this
could, may/might (not)	It's possible
can't, couldn't	It's impossible

Form: present/future
modal + infinitive (without *to*) / *be* + *-ing*
*She **might be** upset.*
*She **should be** ready to serve customers.*
Note: Don't use *must* for future events.

Form: past
modal + *have* + past participle / *been* + *-ing*
*She **couldn't have been checking** messages.*
Note: You can use *could/might have* to criticise someone's behaviour:
*You **might have** phoned me!* (Why didn't you?)
*You **could have** got hurt!* (Why didn't you think first?)

See GRAMMAR DATABASE, page 127.

PRACTISE

3 3.05 **Choose the correct options to complete the conversation. Then listen and check.**

Jake: Excuse me. Have you got these in size 44?
Angie: We (1) *could* / *might* not have any left. I'll just check. No, but we (2) *must* / *should* be getting more on Wednesday.
Jake: OK, I'll just take these then.
Angie: Would you like a bag?
Jake: I think I (3) *'ll* / *may* have one. Yes, I have.
Angie: That's 65 euros then, please. Thanks.
Jake: What's that noise?
Angie: The alarm.
Jake: It (4) *can't* / *mustn't* have been me. I just paid.
Angie: Sorry, it (5) *can* / *'ll* be the security tag. I (6) *must* / *should* have left it on.

4 **Complete the conversation with a present or past modal form. Use different modals.**

Sam: I think that woman over there (1) ______ (follow) us.
Mia: Really? Well, if she is, she (2) ______ (be) a store detective.
Sam: No, she (3) ______ (be) a store detective. She's paying. But did you see that man over there? I think he (4) ______ (put) something in his coat!
Mia: Are you sure? He (5) ______ (take) his glasses out. He's just reading a label.
Sam: Maybe. Where's Tina, by the way?
Mia: She left home half an hour ago, so she (6) ______ (be) here soon. But you never know with Tina.
Sam: Your phone's ringing. That (7) ______ (be) her.
Mia: Yeah. She (8) ______ (phone) to say she's late – as usual.

5 **Complete the criticisms with your own ideas.**

1 'We've been waiting for an hour. You … .'
2 'You shouldn't have left your bag there. It … .'
3 'Oh, no! We're wearing the same top! You … .'
4 'Why did you say your PIN number? Someone … .'

WRITE AND SPEAK

6 **Work in pairs. Speculate about the people in the photos. Who are they? What are they doing? What have they been doing?**

LANGUAGE & BEYOND

»» Make a budget and stick to it

SPEAK AND READ

1 **Work in pairs. Look at the photo. What do you think Carl's thinking? What can you see on the notepad?**

2 a **Match the definitions to words and phrases on the notepad.**

1 Regular costs that don't change.
2 A part-time job delivering newspapers.
3 Costs that change from one month to the next.
4 The money you are given or earn.
5 Money from parents to pay for regular costs and personal things.
6 The amount of money you have to spend on things.

b **Work in pairs. If you made a monthly budget, what similarities and differences would there be with Carl's?**

PHRASE BYTES

Mine would(n't) include ...
I'd need to include money for ...
I think I spend more/less on ...

DO

3 **Calculate the totals and savings in Carl's budget. If he wants to buy trainers costing £45, how long will he need to save?**

4 a **Work in pairs. What can Carl do to cut his costs or increase his income? Add at least two ideas to each list on the right.**

b **Make a class list. Which ideas would help Carl most? Why?**

CUT YOUR COSTS!

1 Prioritise. Do you really need to spend this money now?
2 Wait to buy things in the sales.

BOOST YOUR BUDGET!

1 Sell some old things online.

REFLECT

5 **Discuss these questions with your class. Do you agree with the REFLECTION POINT?**

1 What are the benefits of making a monthly budget?
2 Why can it be difficult to stick to a budget?
3 What are the best ways to make your budget cover your needs?

REFLECTION POINT

Making a budget has many benefits. It makes you aware of how you spend money, and helps you to make better decisions about your spending. It's also good preparation for when you leave home and have to adapt your expenses to your income.

EXTEND

6 **Write your monthly budget. Does your income cover your expenses? If not, what could you do to stick to your budget?**

»» Workbook, page 97

SPEAKING Let's discuss it

Take part in a debate

SPEAK

1 Work in pairs. Look at the photos and speculate about what's happening.

WATCH OR LISTEN

2 3.06 Watch or listen to the scene. Check your ideas from Exercise 1.

Sophie: As you all know, we're going to have to start paying to use this space next month, so we need to discuss how. (1) .... ?
Liam: (2) .... ? I think we should pay a membership fee to be part of the drama group.
Connor: (3) .... ? All other clubs charge a fee.
Sophie: What do you think, Eva?
Eva: I think a fee's a good idea.
Naomi: That's fine if you can afford it but ...
Eva: I'm not saying I *want* to pay ...
Naomi: (4) .... ?
Eva: Sorry, go on.
Naomi: I'd just like to say that if there's a fee, I'll have to stop coming.
Sophie: (5) .... Al, you helped set up the group.
Al: That's right. We spent weeks looking for a place and this was the only free option.
Kalu: (6) .... Maybe it's us who should charge.
Liam: That doesn't make sense! I mean ...
Sophie: (7) .... , Liam. (8) ....
Kalu: We could charge for performances and use ticket sales to pay back our membership fee.

3 a Work in pairs. Complete the debate with the PHRASEBOOK expressions.

b 3.06 Watch or listen again to check or complete your answers. What do you think they should do? Why?

4 Complete the PHRASEBOOK with the headings.

Take a turn	Ask someone to speak	Keep or defend a turn

5 3.07 Listen and repeat the expressions, paying attention to intonation.

PHRASEBOOK 3.08

Let's hear what ... has to say.
What do you think, ... ?
Who'd like to begin?

Can I just add something here?
Perhaps I can say something here.
Shall I start?

Can I just finish what I was saying?
Just a minute, ...
Let him/her finish.

ACT

6 Work in groups. Have a debate.

Your school has announced that the end-of-year trip has been cancelled due to budget cuts. Discuss how the school could save money to pay for the trip and how you could raise money for it if you think that's a better solution.

Workbook, page 95

WRITING On balance ...

>>> Develop an argument

SPEAK AND READ

1 **You've been discussing world trade in class, and your teacher has asked you the question below.**

Today goods can be transported cheaply round the world. On balance, do you think that's a good or a bad thing?

Work in pairs. Add at least one more reason to each list on the right. Then make a class list of reasons.

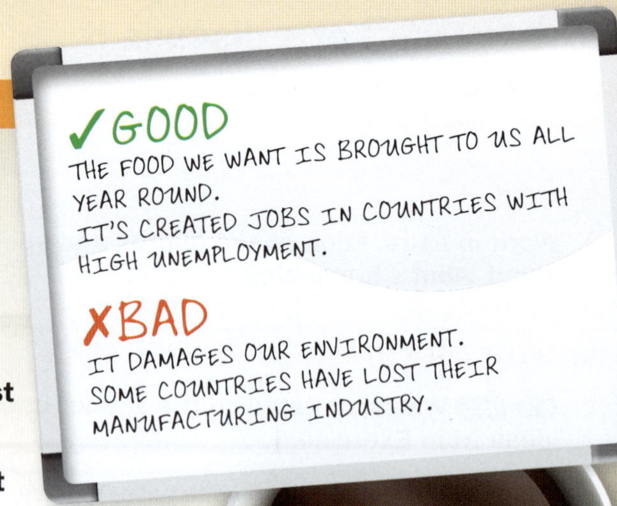

2 **Read the essay. Which opinion does it support? Does it include any of the reasons on your list?**

Over the last half a century, our lives have been transformed by the possibility of transporting goods cheaply around the world. However, despite the obvious benefits, my feeling is that it's done more harm than good.

One reason for that view is the damage that's been done to our environment due to the increase in global traffic. What's more, the huge demand for some products has lead to overfishing and a loss of local crops in favour of food to export.

Another thing that concerns me is the loss of traditional industries in some countries because of competition from other parts of the world.

In addition, I wonder if it's a good thing for us all to be wearing the same things, eating the same food, using the same gadgets. As a consequence, it feels like some of the world's diversity is being lost.

To sum up, global trade brings benefits, but we pay a high price for those benefits. That's why, on balance, I think it's a bad thing.

Get it right

~~the~~ traditional industries

~~the~~ global trade

STUDY

3 **Read the essay again. Write a sentence to describe the role of each paragraph. Then compare with a partner. Do you agree?**

4 a **Read the tips in the HOW TO box.**

HOW TO

develop an argument

- Give your opinions: *My feeling is that*, *I wonder if*, etc. (See page 45.)
- Support your arguments in a clear and logical way.
  - Give reasons: *One/Another reason*, *That's why*, *because*, *since*, *because of*, *due to*, etc.
  - Show consequences: *As a result/consequence*, *so*, *therefore*, etc.
  - Add further arguments: *What's more*, *In addition*, *Moreover*, etc.
  - Contrast your ideas with others. (See page 46.)
- End with a conclusion: *To sum up*, *In conclusion*, *For all the reasons above*, *on balance*, etc.

b **Underline examples of the words and expressions in the essay.**

PRACTISE

5 **Read another paragraph from the essay. Find seven more words and expressions to add to the HOW TO box.**

Furthermore, I suspect that it's multinational companies that really benefit from global trade as it allows them to make bigger profits. I think it allows some of them to pay less tax as well. Also, companies can threaten to move their factories to other places. Consequently, they can keep wages low.

PLAN, WRITE AND CHECK

6 **You're going to write an essay arguing that on balance, it's a good idea that goods can be transported cheaply round the world. Use reasons from Exercise 1, or other reasons, to support your arguments. (You don't need to agree with this opinion.)**

7 **Write your essay. Use expressions from the HOW TO box to help you develop your argument. Then check it.**

SHARE AND REVIEW

8 **Swap your essay with a partner. Read your partner's essay and review it.**

Workbook, pages 96–97

VOCABULARY World trade

1 Match the words in the box to the definitions.

cargo/freight commerce goods industry manufacture motorway railway retailer ship store transport warehouse

Globalisation made easy: World trade

1 __________ : move people and things
2 __________ : move things
3 __________ : keep in a place
4 __________ : make
5 __________ : a wide road for fast traffic
6 __________ : a road for trains
7 __________ : who you buy things from
8 __________ : buying and selling
9 __________ : a big place for keeping things
10 __________ : things we buy
11 __________ : things moved by sea, air or land
12 __________ : the production of things in factories

___ /12

Buying and selling

2 Complete the words. Use words only once, and write the correct form of verbs.

Globalisation: Buying and selling

Companies normally send you a (1) b__________ which tells you what they have (2) c__________ you for their services. This might include the (3) c__________ of (4) de__________ if they send your (5) pu__________ to you. If the company (6) ex__________ something from another country, you might have to pay (7) im__________ (8) t__________ when you receive it. And if the original price was in another (9) cu__________, the bill should tell you the (10) ex__________ r__________ they have used to calculate the price for you.

___ /10

GRAMMAR Passive forms

3 Complete the description with the correct passive form of the verbs.

Globalisation: What is it?

It's the idea that things from around the world (1) __________ (constantly / exchange). It (2) __________ (think) that the container is responsible for the current levels of global trade because things couldn't (3) __________ (send) round the world cheaply before it (4) __________ (invent). As for ideas, exchanging them (5) __________ (made) easier by the internet. But what about the future? When oil runs out, how (6) __________ (we / have / things / send) to us? And although we like (7) __________ (give) free access to websites, will that still be possible?

___ /14

Modal verbs of speculation and expectation

4 Complete with the correct form of the modals.

can't could may might must should will

Globalisation: How does it affect me?

You can't escape it. If you come from a cold country, the bananas you eat (1) __________ (grow) locally, so they (2) __________ (come) from a warmer place. And even if you own a gadget made in your country, it's certain some of the parts (3) __________ (come) from another part of the world. In fact, that gadget (4) __________ (contain) parts from a number of countries, and they (5) __________ (put) the parts together in different countries too. So although you (6) __________ (not like) globalisation and think that it (7) __________ (be) easy to avoid it by looking at the label, it's actually very difficult!

___ /14

Your score: ___ /50

SKILLS CHECK

✓✓✓ Yes, I can. No problem!
✓✓ Yes, I can. But I need a bit of help.
✓ Yes, I can. But I need a lot of help.

I can understand references when I read. ______
I can recognise a speaker's attitude and feelings. ______
I can make a budget and stick to it. ______
I can take part in a debate. ______
I can develop an argument when I write. ______

Workbook, pages 98–99

READ AND COMPLETE

1 Read the article and choose the correct word (A, B, C or D) for each gap.

The Last Word

First it was eggs. They were so good for us we were told we should eat them every day. But the research which that advice was based on (1) .... have been right, because suddenly we had to stop eating eggs because they contained too much cholesterol. But it later turned out that we (2) .... have stopped eating eggs after all. Apparently, they contained cholesterol, but it was the *right type* of cholesterol, so they were actually good for us. It didn't take long before we were all (3) .... to be eating a range of super-healthy 'superfoods' (why does no-one talk about the benefits of those anymore?) and, more recently, research has shown that we could be risking (4) .... illness by eating all that sugar and protein in our diets. The question is, what *can* we eat? I, for one, don't like (5) .... given all these conflicting warnings. Perhaps the old advice is best. Everything's OK – in moderation!

	A	B	C	D
1	**A** must	**B** couldn't	**C** shouldn't	**D** might
2	**A** had	**B** hadn't	**C** would	**D** needn't
3	**A** supposed	**B** thought	**C** suggested	**D** forced
4	**A** the	**B** careless	**C** serious	**D** mysterious
5	**A** be	**B** being	**C** have	**D** to

EXAM TIPS

complete a gapped text with multiple-choice answers

- Quickly read the text. What's it about? Where would you expect to see it?
- Read the text again and look at the words before and after each gap. Think what the missing word might be.
- Look at the answer options. Is your word there? If not, which option fits best?
- Read the whole sentence with your choice in it. Does it make sense? If not, try another option.

identify the tone of a text
See page 74.

understand references
See page 84.

2 For questions 1–5, complete the second sentence so that it has a similar meaning to the first sentence. You must use between two and five words, including the word given. Do not change the word given.

1 Jo said she'd be here by now.
SUPPOSED
Jo .... here by now.

2 Maybe she went to the wrong shop.
HAVE
She .... to the wrong shop.

3 Why didn't you tell me you were going to be late?
TOLD
You .... you were going to be late!

4 Those jeans are a bit long but you could pay someone to take them up.
HAVE
Those jeans are a bit long but you could ....

5 You ought to keep the receipt just in case.
BETTER
You .... the receipt just in case.

Reading and completing: ______ /10

EXAM TIPS

do sentence transformations

- Read the instructions. How many words can you use?
- Read both the given sentence and the incomplete one carefully.
  - Decide what structure you need in order to use the given word.
  - Remember that you can't change the form of the given word.
- Check that the meaning is similar and your spelling is correct.
- Check that you haven't used more words than allowed. Note that contracted forms are counted in full (eg *isn't* = *is not* = 2 words).

LISTEN

3 3.09 **You will hear people talking in five different situations. For questions 1–5 choose the best answer (A, B or C).**

1 You hear a boy inviting a friend to do an activity with him. How does his friend react?
- **A** He wants to go, but he's got other plans.
- **B** He's not interested in the activity.
- **C** He can't decide, and says he'll phone later.

2 You overhear a girl talking on the phone. Where does she arrange to meet her friend?
- **A** At the cinema.
- **B** At the theatre.
- **C** At a concert.

3 You overhear a conversation in a supermarket. Why doesn't the girl let the man go to the front of the queue?
- **A** She's in a hurry.
- **B** The other people in the queue don't want her to.
- **C** She thinks there are other people to consider.

4 You hear part of a debate on the radio. What does Frank say about the internet?
- **A** It's generally been a good thing.
- **B** It's generally been a bad thing.
- **C** It's benefitted everyone except the entertainment industry.

5 You overhear a woman talking to her daughter at an airport. What does the woman decide to do?
- **A** Take things out of her suitcase.
- **B** Pay extra for her suitcase.
- **C** Buy some clothes.

Listening: ______ /10

EXAM TIPS

do a multiple-choice listening exercise (several short audio tracks)

- Read and listen to the question: it identifies the speaker(s) and the situation or topic.
- Listen for the main message and the speaker's attitude or feelings.
- Think about your answer. Then look at the options. Is your answer there?
- Choose an option because of its meaning, not just because it has similar words to the audio.
- When you listen again, check your choices.

understand purpose and intention
See page 76.

recognise a speaker's attitude and feelings
See page 86.

WRITE

4 You've seen this competition on a website. Follow the instructions.

All your films and TV series
FREE
for a year!

Would you like to watch your favourite films and TV series free for a year? Then enter our review competition. All you have to do is write a review of a film or TV programme/series (140–190 words). Remember to include information about the film or TV programme/series, your opinion of it and reasons why other people should (or shouldn't) watch it too.

Writing: ______ / 10

Progress check score ______ /30

EXAM TIPS

write a review

- Read the task carefully. What type of review do you need to write? Who's it for?
- Make a plan. You should include:
  - a description of the film, product, place, etc.
  - general comments about its good and/or bad points.
  - your personal opinion.
  - a summary or conclusion with your recommendation.
- Use appropriate linking words and phrases to make your review clear and easy to read.

make suggestions and express preferences
See page 80.

develop an argument
See page 90.

UNIT 9 MY GENERATION

IN THE PICTURE Generations

»» Talk about young people today and in the past

RECALL AND READ

1 a Match as many of the words as you can to the people and situations in the photos.

careful/less forgetful helpless illegal immoral incapable irresponsible overdressed peaceful reasonable reliable respectable self-centred self-sufficient ultra-modern unaware unusual

b Work in pairs. Explain the reasons behind your choices in Exercise 1a. Which of the people in the photos do you most closely identify with? Why?

2 Read the blog post. Which photos best illustrate Generations X, Y and Z?

WORK WITH WORDS

3 a Complete the table with the words in the box. Use the examples in the blog post to help you.

again bad(ly); wrong(ly) before between many not/without opposite of together

	Prefix	Meaning	Examples
1	co-		collaborative, cooperate
2	dis-		disagree, dislike
3	inter-		interact, interview
4	mis-		misbehave, mistrust
5	multi-		multitask, multilingual
6	non-		non-stop, non-fiction
7	pre-		preconception, prefix
8	re-		rename, reuse

b ▶3.10 Listen and check. Then listen and repeat.

4 Replace the words in bold with words from the *Examples* column in Exercise 3a.

1 Young people today use different digital devices **constantly**.
2 They love to **communicate** with each other.
3 They often **question** official media and use social media.
4 They **don't enjoy** simply consuming. They want to take part.
5 They **use** things **again** rather than throw them away.

Home Blog About me Contact

Don't label me

We love to label people. It's a quick and easy way to 'understand' a person, especially when we see them for the first time. But these labels tend to be based on our **preconceptions** about their age, appearance, accent, and the way they behave or **misbehave**.
Sometimes we give a whole generation a label. People born between around 1965 and 1982 are often called Generation X (or Gen X). They also get called the MTV or 'Me' Generation because they grew up with music videos, personal music players, and are said to be self-obsessed – a label they strongly **disagree** with.
Then there are the Millennials, who were **renamed** Generation Y. They were born between around 1983 and 2001 and are often referred to as 'digital natives' because they were the first generation to **interact** with new technology from a young age. They're **collaborative** people who enjoy working together.
Generation Z covers everyone born after 2001 so that includes me. I guess they'll call us the **multitasking** generation because we're always doing so many things at the same time. Or maybe the **non-stop** generation because we're always busy. Must go!

Follow me

5 THE MOVING PICTURE **Watch the video about 'Generation C'. What five words does the 'C' stand for?**

EXTEND

6 What do the prefixes in bold mean? Use a dictionary to help you.

In the 1960s, hippies were **pro**-freedom and **anti**-war. In the **post**-hippy years, glam rock tried to **out**do everything that had come before it with outrageous clothes, hairstyles and make-up. But no-one was prepared for the **anti**-establishment punk **sub**culture of the 70s.

My generation

We believe in (1) ____________-violence.
We (2) ____________ cycle things.
We're in favour of (3) ____________ culturalism.
We (4) ____________ vene when we see problems.
We believe in (5) ____________ operation.
We don't (6) ____________ judge; we listen first.
We're against (7) ____________ honesty.

We're Generation P

WRITE AND SPEAK

7 a 3.11 **Write the correct prefix to complete the 'Generation P' manifesto. What do you think the 'P' stands for? Listen and check.**

b Work in pairs. Write a manifesto for a new generation. Include some of the prefix words and say what you're *pro* and *anti*. Give your new generation a letter and present your manifesto to other students. Can they guess what the letter in your name stands for?

GO BEYOND

Do the Words & Beyond exercises on page 138.

Workbook, page 100

READING (Do not) share

››› Recognise emphasis

SPEAK AND READ

1 Work in pairs. Look at three common passwords on the internet. Another popular one's missing. What do you think it is?

123456 | qwerty | 12345678

2 ▶3.12 Read the article. Check your answer to Exercise 1. Which one of these things does Heidi feel most strongly about?

1 using one password on different sites
2 keeping written passwords near your computer
3 sharing passwords
4 sharing information

If there's one thing I hate about being a member of Generation C, it's constantly having to think of new passwords for email, banking, online shopping and social media. So when I met digital security consultant Heidi Mellor, the first thing I asked her was how she chose her passwords.

'It's funny. We're repeatedly being warned not to use weak passwords and yet one of the most popular passwords that people choose is the word 'password' itself, which is about as secure as using no password at all!'

Although Heidi admitted that there was no secret formula for creating the perfect password, she did have some tips.

'What I usually advise people to do is create a long password. The longer the password, the more secure it is. If possible, I recommend using at least 15 characters which can consist of letters, numbers, symbols, spaces or just a sentence. And whatever you do, don't reuse the same password for different sites.'

Thinking of different passwords is difficult enough, but how could anyone remember different passwords?

'Write them down somewhere but keep them somewhere very safe indeed. When I asked people in our office where they kept their passwords, the majority of colleagues admitted that they kept them close to the computer. That's not a good idea at all. It's keeping it secret that makes a password good. And that also means not sharing it with other people.'

Heidi went on to explain how she'd been absolutely horrified to discover that her daughter's friends considered sharing passwords to be a sign of trust. Some friends even shared the same password to access their emails, social networks and other accounts.

'My daughter quoted one girl who'd justified sharing passwords with her boyfriend by saying that she had nothing to hide from him and he had nothing to hide from her. That left me speechless.'

But it's not just passwords that Heidi's concerned about. She also thinks we need to be careful about sharing too much information.

'Whenever we use a digital device, we're encouraged to share what we've read, listened to, watched, written, bought or thought with our friends, friends of friends or the whole world. Sharing information may seem like a good idea at the time but it can come back to haunt you. I know from experience that employers often search online for information about potential employees. It's easy to misinterpret something that someone wrote and shared when they were 13 or 14 years old and later regretted.'

In other words –

THINK BEFORE YOU SHARE.

HOW TO recognise emphasis

- Look for:
  - structures like *If there's one … it's …* , *It's … that …* , *What … is …* , *may … but …*
  - *do/did* before a positive verb.
  - reflexive pronouns: *myself*, *themselves*, etc.
  - the addition of *-ever* to *what*, *who*, etc.
  - comparisons: *it's as bad as …*
  - strong adjectives and adverbs: *at all* (with negatives), *terrified*, *speechless*; *repeatedly*, *absolutely*, *even*, *very …*

3 a Read the tips in the HOW TO box.

b Work in pairs. Read the first three sections of the article again and underline one example of each of the six types of emphasis. Then decide what they emphasise.

4 What five pieces of advice does Heidi Mellor give?

REACT

5 Work in pairs. Discuss your answers to Exercise 4. Do you follow Heidi Mellor's advice? Why?/Why not?

GO BEYOND

Make two lists of words and phrases from the article: (1) words/phrases related to being safe online and (2) words/phrases related to giving advice.

››› Workbook, page 101

GRAMMAR Reported speech review

»» Report what people say

READ AND LISTEN

1 3.13 **Read and listen to the conversation. Why's Mina upset with Jack? Did Jack do the right thing?**

Jack: What's up?
Mina: I tried to get onto Andy's page earlier and his password didn't work. When I asked him what was going on, he said he'd changed it. I asked him to tell me the new one, but he told me he couldn't and he **refused** to tell me why. I asked him if there was a problem and he told me not to worry and **insisted** that we were still friends. Then he **apologised** for being secretive … and **blamed** you for making him change his password.
Jack: That's not true!
Mina: So you **deny** telling him not to share his password with me.
Jack: Yes. I **persuaded** him not to share his password with *anyone*. Imagine he used your password on a computer and forgot to log out. Would you forgive him for letting a stranger get into your email account?

STUDY

2 a Complete the first two sections of the explanations with examples from Exercise 1.

Reported speech review

Use: To report what people said in direct speech.

Reported statements and questions

He told me ………………………… .
He said ………………………… .
I asked him if ………………………… .
I asked him what ………………………… .
For changes to pronouns, etc, see page 128.

Reported requests and commands

I asked him ………………………… .
He told me ………………………… .

Reporting verbs

1 **verb + *that*:** *claim, predict,* …………
2 **verb + infinitive (with *to*):** *offer, promise, threaten,* …………
3 **verb + somebody + infinitive (with *to*):** *encourage, remind, warn,* …………
4 **verb + *-ing*:** *admit, suggest,* …………
5 **verb + preposition + *-ing*:** *insist on,* …………
6 **verb + somebody + preposition + *-ing*:** *accuse somebody of,* …………
For other reporting verbs, see page 128.

See GRAMMAR DATABASE, page 128.

b Match each reporting verb in purple in Exercise 1 to one of the six forms.

PRACTISE

3 Write the examples in the first two sections of the study box in direct speech.

1 ' ………………………… ,' said Andy.
2 ' ………………………… ,' Andy said.
3 ' ………………………… ?' I asked him.
4 ' ………………………… ?' I asked him.
5 ' ………………………… ,' I said.
6 ' ………………………… ,' he told me.

4 Work in pairs. For each reporting verb in purple in Exercise 1, write what Andy or Mina might have said.

He **refused** to tell me why.
'I'm not going to tell you why.'

5 Write what the people say in reported speech. Use a reporting verb from the study box and be careful with pronoun and other changes.

1 'You posted that comment on my page, didn't you, Sam?' Sarah said.
Sarah ………………………… .
2 'I want to know why you did it.'
She ………………………… .
3 'I'll stop talking to you if you don't tell me.'
She ………………………… .
4 'Actually, it was me who posted that comment.'
Kevin ………………………… .
5 'It won't take long to tidy up this mess if we all help,' John said to his friends.
John ………………………… .
6 'Why don't we take the bottles to the recycling centre?'
He ………………………… .
7 'I'll clean the floor.'
He ………………………… .
8 'Matt, don't forget to lock the door when you leave.'
He ………………………… .

SPEAK

6 a Work in pairs. Think of examples of at least three of the things below that you've heard over the last week. Tell your partner.

an apology	a request	a command
an accusation	a denial	a refusal
a reminder	a prediction	a suggestion
a promise	a warning	a threat
an offer	a claim	

b Report what your partner told you to another student.

»» Workbook, pages 102–103

LISTENING AND VOCABULARY The elephant in the room

Infer meaning

SPEAK AND LISTEN

1 Work in pairs. Look at the picture and choose the best definition for the idiom *the elephant in the room*.

a The feeling when you've eaten too much and can't move.
b A situation in which you're with someone you don't like.
c A problem that everyone's aware of but doesn't talk about.

2 3.14 Listen to extracts from three television programmes. In which one is there an elephant in the room?

3 a Read the tips in the HOW TO box.

b What's the relationship between the people?

1 Pati and Henry 2 Michael and Angela 3 Evans and Sam

4 3.14 Listen again and choose the correct answer (A or B).

1 The problem started when Pati read an email that ...
A she had sent to her best friend.
B Henry had sent to her best friend.
2 How does Michael view the current situation?
A He thinks it's improving.
B He's sure that it's going to get much worse.
3 How does Sam feel?
A He thinks that Brent is guilty.
B He mistrusts Evans.

5 Which tips in the HOW TO box did you use for help with Exercises 3b and 4? Tick (✓) them.

REACT

6 Work in pairs. What types of TV programme were the extracts from? Name similar programmes in your country.

WORK WITH WORDS

7 a Work in pairs. Complete the idioms with the words in the box.

bridge	chest	end	iceberg	moment
side	stick	tree	tunnel	water

1 look on the bright ______
2 the tip of the ______
3 cross that ______ when we come to it
4 light at the end of the ______
5 at the ______ of the day
6 in the heat of the ______
7 get it off your ______
8 get the wrong end of the ______
9 barking up the wrong ______
10 ______ under the bridge

b 3.15 Listen and check. Then listen and repeat.

8 a Complete the story with idioms 1–5 in Exercise 7a.

Term ends soon. There's (1) ______ . I know we've got an English exam next week but we can (2) ______ . It's the first of many exams so it's just (3) ______ . But afterwards I'll be free! (4) ______ you have to (5) ______ of life, don't you?

b Complete the story with idioms 6–10 in Exercise 7a.

It's good to talk about a problem and (1) ______ . However, people sometimes misunderstand and (2) ______ . I recently said something to a friend (3) ______ . I thought after a couple of days it'd be (4) ______ . But today they said I was (5) ______ if I thought ignoring the issue for a few days would make it go away.

HOW TO infer meaning

- ☐ Identify the context and topic. Keep listening for clues if these aren't immediately obvious.
- ☐ Identify relationships. People say things less clearly or directly when they don't know or trust someone, or when they're unsure how they'll react.
- ☐ Listen to *how* people talk. Their tone of voice can often be a better indication of what they mean or feel than their words.
- ☐ Be aware of irony; saying the opposite of what you mean to make someone laugh or criticise them.
- ☐ Listen for idioms. Think about the image they create, and use the context to work out their meaning.

GO BEYOND

Do the Words & Beyond exercise on page 138.

Workbook, pages 104–105

GRAMMAR Question tags

Ask questions and confirm ideas using question tags

READ AND LISTEN

1 3.16 **Read and listen to the conversation. Who's Ellie? How does Aria know her?**

Aria: You're joining our 9 o'clock English lessons, aren't you? You were introduced to us this morning.
Ellie: Yes, but you weren't taking part in the class this morning, were you?
Aria: I was at the back. You said you moved here from London, didn't you?
Ellie: Yes.
Aria: And you live near the hypermarket.
Ellie: That's right. I'm on the right bus, aren't I?
Aria: Yes. I get off at the stop before you. But let's get off at the same one, shall we? Then I can show you where I live.
Ellie: OK. That sounds good.

STUDY

2 Complete the explanations. Use Exercise 1 to help you.

Question tags

Use: At the end of sentences to make questions.

Form: auxiliary verb + subject

Auxiliary	Tag
negative	....
positive	....
no auxiliary	*do/does, did*
I'm	.... ?
Let's	.... ?

See GRAMMAR DATABASE, page 128.

PRACTISE

3 3.17 **Complete the conversations with question tags. Then listen and check.**

Seth: It was a great match last night, (1) .... ?
Quinn: What match?
Seth: The final! You like football, (2) .... ? I mean, you're wearing a football shirt, (3) .... ?
Quinn: Oh, right. It's just fashion. I hate football.

Ash: This rain isn't going to stop, (4) .... ?
Brock: No. You're going to get soaked, (5) .... ?
Ash: Yes. You haven't got another umbrella, (6) .... ?
Brock: No, I'm sorry.
Ash: I couldn't come under yours, (7) .... ?
Brock: Well, it's a bit small ...

Nell: Someone should tell those boys to be quiet, (8) .... ? They've been shouting non-stop, (9) .... ?
Shea: I hadn't noticed to be honest.
Nell: Let's tell them to stop, (10) .... ?
Shea: I'm fine with the noise, really.

Workbook, page 106

4 a 3.18 PRONOUNCE **The pronunciation of words can change in everyday speech. Listen to the sentences and answer the questions.**

1 Which sound disappears in these phrases?
last night   wasn't it
2 How are the underlined letters pronounced?
don'<u>t you</u>   <u>do you</u>   aren'<u>t you</u>
3 How is 'going to' pronounced?

b 3.19 **Listen and write what you hear.**

5 a Complete the conversation with the correct form of the verbs. Where are the people?

Toni: Excuse me, I think I (1) .... (**sit**) by the aisle, aren't I?
Rob: No, I don't think so.
Toni: But that (2) .... (**be**) A, is it?
Rob: Yes, it is.
Toni: Oh, no. You (3) .... (**mind**) changing with me, would you?
Rob: Sure, no problem.
Toni: This bag (4) .... (**fit**) under the seat, won't it?
Rob: I think so, yes.
Toni: They (5) .... (**let**) us bring much on board, do they?
Rob: No, not much.
Toni: They (6) .... (**say**) we were going to take off late, didn't they?
Rob: Yes, I think that's what I heard.
Toni: That (7) .... (**seem**) to be happening more and more, doesn't it?
Rob: I really don't know.
Toni: I (8) .... (**annoy**) you, am I?
Rob: Well, I was hoping to read a bit.

b 3.20 **Listen and check your answers.**

SPEAK

6 a You're sitting next to someone you don't know on a long train journey. Think of different ways to start a conversation and keep it going. Look below for ideas.

the weather
the train / other passengers
if there's a buffet car (to buy food and drink)
the journey and if the train's on time
something that happened at the station
something on TV last night

b Work in pairs. Have your train conversation.

LANGUAGE & BEYOND

COMMUNICATE & COOPERATE

>>> Prepare for an interview

SPEAK AND READ

1 Work in pairs. Answer the questions.

1 Have you ever been in an interview situation?
YES: When? What happened? How did you feel?
NO: When do you think your first interview will be?
How do you think you'll feel?

2 What advice would you give to someone who's preparing for an interview? Make a list.

2 Read the article. Tick (✓) the advice on your list. What advice isn't on your list?

☐ ***Do some research beforehand.*** Know what the interviewers are looking for. Predict any questions you'll be asked, and think about your answers. Also prepare questions you want to ask. Bring a notepad and pen.

☐ ***Leave yourself plenty of time*** to get to the interview and find the right place. Having to rush will make you nervous.

☐ ***Be polite.*** Shake hands and don't sit till you're asked to. Sit upright and speak clearly, avoiding colloquial language or slang.

☐ ***Know what you want to say,*** but don't learn your words as if they were a script. Be flexible and ready to answer questions you weren't expecting.

☐ ***How you dress*** shows how important the interview is to you. Dress simply, avoiding sandals, trainers, shorts or T-shirts. Look clean and tidy.

☐ ***Be confident,*** but don't come across as overconfident or arrogant. Talk honestly about what you can do, but make it clear you're willing to learn new skills.

DO

3 a Work in pairs. Read the notice. Would you like to be chosen? Why?/Why not?

An international youth organisation is inviting teenagers from round the world to talk about Generation Z. Could *you* represent your school and your generation? If so, tell the school director before the end of the month. Interviews will take place at the start of next month and the student chosen will go on a 14-day, all-expenses-paid trip to Sydney to take part in the conference.

b You've decided to apply for an interview. Do the following tasks.

1 Think of four questions you might be asked.
2 Think about your answers to the questions.
3 Think of at least two questions you would ask.

4 a Work with another partner. Role-play the interview. Then swap roles.

b Discuss the interviews. Did they go well? How could they have gone better?

REFLECT

5 Discuss these questions with your class. Do you agree with the REFLECTION POINT?

1 Why do people feel nervous before interviews? Is it a bad thing?
2 What did you think of the advice in the article? Give details.
3 What did you learn from doing your role-play interviews?

EXTEND

6 Repeat Exercise 4a with a new partner. See if you can make your interview go better.

REFLECTION POINT

An interview is your chance to show someone that you're the right person to take on a job or responsibility. The four Ps are the best way to do that: be **p**repared, be **p**unctual, be **p**olite and be **p**ositive – but without appearing overconfident.

>>> Workbook, page 109

SPEAKING I've got some bad news

9

››› Soften what you say

SPEAK

1 Work in pairs. Look at the three situations. How would you start each conversation?

1 You promised to go to a concert with a friend. You have to tell them that you can't go.
2 A friend has changed their hairstyle. You don't like it. Your friend asks for your opinion.
3 A friend who loves acting has just discovered that they haven't been picked for the school play.

WATCH OR LISTEN

2 3.21 Watch or listen to the scenes. How similar are the conversations to your answers to Exercise 1?

1
George: (1) ....
Connor: Tell me what?
George: (2) ....
Connor: Go for it. I can take it.
George: It's just that I can't go with you to the concert.
Connor: But you promised.
George: I know. I'm really sorry but Mum and Dad won't let me. You don't mind *too* much, do you?

2
Megan: So? What do you think?
Sophie: Wow. (3) ....
Megan: You don't like it, do you?
Sophie: (4) .... It's just … it's so different. What do *you* think?
Megan: I really like it.
Sophie: Well, that's the main thing at the end of the day. Anyway, I'm probably not the best person to ask, am I? Look at my hair.
Megan: I love your hair.

3
Al: Hi Kayla. I'm really sorry about the play. How are you feeling?
Kayla: I'll get over it.
Liam: I just heard the news. (5) ....
Al: Yeah. Better luck next time. (6) ....
Liam: Look on the bright side. You won't have to work with Daniel.

3 a Match the sentence halves. Then complete the conversations with the sentences.

1 It's not that	a feel awful.
2 It's really	b for words.
3 I'm afraid I've	c I don't like it.
4 I'm lost	d how to tell you this.
5 You must	e bad luck.
6 I'm not quite sure	f got some bad news.

b 3.21 Watch or listen again to check your answers.

4 3.22 Listen and repeat the sentences.

5 Write the phrases in Exercise 3a in the correct sections of the PHRASEBOOK.

PHRASEBOOK 3.23

Bring up a difficult topic

....
....
It's just that …
I'm really sorry but …

Give tactful responses

....
....
It's different/original/interesting …
What do *you* think?
Well, that's the main thing.
I'm probably not the best person to ask.

Express sympathy

....
....
I'm really sorry about …
Better luck next time.

ACT

6 Work in pairs. Think of another situation in which you have to bring up a difficult topic, give an opinion and/or express sympathy. Prepare a conversation using some of the phrases in the PHRASEBOOK. Then present your conversation to another pair.

››› Workbook, page 107

WRITING Old friends

⋙ Write an informal email

SPEAK AND READ

1 **Work in pairs. Tell your partner about an old friend you don't see anymore. Why did you stop seeing them? What are they doing now?**

2 **Read the email from Owen. Why is he getting in touch?**

From: owenlovesPunk@tomail.ca
To: Ali
Subject: Old friends

Dear Ali,
I hope you're well. I'm not sure if you remember me. We used to be in the same class at school before my family moved back to Canada three years ago. I'm the slightly odd person who insisted on making you listen to punk music!
I hope you don't mind me contacting you unexpectedly. I found your email address in an old exercise book and I wondered how you were. Is everything going well at school?
Apart from wanting to make contact with you again, I'm also writing to see if you could do me a big favour. Our class teacher has asked us to write about what it's like to be a teenager in another country. Do you think you could help me by saying what young people like and dislike these days where you are? I haven't lived there for a long time, so I imagine things have changed a lot.
I hope you'll write and tell me how you are even if you can't help me with my school assignment.
Best wishes,
Owen
PS I'm attaching a photo of our house so you can see what it's like.
PPS I still like punk music!

Get it right

To add a note to the end of your message, write *PS* (postscript) under your signature. To add another note, use *PPS* (post-postscript).

STUDY

3 a **Read the email again. Draw an arrow on the line to indicate the degree of formality.**

formal ———————————— informal

b **Work in pairs. Compare your answers, giving reasons for where you placed your arrow.**

4 a **Read the tips in the HOW TO box.**

HOW TO

write an informal email

- Think how well you know the other person. How informal can you be?
- To start/end emails to close friends or family members: *Hi*, *Hiya*, *Hey* (US); *Bye*, *See you*, *Love*.
- To start/end emails to people you don't know so well: *Dear …* ; *Best wishes*, *Yours …*
- Use contractions, informal expressions, phrasal verbs and idioms.
- Ask direct questions. Encourage a response from the other person.
- Emphasise your ideas with strong adverbs and adjectives like *completely* and *amazing*.

b **Underline examples of more formal language in Owen's email. Why do you think he's written in this style?**

PRACTISE

5 **Match the informal phrases below to more formal equivalents in Owen's email.**

1 for ages
2 I'm that mad guy
3 How's it going?
4 Anyway, it'd be good to catch up
5 out of the blue
6 Remember me?
7 I guess
8 get in touch with

PLAN, WRITE AND CHECK

6 **You're going to write a reply to Owen's message. Imagine you're Ali and think of the things to include in your reply to your old friend. Make sure you answer his questions and use a more informal tone.**

7 **Write your message. Use the tips from the HOW TO box to help you get the tone right. Then check it.**

SHARE AND REVIEW

8 **Swap your message with a partner. Read your partner's message and review it.**

⋙ Workbook, pages 108–109

VOCABULARY Prefixes

1 Complete the article with the prefixes in the box. You need to use two prefixes twice.

co dis inter mis multi non pre re

MEET GENERATION D (IF YOU CAN FIND THEM!)

After the (1) ______ tasking Generation C, with its (2) ______-stop use of digital devices, a new generation, Generation D, is emerging, teenagers who (3) ______ like everything digital, (4) ______ trust the internet and (5) ______ agree with having to share everything online. It's the 'disconnect' generation. They still want to (6) ______ act with people, but do it face to face. They want to (7) ______ llaborate with others, but not in a society where everything gets thrown away and nothing's (8) ______ used. We travelled to a remote village with no internet to (9) ______ view them and see if the negative (10) ______ conceptions about them in the media are justified.

___ /10

Idioms

2 Complete the missing words in the idioms.

WHAT PEOPLE HAVE BEEN SAYING ABOUT GENERATION D

'If they've got a problem, they should get it off their (1) ch______!'
'The ones on the news are just the tip of the (2) i______.'
'Look on the bright (3) s______. At the end of the (4) d______, at least they have social skills!'
'They could become dangerous, but we'll cross that (5) br______ when we come to it.'
'Talk to us, Johnny! We said what we said in the heat of the (6) m______ and maybe we got the wrong end of the (7) st______. But it's water under the (8) br______ now.'
'The media's barking up the wrong (9) tr______. These kids are heroes. I see them turning off their devices and think there's light at the end of the digital (10) t______!'

___ /10

GRAMMAR Reported speech review

3 Complete the article with the correct form of the verbs. Add any other words that are needed.

I finally found the village. When they realised I was a journalist, they (1) ______ (**refuse** / **speak**) to me and they (2) ______ (**tell** / **destroy**) my recording equipment if I didn't leave. They hated journalists, they said, and (3) ______ (**accuse** / **tell**) lies about them. But eventually I (4) ______ (**persuade** / **talk**) to me by (5) ______ (**promise** / **write**) an objective report about them. We went into a house and they (6) ______ (**tell** / **leave**) my equipment and phone at the door. They (7) ______ (**deny** / **be**) a group of outsiders and (8) ______ (**claim** / **be**) the real outsiders because we could no longer live without technology.

___ /16

Question tags

4 Complete the sentences with question tags.

HERE'S WHAT SOME GENERATION D MEMBERS SAID

'You're here to discredit us, (1) ______?'
'We can't talk face to face anymore, (2) ______?'
'You haven't understood anything, (3) ______?'
'Newspapers want people to misunderstand us, (4) ______?'
'People used to be happy without technology, (5) ______?'
'Let's talk about society's real problems, (6) ______?'
'You weren't recording that, (7) ______?'

___ /14

Your score: ___ /50

SKILLS CHECK

✓✓✓ Yes, I can. No problem!
✓✓ Yes, I can. But I need a bit of help.
✓ Yes, I can. But I need a lot of help.

I can recognise emphasis when I read. ______
I can infer meaning when I listen. ______
I can prepare for an interview. ______
I can soften what I say. ______
I can write an informal email. ______

Workbook, pages 110–111

UNIT 10

WATCH YOUR LANGUAGE

IN THE PICTURE Languages

>>> Talk about languages

RECALL AND READ

1 **Work in pairs. Look at the flags. Write the names of the countries and the official languages associated with each country. Some countries have more than one official language.**

2 **Look at the photos. Which of the people or things can you identify?**

3 **Read the message from the *Beyond* authors and the fact files and check your answers to Exercise 2. Which of the languages would you most like to learn?**

WORK WITH WORDS

4 a **Complete the description of Klingon with the correct form of the phrasal verbs connected to languages and learning verbs. Use the authors' message to help you.**

break down catch on come across die out end up get across get by keep up look up make up pick up try out

A person who (1) ______________ a 'constructed language' is known as a conlanger. Marc Okrand is the conlanger who came up with the grammar rules and vocabulary for one of the most famous constructed languages – Klingon. The Klingons are a warrior species in the *Star Trek* films and TV series. When they speak Klingon, they can (2) ______________ as quite aggressive!
The Klingon language only has around 3,000 words, so it's hard to (3) ______________ a long conversation. Even so, Klingon fans seem to (4) ______________ quite well when they meet up at *Star Trek* conventions to (5) ______________ new words and phrases with other speakers.
If you want to (6) ______________ some basic Klingon, you'll find help on the internet. jIyajbe is a useful Klingon phrase. It's one of many phrases you can (7) ______________ in Okrand's Klingon Dictionary.
Don't forget that Klingons are warriors and often find it hard to (8) ______________ exactly what they mean. If you talk to a Klingon and communication completely (9) ______________, we recommend making a quick exit. Otherwise you might (10) ______________ in big trouble!
Klingon (11) ______________ quickly when it first appeared and it continues to be popular today. It's highly unlikely that it will ever (12) ______________.

b 3.24 **Listen and check your answers.**

Dothraki

This constructed or invented language was **made up** by the linguist David J Peterson for the television series *Game of Thrones*. Starting from examples in George R R Martin's original fantasy novel series *A Song of Ice and Fire*, Peterson's challenge was to work out how to make a new language **come across** as genuine while at the same time be easy for actors to learn. He **ended up** with more than 3,000 words as well as a set of grammar rules. Other constructed languages include Klingon and Vulcan from the *Star Trek* series of TV shows and films.

Authors' message

"Now that you can **get by** in English, how about **trying out** something more unusual? Here are some alternative languages to consider."

Robert, Rob and Rebecca

Esperanto

Sometimes it's hard to **get your message across**, especially if you're trying to communicate with someone from another country. Esperanto was created in 1887 as an easy-to-learn international language that would stop communication from **breaking down**. It never **caught on** in a big way but there are between 500,000 and 2 million Esperanto speakers around the world.

Siletz Dee-ni

Learn Siletz Dee-ni and not only will you **pick up** a new language but, if you **keep it up**, you'll also be helping to keep a language alive. According to the linguist David Crystal, half of the world's estimated 6,000-plus languages are under threat of **dying out** in the next 100 years. Siletz Dee-ni is a Native American language which was once spoken widely in Oregon, USA. If you want to know how to say 'language' in Siletz Dee-ni, **look it up** in the Siletz Dee-ni Talking Dictionary.

5 3.25 **Listen and repeat the phrasal verbs from Exercise 4a.**

6 THE MOVING PICTURE **Watch the video. Then describe what happens at Château de Grésillon in France every summer.**

EXTEND

7 a Some phrasal verbs are intransitive (have no object). Which phrasal verbs in Exercise 4a are intransitive?

b Intransitive verbs don't have a passive form. However, some phrasal verbs have transitive and intransitive meanings. Make two sentences below passive.

1 The talks **broke down** completely.
2 My car **broke down**.
3 The police **broke down** the door.
4 He **broke down** and started crying.
5 We **broke** the problem **down** into small steps.

SPEAK

8 Work in pairs. Complete the tasks.

- Student A: look at page 141. Student B: look at page 142.
- Choose the correct options to complete your questions.
- Ask and answer the questions, making a note of your partner's answers.

GO BEYOND

Do the Words & Beyond exercises on page 139.

Workbook, page 112

READING The teenage multilinguist

>>> Understand what a writer's *really* saying

SPEAK AND READ

1 **Work in pairs. Discuss why some readers write comments on online articles. Do you ever read or write comments? Why?/Why not?**

2 3.26 **Read the article and write a comment on it.**

American teen speaks
23 LANGUAGES

(10) Comments

American teenager Timothy Doner loves learning languages. He became famous after posting videos of himself speaking different languages online. Apart from languages such as French and German, he's also learned Mandarin, Arabic, Hebrew, Farsi, Pashto and Hindi. He now speaks over 23 different languages.

Timothy says knowing so many languages is useful for eavesdropping on other people's conversations. 'I've listened to people insult me in foreign languages and I've actually been able to respond to them,' he says. To help learn a new language, Timothy memorises pop lyrics, watches movies and communicates with people from around the world.

3 **Read the comments on the article. Which one's closest to yours?**

1 **brock17**
Way to go, Tim! Amazing!

2 **fishinthesea**
So they expect us to believe he actually speaks 23 languages. I'm sorry, but real proficiency in a language takes years to acquire.

3 **L800**
Does he speak Russian? That would show if he's as good as he says he is. I've heard it's pretty much impossible to sound like a native.

4 **susi_J**
I've seen a video of Tim speaking Russian. I don't think he wants to speak well enough to sound like a native. He just enjoys learning languages. All credit to him.

5 **JFbrody**
Just what we need! Another person with too much free time. Couldn't he put his talents to better use?

6 **mel770**
These incredible language geeks are called hyperpolyglots. They're born with a natural ability to pick up languages. FYI hyperglots are usually left-handed!

7 **harth**
I'm left-handed and love languages but no way am I a hyperpolyglot. BTW Please don't use the term 'geek'. It's really derogatory!

8 **ilovelingo**
Does anyone know if his parents are from different countries? I grew up bilingual and I know that makes it so much easier to pick up new languages. I can speak five and I could easily learn loads more.

9 **mel770**
Saying *geek* is derogatory shows how little you know about English. Maybe you should master your own language before trying to learn others. If you prefer, I can use the word *nerd*.

10 **Aslan-L**
I am an English student in Turkey. This is such an inspiring story. We should all learn to communicate more but personally I have too little time.

4 **a** **Read the tips in the HOW TO box.**

b **Read the comments again. Which comment or comments:**

1 are positive about Tim's achievements? ....
2 are rude about Tim's achievements? ....
3 respond rudely to another comment? ....
4 defend Tim against criticism? ....
5 could come across as arrogant? ....
6 make a claim about how languages are learned? ....

5 **Which tips in the HOW TO box did you use for help with Exercise 4b? Tick (✓) them.**

REACT

6 **Work in pairs. Discuss your reactions to the comments.**

GO BEYOND

Write a response to two of the comments in Exercise 3.

HOW TO

understand what a writer's *really* saying

- ☐ Identify tone. (See page 74.)
- ☐ Identify rude or respectful attitudes. Respectful writers:
  - – accept ideas, feelings or success they don't share.
  - – use polite language and avoid negative emotions.
  - – avoid sarcasm (saying the opposite of what you think to criticise someone).
- ☐ Think what the writer's words *imply* (suggest without saying something directly).

Workbook, page 113

GRAMMAR Intensifiers

»» Emphasise qualities and quantities

READ

1 What's wrong with the signs? Read the comments to check your answer.

AnneG589
It's so sad to see bad grammar on signs. Would it be too much trouble to correct them?

celebr8!
Correcting them would be way too expensive. ☹

rantinron
Why can so few people use apostrophes properly? They obviously don't teach kids enough grammar!

***?!@eee**
I totally agree. It's utterly appalling that we can't write our own language.

dude004
Why make such a lot of fuss about such a small thing? It's all rather amusing. The errors aren't serious enough to cause misunderstanding so who cares?

STUDY

2 Read the explanations. Then <u>underline</u> the intensifiers in Exercise 1.

Intensifiers

Use: To emphasise qualities and quantities.

Adverbs of degree

rather/remarkably, etc + adjective/adverb
totally/utterly, etc + extreme adjective/verb

so/such ... (that)

so	+ adjective/adverb + *few/many/little/much*, etc + noun
such	+ (*a*) noun / (*a*) adjective + noun + *a lot of* + noun

Use (*that*) + clause to express consequences.

too/(not) enough ... (for/to)

slightly, way, etc	+ *too* + adjective/adverb + *too few/many/little/much* + noun
adjective/adverb + *enough* (*not*) *enough* + noun	

Use an infinitive with *to* to express consequences.

See GRAMMAR DATABASE, page 129.

»» Workbook, pages 114–115

PRACTISE

3 Choose the correct options to complete part of a letter to a newspaper about texting.

I am writing to express how (1) ___ horrified I am by this messaging craze. It is (2) ___ shame that young people are being turned into zombies by their phones. It is clear they spend (3) ___ time on them and not nearly (4) ___ time talking to each other. They are (5) ___ absorbed by them that they don't even notice others around them. And when they speak, they cannot express themselves (6) ___ to get their message across because they have (7) ___ poor language skills. I hear 'innit' such (8) ___ that I am starting to think it is the only word they know!

	A	B	C
1	**A** utterly	**B** remarkably	**C** pretty
2	**A** such	**B** such a	**C** so much
3	**A** too	**B** much too	**C** too much
4	**A** enough	**B** such	**C** too
5	**A** really	**B** so	**C** so much
6	**A** enough clearly	**B** so clearly	**C** clearly enough
7	**A** such	**B** such a	**C** so
8	**A** often	**B** a lot	**C** a little

4 Complete the conversation with the words in the box. What are they talking about?

a lot of	amazing	good	hard	impossible
many	nearly enough	so	such a	way too

Elle: Your level is remarkably (1) ________ already. How do you do it?
Neil: Well, it's not (2) ________ difficult language to learn, is it?
Elle: But look at all those verb endings. There are so (3) ________ . I'll never remember them all! It's (4) ________ complicated for me. I haven't got (5) ________ time to study them all.
Neil: But the pronunciation's (6) ________ easy! Letters are always pronounced the same way. I think it sounds absolutely (7) ________ too. Think about people learning our language. It's very (8) ________ . It's totally (9) ________ to know how you pronounce things because there are such (10) ________ exceptions. All you need is practice. Let's try now. Hola Elle!

WRITE AND SPEAK

5 a Work in pairs. Write a conversation like the one in Exercise 4. Use intensifiers and one of the topics below. Don't say what the topic is.

school subjects   news stories   films   books
video games   sports or games

b Present your conversation to another pair. Can they guess what you're talking about?

>>> Be an active listener

SPEAK AND LISTEN

1 Work in pairs. Answer the questions.

1 In which situations do people usually make or listen to speeches?
2 Have you ever made or listened to a speech? When? What about?
3 Look at the title of Alberto's speech. What do you think it's about?

2 a Read the tips in the HOW TO box.

b Prepare to listen to Alberto's speech. What's your goal? What action's required?

3 3.27 **Listen actively to Alberto's speech. As you listen, think of a question to ask at the end. Then work in pairs. Compare what you've written down.**

4 Which tips in the HOW TO box did you use for help with Exercises 2b and 3? Tick (✓) them.

5 3.27 **Listen to the speech again. Complete the sentences with a word or short phrase.**

1 Alberto says he went to the UK on a(n) .... programme.
2 He describes feeling .... when he met his host family.
3 Alberto claims the phrase 'no worries' originated in ....
4 People use euphemisms to talk about something without .... itself.
5 Finally, Alberto says you .... learning a language.

REACT

6 Work in pairs. Answer the questions.

1 What did you think of Alberto's speech? Give reasons for your answer.
2 Do you know any English slang or colloquialisms? If so, which?

WORK WITH WORDS

7 a Match the words and phrases to their colloquial equivalents.

ALBERTO'S GUIDE TO ENGLISH SLANG

1	thank you	a	mate (UK), buddy, dude (US)
2	Don't mention it.	b	I'm off (UK, US), I'm out of here (UK, US)
3	How are things?	c	crash (out) (UK, US), hit the sack (UK, US), get some 'Z's (UK, US)
4	good	d	shattered (UK), beat (US)
5	man	e	dosh (UK), dough (UK, US)
6	friend	f	No worries. (UK, US), No problem. (UK, US)
7	money	g	chill (out) (UK, US), kick back (US)
8	toilet	h	ta (UK), cheers (UK)
9	tired	i	bloke (UK), guy (UK, US)
10	relax	j	cool (UK, US), awesome (US)
11	I'm going	k	How's it going? (UK, US), What's up? (US)
12	go to bed	l	the loo (UK), the ladies'/mens' room (US)

b 3.28 **Listen and check. Then listen and repeat.**

8 Work in pairs. Complete the tasks.

1 Write a short conversation that includes at least five of the normal words and phrases in Exercise 7a.
2 Swap your conversation with another pair. Rewrite their conversation using colloquial expressions. Then read your rewritten conversations to each other.

LEARNING TO GET BY IN A FOREIGN LANGUAGE
Speech and discussion
English in the real world: a personal journey
Speaker: Alberto Guzmán, Central Academy, Mexico City

HOW TO
be an active listener

- ☐ Before listening, ask: What exactly am I going to listen to? What do I expect to hear (number of speakers, serious or humorous tone, information or anecdotes)?
- ☐ Decide on your goal: to get information, evaluate something, understand feelings or be entertained?
- ☐ Decide what action is required: taking notes, preparing questions, making decisions, understanding jokes?
- ☐ As you listen, be prepared to adapt your goals and actions if your predictions were wrong.

GO BEYOND
Do the Words & Beyond exercise on page 139.

Workbook, pages 116–117

GRAMMAR Inversion

>>> Add emphasis to what you write and say

READ AND LISTEN

1 3.29 **Read and listen to an anecdote from a speech. Why was the speaker embarrassed?**

'Learning colloquial expressions in English is great. Not only do you suddenly understand more, but you also feel you can finally talk like a native speaker. But you need to be careful. One day I was at a friend's house in Liverpool. So proud was I of my colloquial English that I used it all the time. On a sofa sat an old man – my friend's grandfather. I introduced myself and started talking. He asked me about English food. That's when I said something I shouldn't have. Had I known how rude it was, I'd never have said it. No sooner had it left my mouth than I realised it was a mistake because everyone stared at me. Never had I felt so embarrassed in all my life.'

STUDY

2 Read the explanations. Then underline examples of inversion in Exercise 1.

Inversion
Use: To add emphasis to formal sentences.
Negative adverbials and so
Form: *Never (again)/Rarely/Only then* + auxiliary + subject *No sooner* + auxiliary + subject ... *than* *Not only* + auxiliary + subject ... , *but ... also* *So* + adjective + *be ... that*
Third conditional without *if*
Form: *had* + subject + past participle ... , *would have* + past participle
After a prepositional phrase
Form: prepositional phrase + verb + subject
See GRAMMAR DATABASE, page 129.

PRACTISE

3 Complete the anecdote with the words in the box.

also but never not only so sooner than

'This happened in France last summer. My brother and I were on a bus when a woman got on. On her head she wore the funniest hat we'd ever seen. We thought it was hilarious. (1) ________ had we laughed so much in public. In fact, (2) ________ amusing was it that we missed our stop. But no (3) ________ had the bus stopped at the next one (4) ________ she turned to us and said 'I think you two were meant to get off at the last stop.' (5) ________ then did I realise how foolish we'd been. (6) ________ only did she speak English, (7) ________ she'd (8) ________ understood everything we'd said.'

4 Put the words in order to add emphasis to the anecdote.

'Two days later my brother and I left our hotel for a walk, and soon realised we were lost. (1) *did / then / realise / I / only* ________ that I'd left my phone behind. (2) *a / on / stood / nearby corner* ________ a police officer, so I asked for directions. (3) *I / heard / rarely / had* ________ someone speak so fast, but (4) *confident / so / I / was* ________ about my French that I was sure I'd understood him. How wrong I was. Five minutes later, (5) *were / lost / only / not / we* ________ again, but we'd also ended up in a dangerous area. (6) *felt / I / had / never* ________ so frightened in all my life. We had no choice but to hail a taxi.'

5 Rewrite the sentences to add more emphasis.

1 I was so nervous that I couldn't remember my lines.
________ I couldn't remember my lines.

2 If I'd known she could hear, I wouldn't have said it.
________ she could hear, I wouldn't have said it.

3 It rained all day and it was also freezing cold.
________ freezing cold.

4 I'll never cheat in an exam again.
________ in an exam.

5 I'd hardly left the house when I realised I'd left my keys inside.
________ I realised I'd left my keys inside.

6 a 3.30 PRONOUNCE **Speakers usually break up what they say into small groups of words, with stress on the last content word. Listen and mark the word groups and stressed words below.**

Had I known how rude it was, I'd never have said it.

b 3.31 **Listen and repeat the sentence.**

SPEAK

7 a Prepare to tell an anecdote about a time when you were very embarrassed, frightened, nervous, disappointed or happy. Look at the exercises above for ideas and use inversion.

b Tell other students your anecdote. Ask them questions about theirs.

>>> Workbook, page 118

LANGUAGE & BEYOND

a

b

c

d

Be a successful non-native speaker

COMMUNICATE & COOPERATE

SPEAK AND READ

1 The photos above were all taken at an international youth conference. Work in pairs and answer the questions.

1 What language do you imagine the people are speaking? Why?
2 How do you think each person feels?
3 How would *you* feel if you were at the conference?

2 Work in pairs. Read the comments (1–4) from people at the conference and match them to the photos. Give reasons for your answers.

1 *I didn't speak much. I was nervous and couldn't express myself. Everything came out wrong.*

2 *It was hard to understand some people – and they found it hard to understand me.*

3 *One person didn't look me in the eye. Another person kept moving away. I don't know why.*

4 *Somehow I always found a way to get my ideas across. I learned so much from my new friends.*

DO

3 a Work in pairs. What advice would you give each person in Exercise 2?

b Read part of the conference welcome speech. Match the advice to the four comments. How similar is the advice to yours?

A Now you've all met, let me give you some advice. The grammar, vocabulary and pronunciation of your first language influence your English. That's why it can be difficult to understand speakers of different first languages. So be patient, listen carefully and ask people to repeat things. Say things in different ways if they don't understand you at first.

B Also keep in mind that different cultures have different rules about things like eye contact or how close you stand to people. Don't be offended by these differences. Your behaviour may not follow social rules in other places!

C Next, it can be hard to relax when you speak in English, but if you can, you'll find it much easier to express yourself. Don't worry about mistakes. Concentrate on getting your message across.

D And finally, remember that language is a way to meet people and learn new things. Focus on what you can do with it, not on the language itself.

REFLECT

4 Discuss these questions with your class. Do you agree with the REFLECTION POINT?

1 Have you ever used English to speak to a person from another country? When? How did you feel?
2 Which comments from Exercise 2 do you identify most with? Why?
3 Which advice do you think is most important? Why?

EXTEND

5 Work in pairs. Choose two people in the pictures and role-play their conversation. Imagine what they might be saying.

REFLECTION POINT

English has become the world's most common second language – used around the world between people who don't share a common first language. To communicate successfully in English, you need to be patient and search for ways to make communication work. It's also important to recognise and respect cultural differences.

Workbook, page 121

SPEAKING Centre stage

10

»» Describe a picture

SPEAK

1 Work in pairs. Look at the pictures. How many differences can you find?

WATCH OR LISTEN

2 a 3.32 Watch or listen to the scene. Which picture shows the theatre set Al describes?

Al: Well, (1) ________________ of the picture there's the main acting area. There are doors on the right and left and there are two arches (2) ________________ so you can come onto the stage from both sides. Between the two arches there are a few steps (3) ________________ a second acting level. Above that there's what looks like a gangway joining the two upper levels. There are acting areas in the top left- and top right-hand corners. The one on the left is slightly smaller than the other. That's where we'll do the famous balcony scene.

Kalu: Is that a screen in the background? Can we project things onto it?

Al: There is a screen (4) ________________ but there isn't enough space to project anything.

Eva: I think I can see a staircase through the archway at the back. Is that the only way to get up to the upper level?

Al: You can enter and exit the upper level (5) ________________ . And you can move (6) ________________ behind the screen.

Naomi: What's that thing right at the bottom? I can't quite make it out.

Al: Where?

Naomi: (7) ________________ ? I'm not sure what it is. It looks like ...

Al: Very funny. That's Jacquie's signature.

b Which Shakespeare play is the drama group going to perform?

3 3.32 Write the phrases in the conversation. Then watch or listen again to check your answers.

a on either side
b leading up to
c in the bottom right-hand corner
d in the foreground
e at the very back
f towards the back
g from one side to the other

4 3.33 Listen and repeat the phrases.

5 Work in pairs. Use the phrases in the PHRASEBOOK to describe the other picture in Exercise 1.

ACT

6 Work in pairs. Choose any photo from Units 6 to 10 of *Beyond* and prepare a description of it. Role-play a scene in which you both describe and give an opinion about the photo without showing it to the other students. Can the other students find the photo in the book?

PHRASEBOOK 3.34

Describe the position of things

in the top left-/right-hand corner
in the bottom left-/right-hand corner
in the foreground/background
towards the back
at the very back
on either side / on both sides
from one side to the other
the one on the left/right
leading up to
right at the top/bottom

Express uncertainty

I can't quite make it out.
I'm not sure what it is.
it looks like ...
there's what looks like ...

»» Workbook, page 119

WRITING Frankly, it's unacceptable

»» Express strong views

SPEAK AND READ

1 **Think about things that make you angry. Make a list. Then compare lists with a partner. Explain your choices.**

2 **Read Lara's email to a newspaper editor. What's she angry about? Is it on your list from Exercise 1?**

New mail Reply Forward

To the Editor,
I am writing to express my anger at a recent article about instant messaging in your newspaper. Apparently, it is making teenagers incapable of speaking and writing English properly. I am a teenager and never before have I felt so badly misunderstood and misrepresented.
Frankly, it is unacceptable for adults to attack young people in this way. Not only is it unfair, but it also utterly misses the point. When we send messages and talk to each other, of course we use colloquial language and slang, just like older people used to. What is more, we use a lot of symbols and abbreviations because it makes it quicker to get our message across in writing. Admittedly, some of us use this language when we should not, but that does not mean that we cannot use more formal language when we need to. On the contrary, I for one am completely capable of doing both things perfectly well, as this email shows.
It is about time adults stopped criticising all the things we do and started trying to understand why we do them. Unfortunately, it seems most adults are unable or unwilling to do that.
Lara Smith

STUDY

3 **Work in pairs. Read the email again. What do adults say about messaging where you live? Do you agree with Lara?**

4 **a** **Read the tips in the HOW TO box.**

b **Underline different ways of expressing strong views in the email.**

PRACTISE

5 **Complete the email with words and phrases from the HOW TO box.**

I am writing to express my frustration at recent comments about teenagers' poor social skills. (1) ____________ , we spend so much time looking at our phones that we have lost the ability to talk to each other. (2) ____________ , we have a lot more access to digital devices now than we have ever had before, but they have not replaced real relationships. (3) ____________ , we use those devices to have more contact with each other. (4) ____________ , adults seem to ignore this fact. Maybe because they are too busy looking at their own phones to see what is really going on. (5) ____________ , I am tired of being told how useless teenagers are. (6) ____________ we heard more about the positive things we do.

PLAN, WRITE AND CHECK

6 **You're going to write an email to the editor of a newspaper about something that makes you angry. Choose something from your list in Exercise 1, or think of something else.**

7 **Write your email. Use the tips from the HOW TO box to help you express your views. Then check it.**

SHARE AND REVIEW

8 **Swap your email with a partner. Read your partner's message and review it.**

Get it right

Put adverbs after objects:

- ... incapable of writing ~~properly~~ English properly.
- ... capable of doing ~~perfectly well~~ both things perfectly well.

HOW TO

express strong views

- Use formal language so that people will take your views seriously.
- Use intensifiers and inversion for emphasis. (See pages 107 and 109.)
- Use adverbs to emphasise what you think, eg:
  - *Frankly* before your main view.
  - *Apparently* before an opinion you disagree with.
  - *Admittedly* to partly accept another opinion.
  - *Unfortunately* before something disappointing.
  - *On the contrary* before saying why something isn't true.
- Use the negative form of words: *unacceptable*, *unfair*, *injustice*, etc.
- State what action you think is needed: *It is about time* + past simple.

»» Workbook, pages 120–121

VOCABULARY Phrasal verbs: languages and learning

1 Complete the advert with the verbs in the box.

break catch come die get get
keep look make pick try work

GROK School of Unusual Languages

Special offer! This month you can (1) .... out one of our new courses before you pay!

Body Language – Perfect if you find it hard to (2) .... across exactly what you want to say in words. It's easy to (3) .... up and there are no grammar rules to (4) .... out.

Martian – While some languages (5) .... out, others are born. Experts predict we'll be going to Mars soon and will need a new language. You can help us (6) .... up this exciting new language. We predict it'll (7) .... on in a big way.

Gobbledygook – Communication can (8) .... down and fail for many reasons. Official messages can often (9) .... across as incomprehensible because of obscure language. Learn Gobbledygook and you won't have to (10) .... up every word in a dictionary.

Grok's club – You don't need to study for years in order to (11) .... by in a language but you need to practise. Join our club to (12) .... up your conversation skills.

___ /12

Colloquial phrases

2 Write the words or phrases with the same meaning.

cool crash dough guy kick back
I'm off loo mate no problem
shattered ta what's up

Grok's Colloquial English Exam

1 awesome = ...
2 beat = ...
3 bloke = ...
4 buddy = ...
5 cheers = ...
6 chill out = ...
7 dosh = ...
8 hit the sack = ...
9 How's it going? = ... ?
10 I'm out of here = ...
11 men's room = ...
12 no worries = ...

___ /12

GRAMMAR Intensifiers

3 Choose the correct options.

GROK School of Unusual Languages

At the Grok School of Unusual Languages there are (1) *so many* / *such* unusual languages to learn that I'd be (2) *extremely* / *absolutely* surprised if you didn't find one for you. In my opinion, there aren't nearly (3) *enough opportunities* / *opportunities enough* to learn unusual languages. These languages are (4) *much too* / *so* important to be taught by just anyone. That's why we employ (5) *such a* / *such* highly qualified, hard-working teachers. I'm (6) *remarkably* / *utterly* convinced that our school is the best.

Maddie Grok

___ /12

Inversion

4 Match the sentence halves.

1 Not only are the courses great value,
2 Had I known how cool the course would be,
3 No sooner had I finished my first class
4 Never before have I had
5 So happy were the students
6 In the classroom
7 Rarely have I felt

a such a good time.
b so excited about learning a language.
c stood Maddie Grok herself!
d but the teachers are also amazing.
e than I was speaking basic Martian.
f that they applauded at the end of the class.
g I'd have signed up earlier.

___ /14

Your score: ___ /50

SKILLS CHECK

✓✓✓ Yes, I can. No problem!
✓✓ Yes, I can. But I need a bit of help.
✓ Yes, I can. But I need a lot of help.

I can understand what a writer's really saying. ....
I can be an active listener. ....
I can be a successful non-native speaker. ....
I can describe a photograph. ....
I can express strong views when I write. ....

Workbook, pages 122–123

READ

1 Read the short story and the questions below. For each question, choose A, B, C or D.

The Interview

I got the call at around 10pm. I'd been playing Funny Bird most of the evening (after I'd finished my homework, of course) and I was about to hit the sack.

'Hello. Is that Karl?' It was a woman's voice. She sounded as if we were best friends and yet I had no idea who she was.

'I'm calling about the job interview,' she continued. 'It's 10am tomorrow morning.'

She must've sensed my surprise because she added: 'You do remember that you're coming for an interview, don't you?'

By this time I was totally confused. Maybe some classmates were playing a joke. But then I realised that this was no joke.

'Karl,' she said slowly. 'It would be so much better if you'd cooperate.'

There was something slightly menacing in her voice and I felt a sudden sense of panic.

'But I don't understand!' I said a little too loudly.

'Karl. Listen to me. Did you or did you not download the Funny Bird app at 6:45pm today?'

'Yes, I did,' I said. The new games app had just been launched and I wanted to be one of the first to play it.

'And when you opened the app, did you or did you not click on the box that says "I have read and accept the terms and conditions of using this app"?'

'Yes, I think so.'

'So that means you read the terms and conditions, didn't you?'

'I'm not sure,' I lied. Nobody ever reads the terms and conditions.

The average person spends 1.75 seconds reading them!

'When you read the terms and conditions, I'm sure you noticed clause 84.2 in which you agreed to work full-time for the Funny Bird organisation for the rest of your life subject to our approval at the job interview tomorrow.'

I was lost for words.

'Look on the bright side,' she said. 'You'll be able to play Funny Bird whenever you want. See you tomorrow.'

1 What was Karl doing when he received the phone call?
   - A He was doing some schoolwork.
   - B He was playing a computer game.
   - C He was preparing to go to bed.
   - D He was looking for his phone.

2 What was Karl's initial reaction?
   - A He was totally confused.
   - B He was surprised.
   - C He wished he hadn't answered the phone.
   - D He thought she was a classmate.

3 Which of these statements is most correct?
   - A He didn't read the conditions.
   - B He didn't understand the conditions.
   - C He looked at the conditions for a few seconds.
   - D He didn't see any link to the conditions.

4 How does the woman's attitude change?
   - A She becomes increasingly friendly.
   - B She grows increasingly angry.
   - C She becomes more cooperative.
   - D She becomes more threatening.

5 What do you think the author's message is?
   - A Don't speak to strangers on the phone.
   - B Always use a secure internet connection.
   - C Study rather than play digital games.
   - D Know what you're agreeing to first.

Reading: ______ /10

EXAM TIPS

do a multiple-choice reading exercise

- Read the whole text first.
- Read each question or the first part of the sentence carefully.
- Find the correct place in the text and choose the best option.
- Check that the meaning of the answer or the completed sentence matches the text.

recognise emphasis

See page 96.

understand what a writer's *really* saying

See page 106.

LISTEN

2 (3.35) **You will hear an interview with a music star. For each question, choose A, B or C.**

1 How old was Cool Buddy II when he became successful?
  A 14
  B 16
  C 18
2 Why is Helen slightly worried about interviewing him?
  A He has a reputation for being aggressive in interviews.
  B He doesn't like being interviewed.
  C He once behaved badly during a television interview.
3 Cool Buddy thinks it's important for people to ...
  A be themselves.
  B read the papers.
  C buy his new album.
4 The title of his new album is ...
  A *Buddies.*
  B *In the Heat of the Moment.*
  C *Barking up the Wrong Tree.*
5 What's 'Karulakool'?
  A A word he invented when he was a child.
  B The name given to describe his fans.
  C A collection of made-up words and phrases.

Listening: ______ /10

WRITE

3 You have received a letter from a magazine editor asking you to write an article. Read the letter. Then write an article (120–150 words) including the points in the letter.

We'd like you to write about your language-learning experience.
What has been the greatest challenge for you? What have you enjoyed most? Do you think someone from another country would find it more or less difficult to learn your language? Why?

Writing: ______ / 10

Progress check score ______ /30

EXAM TIPS

do a multiple-choice listening exercise (one long audio track)
See page 71.

infer meaning
See page 98.

be an active listener
See page 108.

EXAM TIPS

Write an article

- Read the task carefully. What's the article about? Underline information you need to include.
- Think about your audience. Where will the article be published? Who will read it?
- Make a plan. You should include:
  - a short introduction to get the reader's attention.
  - two or three paragraphs to develop the topic.
  - a conclusion with a personal comment.
- Give your article an interesting title that will make people want to read it.

express strong views
See page 112.

EXTRA READING Middlemarch

BEFORE YOU READ

1 Look at the cover of the book and read the introduction. Does the woman come from a rich or a poor family? What do you think that tells us about her education, work, marriage and future plans?

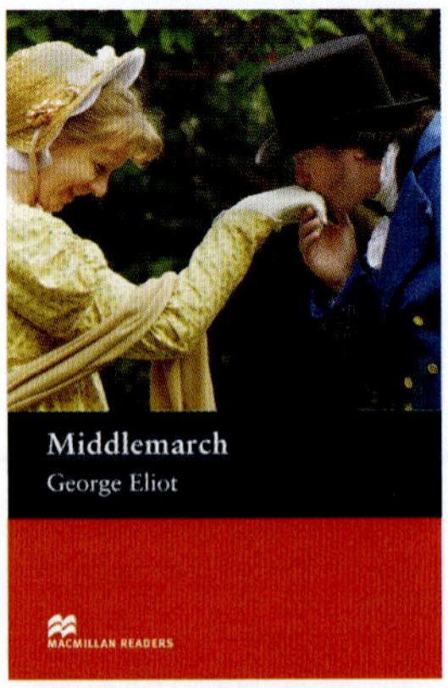

Middlemarch was written between 1871 and 1872 and first published in eight monthly parts. It was a great success and was published as a complete book in 1874.
The novel is set between 1829 and 1833 in the fictitious English town of Middlemarch. The town was based on Coventry (now a major city), where Eliot once lived. The heroine, Dorothea, is very beautiful. She lives with her wealthy uncle, Mr Brooke, and her younger sister, Celia, in a big old house in the countryside near Middlemarch.

WHILE YOU READ

2 (3.36) Read the extract from *Middlemarch.* Was your answer to Exercise 1 correct?

HOW TO
deal with new vocabulary when you read
See page 18.

HOW TO
understand opinions
See page 40.

Dorothea and Celia had been orphans for more than seven years. Their uncle, Mr Brooke, who had never married, was their guardian. He had sent his nieces to live with good families in England and Switzerland. There they had been taught by governesses until their uncle decided that they were old enough to live with him at Tipton Manor.
Mr Brooke was very fond of Dorothea and Celia and although he knew very little about women, he was happy to look after his nieces.
Both girls had inherited a little money from their parents. As Dorothea was the elder sister, any future son she might have would inherit Mr Brooke's wealth too. Of course, the Brooke sisters were expected to make good marriages to rich men who owned land and had a big house and many servants. The girls' lives would be spent looking after their husbands and, later on, their children.
Neither of the girls was well educated. Very few women received a good education in 1829. Yet everyone agreed that Dorothea was clever. She was beautiful too, with long dark hair and large dark eyes. She always dressed very plainly and she wore her hair in an old-fashioned way, but somehow that only made her look even more lovely.
Dorothea had very strong opinions about many things and she sometimes had strange ideas too. She wanted to use her mind and think for herself, but she also tried to learn as much as she could from other people. She wanted to use her money to make the little world of Middlemarch a better place.
Celia Brooke was very pretty, with light brown hair and brown eyes. She enjoyed wearing fashionable clothes and curling her hair. She was not as serious as her elder sister. But everyone said that Celia was more sensible than the beautiful Dorothea.

Mr Brooke had invited two guests to dinner that evening – the Reverend Mr Casaubon of Lowick Manor, who was a scholar, and Sir James Chettam, who lived at Freshitt Hall.
Celia wore amethysts with a new white dress and she looked very pretty. Dorothea did not wear any jewellery and her dress, as usual, was very plain. But this made her look more beautiful than ever.
Sir James was a handsome young man, who was often a guest at Tipton Grange. Like Mr Brooke, Sir James owned a large estate and a fine house. And, like Mr Brooke, Sir James was a very wealthy man. He had decided that he would ask Dorothea to marry him and he was sure that she would say yes. Mr Brooke was fond of his young neighbour and he hoped that Dorothea would agree.
However, Dorothea was not at all interested in Sir James. She believed that he came to Tipton to see her sister, Celia. Dorothea did think of marriage, of course, but not to a young man. Her idea of a husband was an intelligent, older man who would guide her and teach her, like a father.
Dorothea had never met Mr Casaubon before but she had immediately become interested in his serious conversation. By the side of Sir James, Mr Casaubon looked old and pale. His hair was partly grey and his eyes had deep shadows under them. But Dorothea, listening to the older man's slow careful voice, took no notice of these things.
In answer to a question from Mr Brooke, Mr Casaubon was speaking about his own work.
'I am happy to tell you about it,' he said with a smile. 'I have been studying the subject for many years. In preparation, I have read all the Latin and Greek authors and others too, of course. My aim is to put together all the greatest thoughts on the myths and

world religions. I plan to show that they are all part of the same knowledge – of one great plan. My book will be called "The Key to All Mythologies"'.
Then Mr Casaubon sighed. 'I still have a great deal of information to put in order before I start writing the book,' he added. 'My health is not always good and I sometimes think that I will die before my work is finished.'
'That would be terrible!' Dorothea said quickly. 'Perhaps you need a secretary to help you arrange your notes. I try to put my uncle's papers in order sometimes, but he won't let me.'
'Well, a woman's mind, you know,' Mr Brooke said with a laugh. 'Women are not trained to do these things, are they, Mr Casaubon?'
When the two girls were alone, after dinner, Celia said:
'How very ugly Mr Casaubon is with his pale face and thin grey hair! He must be at least 45 years old. He moves his head up and down when he speaks and his voice is so unpleasant.'
'You mustn't talk about Mr Casaubon like that, Celia!' Dorothea cried. 'He is a scholar and he has a very fine mind. I wish that I could help him with his work!'
'To do that, you would have to marry him. What would Sir James Chettam think about that?' Celia replied with a smile.
'Sir James? What do you mean?' Dorothea asked quickly.
'You know what I mean, Dorothea. Sir James wants to marry you,' her sister replied. 'Why do you think that he visits our uncle so often? And why is he so interested in your drawings for the new cottages in Freshitt village? I know that you are very clever, Dorothea, but you don't understand people at all.'

AFTER YOU READ

3 **Copy or download the organiser. Then read the first part of the extract and make notes about the two sisters. What do they have in common? In what ways are they different?**

Title: ____________________

Dorothea	Both sisters	Celia

4 **Write the answers to the questions in your own words.**

1 Why does Sir James visit Tipton Manor so often?
2 How does Dorothea feel about Sir James and Mr Casaubon?
3 Why does Celia tell Dorothea that she doesn't understand people at all?

HOW TO
understand referring words
See page 32.

5 **3.37 Listen to an audio extract from a later part of the novel and answer the questions below.**

1 Who does Dorothea marry?
2 What do the sisters think of Mr Casaubon's house?
3 How is Will Ladislaw related to Mr Casaubon? Do they get on well together? How do you know?

HOW TO
deal with new vocabulary when you listen
See page 54.

6 **Read about *Middlemarch* and answer the questions.**

There are many themes in *Middlemarch*, but the most important one is that of marriage and what men and women of that time expected from it. Eliot also showed how unkind and mean people can be to others who are different from themselves. Although Eliot wrote about a different time and a different society in *Middlemarch*, the book is still popular today.

1 Why do you think *Middlemarch* is still popular today?
2 George Eliot was the pen name used by Mary Ann Evans. Why do you think she used it? Do you think women authors still use male pen names today? Why?/Why not?
3 The story of *Middlemarch* is told in the third person. What are the advantages of telling a story in the third rather than first person?

EXTRA READING Moby Dick

BEFORE YOU READ

1 Look at the cover of the book and read about its author. Which of Melville's jobs do you think influenced his writing? In what ways?

The American writer, Herman Melville, was born in New York in 1819. His father died when he was twelve years old, and a year later he left school and began working in a bank to help support his family. This was followed by jobs as a teacher and newspaper reporter. Then, at the age of nineteen, he worked as a sailor on a merchant ship going to England. *Moby Dick* was published in 1851 but it wasn't until the 1920s that it was recognised as a classic American novel. It is now considered to be one of the greatest novels of all time.

WHILE YOU READ

2 3.38 Read the extract from *Moby Dick* and match it with the correct chapter title.

a Elijah's warning b 'Man Overboard!' c The Five 'Ghosts'

HOW TO
understand references

See page 84.

It was night time. I was on deck when I heard two sailors talking.
'Listen! Did you hear that noise?' said one man.
'What noise, Archie?' asked the other man.
'There it is again – below deck! Do you hear it? It's someone coughing,' said Archie.
'I don't hear anything,' said Cabaco.
'And again!' said Archie. 'Listen! It's the sound of two or three men moving in their beds. I think there are some other men hidden below deck, and we haven't seen them yet. And I suspect our captain knows something about it.'
After his talk with the crew, our captain had spent most of his nights studying charts and maps. He knew about sperm whales' feeding habits and was able to make quite good guesses at the times and places where he might find Moby Dick.
At the same time, his men told each other many stories about the great white whale. Some were true, some imagined. To believe them all meant that Moby Dick must have been in ten places in the world at the same time.
Already, many men had died trying to catch Moby Dick. On one occasion, a whaling captain had jumped on his back and attacked him with a knife. But the whale had simply turned his great head and bitten off the captain's leg. That man was Captain Ahab. His shipmates had pulled him from the water and he was screaming with pain. For weeks after that, he was like a madman and the crew had to tie him to his bed.
Now this crazy gray-haired old man was chasing the same whale around the world. Would his hatred for Moby Dick drive us all to our deaths?
It was a cloudy, warm afternoon. Sailors were half asleep on the decks or staring out to sea. I was sitting with Queequeg. Suddenly, there was a shout from the top of the main mast.
'There she blows! Whales! Lots of them!' It was Tashtego pointing out to sea with his left hand.
Immediately, every man on the ship began to move. Tashtego came down from the mast and we helped the crew put the whaleboats over the side of the ship.

At that moment, we heard a sound behind us and turned around. Captain Ahab was standing there with five men. They stood like ghosts around Ahab. Then four of them went to one of the spare whaleboats and put it over the side of the ship. The fifth man was the chief of the others. He wore black cotton trousers and a black cotton jacket. He had one white tooth, and his hair was fixed high on his head like a tall hat.
'Are you ready, Fedallah?' Ahab asked him.
'I'm ready,' was the whispered reply.
'Then lower the boats!' Ahab shouted.
The other men and I jumped into our three boats and they were lowered quickly into the sea. I was in Starbuck's boat. We were rowing away from the ship when the fourth boat came from the other side of the ship. The five strangers were rowing it, and Captain Ahab stood behind them.
'Move out!' Ahab shouted to the three boats captained by Starbuck, Stubb and Flask. 'Spread yourselves!'
'Captain Ahab – ?' began Starbuck, staring at the strange men.
'Flask, pull away to your left!' shouted Ahab.
'Yes – yes, sir!' shouted Flask. 'Don't worry about the captain's new crew,' he told his men. 'Row, boys, row! There she blows! There she blows!'
Soon Stubb's and Starbuck's boats were passing each other and Stubb spoke to the first mate.
'Mr Starbuck, sir!'
'Yes, Stubb?' answered Starbuck.

'What do you think about those new men?'
'They came on board secretly before the ship left Nantucket,' replied Starbuck. I'm sure of it.'
'But why are they here?' asked Starbuck.
'It's all because of the white whale,' answered Stubb.
The arrival of these five strangers did not frighten the rest of the crew. Archie had already told them about what he had heard, so they were not as surprised as they might have been. But this did not stop them from wondering about them. Where had Ahab found them? How had he persuaded them to come on the voyage? Wild stories would spread about the men, but nobody knew the truth.
I remembered the strange shadows in the mist the day that Queequeg and I had come aboard. 'These strangers must be the men I saw,' I thought.
Then I remembered Elijah's mysterious warning.
Captain Ahab's boat was far ahead of the others. Fedallah had thrown off his black jacket and now stood holding his harpoon. Suddenly, Ahab put up his hand. It was a signal for every man to stop rowing.
'Queequeg, stand up and look out,' Starbuck ordered.
Queequeg stood up in the boat and looked around for the whales. Across from us, Flask was also looking from his boat. For a moment everything had gone silent and still. Then Starbuck suddenly shouted, 'Row, boys, row!'
Great waves lifted us up, then threw us down again. The boats separated, and our boat began to chase after three whales. Our sail was up and, with the strong wind, we rushed through the water.
'Pull, boys, pull!' said Starbuck. 'We must kill them before the wind gets too strong for us. Stand up, Queequeg!'
Queequeg jumped up at the front of the boat. His harpoon was ready in his hand. We all waited. Then there was a sudden loud noise as one of the whales came up through the waves.
'That's him!' said Starbuck.

AFTER YOU READ

3 **Copy or download the organiser. Look for time expressions in the extract and make notes about what happened at the different times.**

Time:	Time: ....
Event:	Event: ....

4 **Write the answers to the questions in your own words.**

1 Why was Ahab looking for Moby Dick?
2 The narrator mentions a character called Elijah who'd given him a mysterious warning before the voyage. What do you think the warning was?
3 What do you think the phrase 'There she blows!' means?

5 3.39 **Listen to an audio extract from another part of the story and answer the questions.**

1 What dangers do the sailors face? How do they deal with them?
2 How does the narrator describe the moment in the illustration?

HOW TO
be an active listener
See page 108.

6 **Read about *Moby Dick* and answer the questions.**

Moby Dick is an adventure story inspired by real news stories of the period. 'Mocha Dick' was a famous whale who was named after the sailor who eventually killed him. But the novel is more than an account of whaling in the 1800s. It's also the story of an individual's struggle against fate or against nature and about the battle between good and evil. It's a book that can be read on many levels.

1 What does the last sentence of the article mean?
2 In *Moby Dick*, who do you think represents good and who represents evil?
3 What techniques does the author use that are common in films and TV series?
4 *Moby Dick* is sometimes called the greatest American novel. What's an equivalent novel in your country and what makes it so special?

Present tenses review

Present simple

- Use the present simple to talk about habits, routines and facts:
  *I **check** my emails when I **get** home from school.*
  *Hurricanes **form** in the north Atlantic or north-east Pacific.*
- Use adverbs of frequency such as *usually*, *always*, *hardly ever* and expressions of frequency such as *every day*, *from time to time* and *once a week* with the present simple:
  *She **usually chats** online in the evenings.*
  ***From time to time** strong winds **batter** the coast.*

Present continuous

- Use the present continuous to talk about things in progress now or around now:
  *The waves **are crashing** onto the beach.*
- Use time expressions such as *now*, *right now*, *at the moment* and *these days* with the present continuous:
  *People **are evacuating right now**.*
  ***Are** you still **living** in Hawaii **these days**?*
- Use the present continuous to talk about temporary or changing situations:
  *The temperature**'s rising**. It**'s getting** really hot.*
- Use the present continuous with *always* to criticise someone's habits:
  *My sister**'s always borrowing** my clothes.*

Present perfect simple

- Use the present perfect simple with *ever/never* for past actions when you don't say an exact time:
  ***Have you ever been** at sea during a storm?*
  ***I've never seen** such strong winds before.*
- Use the present perfect simple for recently completed actions with *just*, *already*, *so far*, *yet*, etc:
  *The authorities **have just ordered** everyone to evacuate.*
  ***So far** the storm **hasn't caused** too much damage.*
- Use the present perfect simple with *for/since* for actions in a period that started in the past and continue to now:
  *The current hurricane naming system **has been** in use **since** 1953.*

Present perfect continuous

- Use the present perfect continuous with time expressions such as *recently*, *lately* and *all day/afternoon/week* to describe actions in progress recently:
  *I**'ve been watching** the waves from my window **all morning**.*
- Use the present perfect continuous with *for/since* for actions in progress from a time in the past until now:
  *The storm **has been strengthening** in the Atlantic **for** weeks.*
  *People **have been leaving** the town **since** this morning.*

WATCH OUT! State verbs

We usually use the simple form with **state verbs**. State verbs often express mental states and opinions (eg *believe*, *feel*, *know*, *think*, *remember*, *understand*, etc) and preferences (eg *like*, *love*, *hate*, *need*, *want*, etc):
*She **feels** scared.* (NOT ~~*She's feeling*~~ *...*)
*I **want** to go home.* (NOT ~~*I'm wanting*~~ *...*)
However you can use a continuous form if the same verb describes an action (eg *thinking* = *considering*, *having* = *eating* and *being* = *behaving*):
*I**'m thinking** about getting my hair cut.*
*She**'s having** cereal for breakfast.*
*Ali**'s being** really annoying.*

Articles and other determiners

USE

- Use articles to show if you're referring to something specific or general.

FORM

- Use *a(n)* before one example of a thing:
  *I've got **a** really **bad memory**.*
- Use *the* before a specific thing:
  *What did you think of **the history test** in class this morning?*
- Use *the* before a unique thing such as *the moon*, *the sky*, etc:
  *Who invented **the internet**?*
- Use *the* before plural names of people and places:
  *Have you met **the Johnsons** who live next door?*
- Use *the* before rivers, oceans, seas and deserts:
  *Which is the longest river – **the Amazon** or **the Nile**?*
- Use *the* before a group of people, eg *the English*, *the poor*, etc.
- Use no article before plural and uncountable nouns with a general reference: ***Children** have wonderful **imaginations**.*
- Use no article before abstract ideas such as *love*, etc:
  ***Friendship** and **happiness** are more important than money.*
- Use no article before singular place names, streets, etc:
  *New York's **Central Park** was first opened in 1857.*

Other determiners

USE

- Use determiners to show how many or which things you're referring to.

FORM

- Use *all*, *most*, *some* and *no* before plural and uncountable nouns:
  ***Some** students struggled. (= approximately 30% of students)*
  *But **no** students failed. (= 0% of students)*
- Use *both* (for two things) and *many* before plural nouns:
  ***Both** rivers are long.*
  ***Many** cars are made in Japan.*
- Use *a few* (several or some) and *few* (= a very small number) before plural nouns:
  *I had **a few** problems. **Few** people passed the test.*
- Use *no*, *either* and *neither* before singular countable nouns. *Either* means 'one or the other' and *neither* means 'not one and not the other':
  *You could buy **either** dictionary. **Neither** dictionary is expensive.*
  *But **no** dictionary contains every word in the English language.*
- Use *each* when referring to two or more things separately:
  ***Each** dictionary has got a pronunciation guide at the back.*
- Use *every* when referring to three or more things together:
  ***Every** student in the class will receive a letter to take home.*
- Use a determiner + *of* + *the/our/us*:
  ***Most of us** knew the answer to question 1.*
  ***None of the students** knew the name of the world's largest lake. (= no students knew)*
- Use *none* not *no* with *of*.

WATCH OUT!

Neither has a negative meaning but use a positive singular verb after it:
*We watched two DVDs but **neither** film **was** very funny.*

Narrative tenses review

Past simple

- Use the past simple for completed actions in the past:
  *A long time ago, a young fisherman named Urashima Taro **lived** in a small coastal village.*
  *Taro **saw** a group of children shouting.*

Past continuous

- Use the past continuous for actions in progress at a particular time in the past, often interrupted by events in the past simple:
  *One day, while he **was walking** along the seashore, Taro saw a group of children shouting …*
  *After a few days, he **was fishing** by the seashore when suddenly a big turtle appeared from out of the waves.*
- You usually use *while* before the past continuous:
  *… **while** he was walking …*
- You usually use *when* before the past simple:
  *… **when** suddenly a big turtle appeared …*

Past perfect simple

- Use the past perfect simple to show that an action happened before another action or time in the past. Use the past simple for the other more recent action/time:
  *Once the children **had gone**, Taro **took** the turtle to the water's edge and set it free.*
- You often use the past perfect with the time expressions *by* + time/age, *before*, *just*, *once*, *yet*, *after* and *already*:
  ***After he'd returned** the turtle to the water, it swam out to sea.*
- You often use the past perfect with *because* to give an explanation:
  *The children stopped throwing stones at the turtle **because** Taro **had offered** them money.*

WATCH OUT!

The past perfect simple (and the present perfect simple) is formed with past participles. Many of these are irregular. See page 140 for a list of irregular past participles.

Past perfect continuous

- Use the past perfect continuous for actions in progress up to a time in the past:
  *Before Taro arrived, the children **had been kicking** and **throwing** stones at a small turtle.*
- You often use the past perfect continuous with the time expressions *all morning/day*, *for* and *since*:
  *Taro **had been fishing all morning**, when he saw a strange sight.*

Past perfect simple or continuous?

- Use the past perfect simple for a finished action and the past perfect continuous for an action in progress:
  *Taro **had been fishing** by the sea when a big turtle suddenly appeared.*
  *It was the same turtle whose life he **had saved**.*

WATCH OUT! State verbs

You don't often use the past continuous and the past perfect continuous with state verbs such as *like*, *need*, *want*, *know*, *think* and *understand*.
*Taro **felt** scared when the big turtle appeared.* (NOT *~~Taro was feeling~~ …*)
*I'**d known** him for a long time.* (NOT *~~I'd been knowing~~ …*)
However you can use a continuous form if the same verb describes an action (eg *thinking* = *considering*, *having* = *eating* and *being* = *behaving*). Also see Grammar Database 1 Watch out! State verbs.

Used to and *would*

USE

- Use *used to* to talk about habits or states in the past:
  *I **used to** keep a journal when I was younger.*
  *She **used to** have terrible handwriting but now she writes beautifully.*

FORM

- Use *used to* + infinitive to talk about habits or states in the past:
  *Good handwriting **used to be** considered a measure of intelligence.*
- The negative form of *used to* is *didn't use to* + infinitive:
  *People **didn't use to write** down folk tales.*
- To form questions, use *did* + subject + *use to* + infinitive:
  ***Did people use to** read more?*
  Yes, they did. / No, they didn't.
- Don't use *used to* in the present; use adverbs of frequency:
  *I **usually cook** at the weekend.*

WATCH OUT!

Don't use *used to* in negative and question forms:
*I didn't **use** to like chocolate* (not *~~I didn't **used** to like chocolate~~*.)

Would

USE

- Use *would* to talk about habits (NOT states) in the past:
  *People **would** write letters by hand.*
  *Many fairy tales **would** be told orally in the past.*
- *Would* is more common in written descriptions than in speech.
- Don't use *would* when talking about past states:
  *We **used to** have a pet cat but we don't anymore.* (NOT *~~We would have~~ a pet cat …*)

FORM

- Use *would/wouldn't* + infinitive without *to*:
  *When I was younger I **would go** and stay at my grandmother's house and she **would read** me lots of fairy tales.*

Futures review

USE

- Use different future forms to express different ways of talking about the future.

Present simple

- Use the present simple for events on a timetable or a schedule:
  The website competition ***closes*** *at the end of the month.*

Present continuous

- Use the present continuous for future arrangements:
  *I'****m leaving*** *school at the end of the academic year.*

be going to **(1)**

- Use *be going to* + verb for future plans and intentions:
  *I'****m going to start*** *my own business.*

be going to **(2)**

- You can also use *be going to* + verb for predictions based on present evidence, or for which you have reliable information (eg statistics/research/reports):
  *My mobile phone'****s going to run out of*** *battery soon.*

will/won't **(1)**

- Use *will/won't* + verb for facts:
  The app ***will show*** *you how to achieve your goals.*
  *You'****ll find*** *more information on the website.*
  You ***won't have to*** *write any of the content for the website.*

will/won't **(2)**

- Use *will/won't* + verb for predictions about the future:
  *Don't miss out – it'****ll be*** *fun!*
  Starting up your own business means you ***won't have to*** *look for a job in the future.*
- Use *will definitely* when you're 100% sure:
  Running your own business ***will definitely*** *be hard work.*
- Use *will probably* when you're 75% sure:
  *It'****ll probably*** *be a big success.*
- In affirmative sentences with *will*, the adverb (*probably/ definitely*) comes AFTER *will*:
  *I'****ll probably*** *employ other people too.*
- In a negative sentence, the adverb comes BEFORE *won't*:
  It ***probably*** *won't make a lot of money.*

will/won't **(3)**

- Use *will/won't* for promises and decisions made at the time of speaking:
  *I'****ll*** *download it now!*

be likely to

- Use *be likely to* + verb to talk about things that will probably happen:
  Young people ***are likely to*** *use the app the most.*

be about to

- Use *be about to* to talk about things that will happen soon:
  Developers ***are about to*** *start work on the app.*

will be able to

- Use *will be able to* to talk about future ability:
  *You'****ll be able to*** *buy the app soon.*

Future continuous and future perfect

USE

- Use the future continuous to talk about things in progress at a time in the future:
  *We'****ll be handing*** *in our essays next week.*
- Use the future perfect simple to talk about things completed before a time in the future:
  I hope I ***will have finished*** *my essay by the weekend.*
- Use the future perfect continuous for actions in progress before a time in the future, often with *for* and *since*:
  By Saturday I will have been working on it for ten days.

FORM

- Form the future continuous with *will/won't* + *be* + verb + *-ing*:
  *I'****ll be doing*** *my homework at 8pm.*
- Form the future perfect simple with *will/won't* + *have* + past participle. You often use *by* + time expression with the future perfect:
  I ***will have finished*** *my homework* ***by*** *9pm.*
- Form the future perfect continuous with *will/won't* + *have* + verb + *-ing*:
  I ***will have been studying*** *all week.*

Conditionals

First conditional

USE

- Use the first conditional to talk about possible situations in the future and their results. The *if*-clause describes a possible action. The other clause describes its predicted result:
  *If you **don't hand** your essay in on time, you'**ll lose** marks.*

FORM

- Use the present simple in the *if*-clause and *will* (*not*) + infinitive in the result clause:
  if-clause (action) result clause
  ***If** you **come** to the concert tonight, **you'll have** a great time.*
- Use the present simple in the *if*-clause and *may* or *might* (*not*) + infinitive in the result clause if you are not sure about the result:
  ***If** I **go** for coffee, I **may** be late home.*
- You can also use other modal verbs such as *must* (*not*) + infinitive in the result clause:
  ***If** you **use** sources for your essay, you **must** credit them.*
- Use *unless* with a positive verb in the *if*-clause to mean '*if … not*':
  *We won't improve **unless** we learn from our mistakes.*
- Use *as/so long as* or *providing/provided* (*that*) instead of *if* to mean 'on condition that':
  ***Provided** she studies hard, she will pass her exams.*
- Use imperatives instead of *will* in the result clause to give commands:
  *If you see Dan later, **tell** him I need my history book back.*

Second conditional

USE

- Use the second conditional to talk about unlikely or imaginary situations in the present or future and their results:
  *If we **recycled** more, we **wouldn't produce** so much waste.*

FORM

- Use the past simple after *if* in the *if-clause*. Use *would* (*not*) + infinitive without *to* in the result clause. The contracted form of *would* is *'d*.
  if-clause (action) result clause
  *If we **banned** cars, we**'d reduce** pollution levels.*
- To form questions, use *would* + subject + infinitive without *to*.
  ***Would you work** for a charity **if you had** the chance?*
- You can use *If I was* or *If I were* for the first person.
  *If I **was/were** in charge, I would make fares cheaper.*

Third conditional

USE

- Use the third conditional to talk about imaginary situations in the past and their results. Use the *if*-clause to imagine a change to what really happened in the past. Use the other clause to imagine the result of that change:
  *If **I'd known** there was a test today, I **wouldn't have stayed** up so late last night.*

FORM

- Use the past perfect after *if* in the *if-clause*. Use *would(n't) have* + past participle in the result clause:
  if-clause (action) result clause
  *If they **hadn't cut down** so many trees, they **wouldn't have destroyed** their main food source.*
- In the result clause, you can use other modals like *should*, *could* and *might*:
  *They **might** have survived if they'd respected their environment.*
- To form questions, use *would* + subject + *have* + past perfect:
  ***Would they have survived** if the settlers hadn't arrived?*
  Yes, they would. / No, they wouldn't.

Mixed conditionals

USE

- Mix second and third conditionals to connect the past with the present:
  *I **wouldn't be** so hungry now if I **had eaten** my breakfast.*
- The first clause in the above sentence is the second conditional and is about an unlikely situation in the present. The second clause is the third conditional and is imagining a change in the past.

WATCH OUT!

With all types of conditional sentences, you can start the sentence with either clause:
If you work hard, you'll get good marks.
You'll get good marks if you work hard.
Remember: if the *if*-clause comes second, don't use a comma.

Wishes and regrets: *I wish/If only*

USE

- Use *I wish* or *If only* to express unhappiness with a situation in the present or in the past, or with a future plan:
  I wish I could play** the guitar.* (= ***I can't play the guitar but I'd like to be able to play it.)
  ***If only I hadn't lost** touch with my best friend from primary school.*
  ***I wish I didn't have to** babysit my little sister tonight.*

FORM

- Use *I wish* or *If only* + past simple to express unhappiness with a situation in the present, or with a future plan:
  ***I wish I was** taller. **If only I could go** out tonight.*
- Use *I wish* or *if only* + past perfect to express unhappiness with a situation in the past:
  ***If only I hadn't been** so angry with her.*
  ***I wish I'd revised** harder for the history test.*
- Use *I wish* or *If only* + *would* + infinitive without *to* to complain about annoying behaviour:
  ***I wish my sister would stop** borrowing my clothes.*
- You can use *were* instead of *was* after *if only* and *I wish*:
  *If only I **were** taller.* (or *If only I **was** taller.*)
  *I wish it **were** the weekend.* (or *I wish it **was** the weekend.*)

Verbs followed by *-ing* and/or infinitive

- Use the *-ing* form after these verbs:

enjoy keep mind practise admit deny suggest

Do you ***enjoy working*** *in a team?*

- Some verbs with prepositions take the *-ing* form, such as:

succeed in dream about look forward to

I'm ***looking forward to seeing*** *you soon.*

- Use the infinitive with *to* after these verbs:

choose hope manage

He's ***managed to get*** *into the football club's youth team.*

- Some verbs can be followed by object + infinitive with *to*:

ask help want would like/love/hate/prefer

Do you ***want*** *<u>me</u>* ***to help*** *you?*
*We'****d like*** *<u>you</u>* ***to be*** *part of it.*

- But they don't always need an object:
*I'****d love to go*** *to the new art exhibition in town.*
- Some verbs are always followed by object + (*not*) infinitive with *to*:

advise encourage invite teach tell warn

She ***encouraged*** *<u>me</u>* ***to take*** *part.*
He ***warned*** *<u>me</u>* ***not to go****.*

- Modal auxiliary verbs such as *can*, *could*, *should*, *will* and *would* are always followed by infinitive without *to*:
You ***should go*** *and* ***see*** *the new exhibition at the museum.*
- *Used to* (for past habits) is followed by infinitive without *to*:
I didn't ***use to enjoy*** *speaking in public but now I feel much more confident.*
- Some verbs such as *make* and *let* are followed by object + infinitive without *to*:
My parents ***let me go*** *to the football match.*
- Some verbs can be followed by either *-ing* or the infinitive with *to* and have a similar meaning:

like love hate prefer begin continue start

I ***hate doing*** *the washing-up. = I* ***hate to do*** *the washing-up.*

- Some verbs can be followed by either *-ing* or the infinitive with *to* but have a different meaning in each case:

stop forget remember try mean

I ***forgot to feed*** *the cat.* (about an action that needs to be done)
I'll never ***forget going*** *to London for the first time.* (about an action in the past that was done)
I ***meant to tell*** *you yesterday but I didn't have time.* (*mean = intend*)
If you want to be in the school play, it will ***mean going*** *to rehearsals every day.* (*mean = involve/have a result*)

Comparisons

Comparatives, superlatives, (*not*) *as … as …*

USE

- Use comparatives to compare two things:
I prefer this painting – the colours are ***brighter*** *and* ***more intense****.*
- Use superlative adjectives and adverbs to compare one thing with all the others in a group:
John is ***the most confident*** *person I know.*
- Use (*not*) *as* + adjective/adverb + *as* to say that two things are (or are not) the same:
Red isn't ***as popular as*** *pink.*
- (*not*) *as … as* is more common than *as … as*. We tend to use *just* in *as … as* comparisons:
He's ***just as tall as*** *me.*

FORM

WATCH OUT! **Some comparative and superlative adjectives and adverbs are irregular:**

adjective/adverb	comparative adjective	superlative adjective
good/well	better	the best
bad/badly	worse	the worst
far	further	the furthest

- Use *more* and *most* for the comparative and superlative forms of most adverbs:
Can you talk ***more slowly*** *please?*
- *Less* + long adjective is the opposite of *more*. Only use *less* with long adjectives:
During the Roman Empire, people who wore blue were considered ***less worthy*** *than their richer counterparts.*
- *The least* + long adjective is the opposite of *the most*. Only use *the least* with long adjectives:
He's ***the least friendly*** *person I know.*

Comparing nouns

- Use *more/less/fewer* to compare the number of things.
- Use *less* with uncountable nouns and *fewer* with countable nouns:
I ran ***fewer miles*** *today because my foot was hurting.*
I've got ***less time*** *for football training because I've got exams.*
- Use *more* with **both** countable and uncountable nouns:
We've received ***more money*** *to spend on* ***more books****.*

Intensifiers

- Use *a lot*, *far* or *much* with adjectives to make a contrast stronger:
It wasn't until ***much later*** *blue started to increase in popularity.*
- Use *a bit*, *a little* or *slightly* with adjectives to make a contrast weaker:
If you'd rather collect something ***slightly more mundane****, then find a theme for your collection.*

Repeated comparatives

- Use comparative + *and* + comparative to say something is changing:
I stood next to the pitch getting ***colder and colder****.*
- Use *the* + comparative … *the* + comparative to show how one action affects another:
The more unusual *and* ***quirky*** *your collection is,* ***the more interesting*** *it'll be.*

Relative clauses

Defining relative clauses

USE

- Use defining relative clauses to identify or describe people, things and places:
  It's a process ***which*** *was discovered about 50 years ago.*

FORM

- Use *who* for people, *which* for things, *where* for places and *when* for times:
  The scientists ***who*** *discovered DNA won a Nobel Prize.*
  We only have one heart ***which*** *needs to be on the left-hand side of the body.*
  I can't remember the name of the university ***where*** *Sara is studying.*
- You can also use *that* instead of *who* or *which* in defining relative clauses:
  Is this the book ***that/which*** *you were looking for?*
- Use *whose* for possessions:
  Sponges are the only living organisms ***whose*** *bodies are completely asymmetrical.*
- Use *what* for 'the thing(s) that':
  She told me ***what*** *she knew.*
- *whom*, the object of *who*, is sometimes used in formal English:
  Those are the students ***whom*** *I addressed.*
- In defining relative clauses, when *who*, *which*, *that* and *where* are the object of the verb, they can be left out:
  *It's a quality (****that****) we share with almost all other animals.*
- Prepositions sometimes come before *which* or *whom* in formal English:
  It's an organ ***about which*** *we know little.*

Non-defining relative clauses

USE

- Use non-defining relative clauses to give extra information about people, things and places:
  The male brain, ***which has*** *blue connections, is on the left.*

WATCH OUT! **Defining or non-defining?**

A defining relative clause tells us exactly which person, place or thing we are talking about. The sentence does not make sense without it.
A non-defining relative clause gives us extra information about a person, place or thing. The sentence still makes sense without it. It uses commas to separate the clause from the main part of the sentence.

FORM

- You can't leave out the relative pronoun in non-defining relative clauses:
  For about 1 in 20,000 people this process works in reverse, ***which*** *means their heart is on the right.*
- Non-defining relative clauses can go in the middle or at the end of a sentence. Use a comma before the pronoun.
- Non-defining relative clauses don't start with *that.*
  The photo above, ***which*** *was created using computer technology, shows how strange perfect facial symmetry would look.*
- You can use a quantifier such as *all/both/some*, etc + *of* + *which/whom* in non-defining relative clauses:
  The scientists, ***some of whom*** *studied at Oxford University, have won an award for their groundbreaking research.*

WATCH OUT! **Defining or non-defining?**

Non-defining relative clauses have a comma before the relative pronoun.
But don't use commas with defining relative clauses.

-ing and *-ed* clauses

-ing clauses

- Use *-ing* clauses with a main clause (subject + verb) when the subject of both clauses is the same.
  For two actions at the same time:
  I was online ***looking*** *for information. (= and I was looking)*
  I'd forgotten how I felt ***growing up****. (= when I was growing up)*
  To explain something:
  Not knowing *where to go for advice, I looked online. (= because I didn't know)*
  Being *a girl, she didn't always see things from a guy's perspective. (= because she was a girl)*
  After *when*, *while*, *before* and *after*:
  After writing *for a few weeks, I started getting comments from other teens. (= after I'd written)*
  After *by* to say how to do something:
  By reading *the blog, parents can see the points of view of teenagers.*

-ing and *-ed* as relative clauses

- Use *-ing and -ed* clauses as a reduced form of a relative clause.
- *-ing* clauses have an active meaning:
  The book is aimed at parents ***finding*** *it hard to understand their teenage children. (= who are finding)*
- *-ed* clauses have a passive meaning:
  This is a book written for parents by teenagers. (= which is written)

Modals of obligation, prohibition and advice

Obligation

USE

- Use *have/has to* and *must* + infinitive without *to* to talk about obligation and to say something is necessary, important or strongly recommended:
  Arriving late at the cinema means you **have to** *find a seat in the dark.*
  Here are five things you **must** *remember to do when you go to the cinema.*
- In formal contexts, *must* and *have to* mean the same.
- Use *have to* when a situation makes it necessary to do something and there is no choice:
  You **have to** *book your seat in advance.*
- *Must* is more common for personal decisions:
  I really **must** *try and do more exercise.*

FORM

- The past form of both *must* and *have to* is *had to*:
  I **had to** *stay at home and help my mum yesterday.*
- Use *will have to* to talk about future obligation:
  You'll **have to** *be very quiet at school tomorrow – there are lots of exams happening.*
- There is no future form of *must*, but you can use *must* and *mustn't* to give orders or instructions for the future:
  You **mustn't** *forget to turn off your phone in the cinema later.*

No obligation

- Use *don't have to* and *needn't* when there is no obligation to do something:
  You **don't have to** *be a member to use the gym.*

FORM

- Use *didn't have to* + verb or *needn't have* + past participle to talk about no obligation in the past:
  He **didn't have to** *turn off his mobile – it had already run out of battery!*
  You **needn't have** *rushed – there's plenty of time before the film starts.*
- *Didn't have to* can mean an action wasn't necessary and it wasn't done whereas *needn't have* can mean an action wasn't necessary but it was done.
- Use *won't have to* or *won't need to* to talk about no obligation in the future:
  You **won't have to** *buy a ticket for this event – it's free!*
  If you book your tickets online, you **won't need to** *queue at the box office.*

Prohibition/no permission

- Use *mustn't* and *can't* + infinitive without *to* to say something is prohibited or to give no permission:
  And please – you **mustn't** *slurp your drink or rattle your ice!*
  What's in that bag? I **can't** *tell you – it's a surprise!*

FORM

- The past form of *mustn't* is *wasn't allowed to*.
- The past form of *can't* is *couldn't*.
- Use *won't be able to* + verb to talk about prohibition or no permission or possibility in the future:
  You **won't be able to** *watch the film tomorrow – the cinema is closed.*

Advice

- Use *should (not)* or *ought (not) to* + infinitive without *to* to say something is a good (or a bad) idea:
  You **should** *try it!*
  You **ought not to** *eat too much popcorn.*
- *Should (not)* and *ought (not) to* have the same meaning but *should (not)* is more common and stronger.
- Use *had better (not)* + infinitive without *to* to say something is a good (or a bad) idea in a particular situation, not in general:
  *You***'d better** *find out what time the film starts.*
- You usually use *had better* in speech or informal writing.

FORM

- There are no past forms of *should (not)* / *ought (not) to* but you can use *should(n't) have done* or *ought(n't) to have done* to talk about things which were supposed to happen but didn't:
  I'm sorry – I **should have told** *you I was going to be late.* (*= I didn't phone*)
- You can use a contracted form of *had* in *had better* (*'d*) but you cannot contract *not*.
  *You***'d better not** *forget to phone your dad later.*
- You use *had better (not)* to talk about the present or the future. There is no past form of *had better (not)*.
- There is no future form for *should*, *ought (not) to* and *had better (not)*, but you often use these modal verbs to give advice about the future:
  When you go to London, you should visit the IMAX cinema.

Future in the past

USE

- Use the 'future in the past' to talk about future events seen from the past which had not yet happened:
  Everyone thought **it would** *be one of the most successful films of 2001.* ('*It will be one of the most successful films …*')
  Johnny Depp **was going to** *star in it.* ('*Johnny Depp is going to star in it.*')

FORM

- Use the past form of different future forms to talk about future events seen from the past.
- For *be going to*, use *was/were going to*:
  Someone else **was going to** *make* The Lord of the Rings *before Peter Jackson made his famous version.*
- For *will*, use *would*:
  Tolkien thought the film **would** *be a total disaster.*
- Use *was about* + infinitive with *to* to say something was going to happen very soon:
  Filming **was about to start** *when they had to abandon it.*
- Use *was supposed/meant/expected* + infinitive with *to* to talk about something in the past which was expected to happen but didn't:
  The film **was expected to be** *a massive hit but it was never made.*

Passive forms

Different tenses

USE

- Use passive forms to focus on the action, when the action is more important than the 'agent' (person/thing that does it):
  *Goods **are transported** all over the world in containers.*

- Use the correct tense of *be* + past participle (+ *by* + agent):
  *Space **is provided** in warehouses in the e-commerce zone.*
  *Container ships **were invented** by an American trucking company owner.*
  *The container ship **has** just **been unloaded**.*
  *The shipping containers **are being transferred** onto the trucks right now.*
  *The goods **will be sold** in shops across Europe.*
- If a verb has two objects, such as *send* and *give*, both can be the subject:
  ***The inventor** was given a reward.*
  ***A reward** was given to the inventor.*
- *Get* can replace *be* in informal contexts:
  *There was an accident at the docks but nobody **got** hurt.*

Passive infinitives and gerunds

- Use a modal verb + *be* + past participle:
  *Until the 1960s, **ships had to be unloaded** by hand.*
- Use a modal verb + *have been* + past participle to talk about possible and hypothetical events in the past:
  *The goods **could have been flown** by cargo plane but it would have been too expensive.*
- Some verbs, such as *want* and *choose* use the passive infinitive *to be* + past participle:
  *She didn't **want to be left out**.*
- Some verbs, such as *enjoy*, *keep* and *tell* use the passive gerund *being* + past participle:
  *He **kept being told** to study harder but he wouldn't listen.*

have/get something done

USE

- Use *have/get* something done to talk about things you pay or ask someone to do for you:
  *I **had** my hair **cut** yesterday. (= A hairdresser cut it.)*

FORM

- Use the correct tense of *have/get* + object + past participle:
  *You look nice. **Have** you **had** your hair cut?*
  Have and *get* mean the same, but use *have*, not *get*, in more formal contexts.

WATCH OUT!

The past participle comes *after* the object:

object — past participle

*I'm going to **get my nails done** for the party.*

believe, know, say, think

- Use *it* + passive form of *believe*, *know*, *say* and *think* to talk about general opinions:
  ***It is believed** that the ship sank off the coast of Ireland.*

Modal verbs of speculation and expectation

USE

- Use modals of speculation and expectation to give possible explanations for things based on evidence:
  *That **can't** be my jacket. Mine has got a tear in the pocket.*
  *You **should have known** how to use the phone. It's similar to yours.*

Present and future events

- Use modal + infinitive without *to* and modal + be + *-ing* to talk about present or future events.
- Use *will/won't* and *must* when you're sure an explanation is true:
  *She**'ll be walking** to school by now.*
  *There **must be** some kind of a mistake.*
- Don't use *must* for future events.
- Use *should(n't)* when you expect something to happen or not to happen:
  *It **shouldn't be snowing** now – it's May!*
- Use *could/may/might (not)* when you think something is possible:
  *Who's that at the door? It **might be** Dani. She hasn't got her key.*
- *Use can't* or *couldn't* when you think something is impossible:
  *It **can't be** Dani. She's at netball practice.*

Past events

- Use *will/won't, can't have, could have, may have, might have* and *must have* + past participle to talk about possible explanations for things in the past that are based on evidence.
- Use *will/won't have* to talk about something you are sure has happened:
  *He**'ll have gone** home by now.*
- Use *could have, may have* and *might have* when you think an explanation is possible for something that happened in the past:
  ***Could** you **have given** us the wrong address?*
  *He **might have left** his mobile on the bus.*
- You can also use *could/might have* to criticise someone's behaviour:
  *You **could have** warned me! (Why didn't you?)*
- Use *must have* when you're sure an explanation is true:
  *Why is my phone bill so high? You **must have had** roaming switched on.*
- Use *can't have* or *couldn't have* when you're sure an explanation is impossible:
  *I **can't have been** out. I work at home.*
- Use *may not have* or *might not have* when you're unsure if something happened:
  *She **might not have** got your text.*
- Use *should(n't) have* + past participle to talk about an event that was supposed to happen:
  *You **should have been sent** a warning when you'd spent 50 euros.*
- You can also use *should(n't)* to express criticism or regret about something that did or did not happen:
  *You **shouldn't have made** so many calls on your mobile.*

Reported speech review

Reported statements and questions

USE

- Use reported speech to report what people said in direct speech:
  'I'll phone you later.' > He said he would phone me later.

FORM

Reported statements

- Use *said* or *told* in reported speech. You can use reported speech with or without *that*:
  He said (**that**) *he'd sent me an email.*
- Use *told* + object pronoun to say who the person was talking to: *He told* **me** *that he'd sent me an email.*

Reported questions

- Form reported *yes/no* questions with *asked* + person + *if/whether* + *I/you*, etc + verb:
  He asked me if I had changed my email address. (*'Have you changed your email address?'*)
- *Whether* is more common in formal English.
- Form reported *wh-* questions with *asked* + person + question word + *I/you*, etc + verb:
  I asked her how she chose her passwords. (*'How do you choose your passwords?'*)
- The word order in reported questions is different to direct questions. In reported questions, the verb comes *after* the subject:
  He asked me what time ***I was*** *going.* (*'What time* ***are you*** *going?'*)

Reported requests and commands

- Form reported requests with *asked* + object + (*not*) *to* + infinitive without *to*:
  She asked me to open it. (*'Can you open it?'*)
- Form reported commands with *told* + object + (*not*) *to* + infinitive without *to*:
  He told me not to tell anyone. (*'Don't tell anyone.'*)
- Tenses 'move back' one tense in reported speech:

Direct speech	Reported speech
present simple	past simple
present continuous	past continuous
present perfect / past simple	past perfect
future with *going to*	*was going to*
future with *will*	*would*
can	*could*
may	*might*

- Expressions of time and adverbs of place change in reported speech:

Direct speech	Reported speech
now	*then*
today	*that day*
here	*there*
tonight	*that night*
yesterday	*the day before / the previous day*
tomorrow	*the next / following day*
last week	*the week before / the previous week*
next week	*the following week*

Reporting verbs

- Reporting verbs such as *claim* and *predict* follow the structure verb + *that*:
  He ***predicted that*** *the government would lose.*
- Reporting verbs such as *agree*, *offer*, *promise*, *refuse* and *threaten* follow the structure verb + (*not*) + infinitive with *to*:
  She ***promised not to tell*** *anyone.*
- Reporting verbs such as *encourage*, *invite*, *remind*, *persuade*, *warn* follow the structure verb + object + infinitive with *to*:
  She ***warned people not to share*** *their passwords.*
- Reporting verbs such as *admit*, *deny*, *recommend* and *suggest* follow the structure verb + *-ing*:
  Some people ***admitted sharing*** *their passwords.*
- You can also use (*that*) + subject + verb after the verbs *admit*, *ask*, *deny*, *recommend* and *suggest*:
  Some people ***admitted (that) they shared*** *their passwords.*
- Reporting verbs such as *insist on* and *apologise for* follow the structure verb + preposition + *-ing*:
  She ***insisted on walking*** *me home.*
- Reporting verbs such as *accuse* (*somebody*) *of*, *blame* (*somebody*) *for* and *congratulate* (*someone*) *on* follow the structure verb + object + preposition + *-ing*:
  He ***accused me of reading*** *his emails.*

Question tags

USE

- Use question tags at the end of sentences to make questions.

- If the sentence has an auxiliary verb, use the auxiliary verb (*can*, *have*, *is*, *will*, etc) + subject in the question tag:
  The students ***weren't listening*** *carefully,* ***were*** *they?*
- Put a comma before the question tag and a question mark at the end.
- If the sentence doesn't have an auxiliary verb, use *do(n't)/ does(n't)* and *did(n't)* + subject:
  You ***know*** *Ellie,* ***don't*** *you?*
  For sentences using the verb *be* as the main verb, use *be* in the question tag too: *You****'re*** *new here,* ***aren't*** *you?*
- Use a negative question tag with a positive sentence:
  It's a lovely day today, ***isn't*** *it?*
- Use a positive question tag with a negative sentence:
  You ***weren't*** *in class today,* ***were*** *you?*
- Use the tag *shall we* after *Let's*:
  Let's *look on the bright side,* ***shall we?***
- The intonation goes down when the speaker wants confirmation or agreement:
  You're a friend of Cathy's, aren't you?
- The intonation goes up when the speaker doesn't know the answer and is checking something:
  But you weren't at her party, were you?

WATCH OUT!

Use *aren't I* for *I'm*: ***I'm*** *wrong,* ***aren't I?***
But use *am I* for *I'm not*: ***I'm*** *not angry,* ***am I?***

Intensifiers

USE

- Use intensifiers such as adverbs of degree, *so/such … that* and *too / (not) enough … (for/to)* to emphasise qualities and quantities:
  *That's **really** impressive.*
  *It's **totally** absurd that people are making **such** a fuss.*
  *He doesn't want to speak **well enough to** sound like a native.*
- Use *too* to mean 'more than is necessary/enough':
  *I can't afford it. It's **too** expensive.*
- Use *(not) enough* to mean '(not) as much as is necessary':
  *Don't give the cat any more to eat. She's got **enough** food.*
  *I have**n't** got **enough** money.*

Adverbs of degree

- Use *rather, really, remarkably, pretty* + adjective/adverb for emphasis:
  *Where is he? He's **rather** late.*
  *Please don't use that term. It's **really** derogatory!*
- *Rather* and *pretty* have less emphasis than *really* and *remarkably.*
- Use *absolutely, completely, totally* and *utterly* with extreme adjectives and verbs:
  *It's **absolutely** freezing today!*
  *The state of some people's grammar **completely** horrifies me.*

so/such … (that)

- Use *so* + adjective/adverb:
  *I'm **so tired.***
  *He speaks **so quickly.***
- Use *so* + *few/many* + countable noun:
  *I'm really stuck with this essay. I've got **so few** ideas.*
  *Why **are there so many** people here today? There's nowhere to sit!*
- Use *so* + *little/much* + uncountable noun:
  *There was **so little** time left that I didn't finish the exam question.*
  *We had **so much** food left over at the end of the party we gave it away to our guests.*
- Use *such a/an* + adjective + singular countable noun:
  *This is **such an** inspiring story.*
- Use *such* + adjective + uncountable noun/plural noun:
  *It was **such cold weather.***
- You can use also *such* + noun without an adjective:
  *It's **such a pity** that he can't come.*
  *The party was **such a success** we want to do it again!*
- Use *such* + *a lot of* + noun:
  *Why did you buy **such a lot of** food for the party?*
- Use *that* + clause to describe the consequences of the qualities/quantities:
  *It was such cold weather **that we decided to go home.***

too/(not) enough … (for/to)

- Use *too* + adjective/adverb:
  *I can't eat this soup – it's **too hot.***
  *You're talking **too quickly** – slow down!*
- Use *too few/many* with countable nouns:
  *I can't go out tonight. I've got **too many** jobs to do at home.*
- Use *too little/much* with uncountable nouns:
  *He's obviously got **too much** free time.*
- Use *slightly* before *too* to mean 'a small degree':
  *We've got **slightly too few** plates for the party – could we borrow some?*
- Use *way* before *too* to mean 'a large degree':
  *This is **way too difficult.** I'll never be able to do it.*
- *(Not) enough* goes after an adjective/adverb:
  *I'd like to be in the netball team but I'm **not good enough.***
- *(Not) enough* goes before a noun:
  *We have**n't** got **enough chairs** for everybody.*
- Use infinitive with *to* or *for* + something to express consequences:
  *It's too early **to go** to bed yet!*
  *This isn't important enough **to worry about.***
  *This is too difficult **for me.***
  *It wasn't warm enough **for us** to swim in the lake.*

WATCH OUT!

too few/little means the same as *not enough*:
*I have**n't** got **enough** money for the cinema ticket. = I've got **too little** money for the cinema ticket.*
Not enough is more common.

Inversion

USE

- Use inversion to add emphasis to formal sentences:
  ***No sooner had I** stepped off the plane than I realised everyone was speaking an unknown language.*
  ***Had I realised** how much fun I would have, I wouldn't have been so nervous.*

Negative adverbials and so

- Use *Never (again)/Rarely/Only then* + auxiliary + subject:
  ***Never had I** felt so relieved.*
  ***Never again will I** watch that film!*
  ***Rarely does anyone** ask me how I am.*
  ***Only then did I** realise what the problem was.*
- Use *No sooner* + auxiliary + subject … *than*:
  ***No sooner had she** put the washing out **than** it started raining.*
- Use *Not only* + auxiliary + subject … , *but … also*:
  ***Not only could I** not understand what anyone was saying, **but** I had **also** lost all confidence.*
- Use *So* + adjective + *be* … *that*:
  ***So pleased was** I about my exam results **that** I shouted with joy.*

Third conditional without *if*:

- Use *had* + subject + past participle … , *would have* + past participle:
  ***Had I known** more about the language, then I **would have been** more prepared for my trip.*
- Do not contract negatives in inverted conditional clauses:
  Had I not heard … (not ~~*Hadn't*~~ *I heard …*)

After a prepositional phrase:

- Use prepositional phrase + verb + subject:
  At my feet was a large snake. I screamed.
- Use this when the subject is being introduced for the first time.

WORDS & BEYOND

UNIT 1

Pages 6 and 7

NAMES

alias
assumed name
brand name
domain name
household name
initials
maiden name
nickname
pen name/pseudonym
stage name
title
username

EXTEND: 'NAME' EXPRESSIONS

be a big name in something
be named after somebody
call somebody names
give somebody/something a bad name

GO BEYOND

1 **Choose six of the name types and write an example that's connected to you in some way, eg: *Carmody = my mother's maiden name*.**
2 **Show just the names to someone else. Can they guess what type of name each one is and who it belongs to?**

EXTEND YOUR VOCABULARY

TIP: When you learn a new expression based on a word, look up other expressions based on the same word in a dictionary.

TASK: Try and complete the sentences with the 'name' expressions. Check your answers in a dictionary.

by name   made a name for herself   name names
put a name to the face   under the name of

1 I've seen that girl before, but I can't ________ .
2 We never address our teacher ________ .
3 JK Rowling published *The Cuckoo's Calling* ________ Robert Galbraith.
4 I know who painted this graffiti, but I'm not going to ________ .
5 Actor Salma Hayek first ________ as a gymnast.

Page 10

WORD FAMILIES

Verb	Noun	Adjective
appear	appearance	apparent
exaggerate	exaggeration	exaggerated
forget	forgetfulness	forgetful
imagine	imagination	imaginative
improve	improvement	improved
mean	meaning	meaningful
memorise	memory	(un)memorable
practise	practice	practical
sleep	sleep	sleepy
strengthen	strength	strong
succeed	success	successful
train	training	trained

GO BEYOND

Write sentences, with each one containing a verb, noun and adjective from the lists. How many can you write?

NEW WORDS IN UNIT 1

birthplace
change your mind
compile
cyclone
downgrade
establish priorities
feminist groups
hurricane
hotly debated
indigenous
keep things in perspective
make landfall
matronymic
moist
mononym
negative impact
patronymic
storm surge
sustained
typhoon
vast majority
vulnerable (to)
warm-blooded

Pages 16 and 17

TYPES OF STORY

epic
fable
fairy tale
folk tale
legend
myth
saga
tale
tall story (UK)/tall tale (US)
urban legend/myth

EXTEND: COLLOCATIONS

a likely story
a long story
a sob story
the same old story

GO BEYOND

1 **Think of an example from your own culture for each type of story and make a list.**
2 **Show your list to someone else. How many of the stories could they tell?**

EXTEND YOUR VOCABULARY

TIP: Use an online collocations dictionary to find out what words are commonly used together.

TASK: Look at the collocations (eg *true story*, *made-up story*, etc). What do you think they mean? Check your answers in a dictionary.

true	made-up	tragic	life	success	bedtime	+ story
official	hard-luck	short	horror	full	front-page	

Page 20

CHARACTER ADJECTIVES

creative
inventive
open
outgoing
practical
reserved
sensible
sensitive
tactful
temperamental

GO BEYOND

Write a short description of two friends who are very different using as many of the character adjectives as you can.

NEW WORDS IN UNIT 2

a blast (of air)
amazement
ancestor
backstory
beep
bump into someone
clay tablet
coral
creep
cruise
cursive letters
deceive
Declaration of Independence
depict
flea market
frame
jewel encrusted
lobster
longing
memorabilia
moral
mother ship
plunge
reward
savage
seashore
set free
slope
spot someone/something
stretch limo
sway
the back of beyond
you're kidding (= you're not serious)

WORDS & BEYOND

Pages 28 and 29

PHRASAL VERBS: GOALS AND ACHIEVEMENTS

carry on
come up with
get round to
give back
give up
miss out on
put off
sign up for
start up
take over
take up
work out

EXTEND: OBJECTS WITH PHRASAL VERBS

come up with an idea / come up with it
start up a company / start a company up / start it up

GO BEYOND
Write at least four sentences about things you've achieved recently or in your life. Use a different phrasal verb from the list in each one.

EXTEND YOUR VOCABULARY

TIP: When you learn a new phrasal verb, notice what the preposition or adverb adds to the verb's meaning. This can help you to guess the meaning of new phrasal verbs.

TASK: Match what *up* in each phrasal verb adds to its meaning (a–f).

1 We started **up** a new company.
2 I gave **up** playing the piano.
3 She always gets **up** early.
4 We need to build **up** our business.
5 Phone later. Your voice is breaking **up**.
6 If we walk faster, we might catch **up** with the others.

a awake, out of bed, upright
b into parts or pieces
c approach, reach
d create, start, appear
e finish, complete
f increase, improve

Page 32

ADJECTIVE + PREPOSITION

annoyed with
aware of
famous for
proud of
responsible for

VERB + NOUN + PREPOSITION

get ready for
keep an eye on
take charge of
take pride in
take responsibility for

GO BEYOND
Look at the phrases. For each one, write down the name of a person or thing that could follow the expression.

NEW WORDS IN UNIT 3

addictive
assure
coding
creative force (behind)
entrepreneur
flair
foolish
from scratch
investor
long-term
panel
pitch (an idea)
postpone
roommate
short-term
sponsor
spread the word
staff
start-up
ultimate (goal)

Pages 38 and 39

BUILDINGS AND ARCHITECTURE

Buildings	Features
office block	arch
palace	column
pyramid	dome
skyscraper	façade
temple	spire
tower block	steps

EXTEND: BUILDING IDIOMS

be just a façade
get on like a house on fire
hit the roof

GO BEYOND

1 **Choose four words from each list and write what you think the world's most famous example is.**
2 **Show your list to someone else. Do they agree with you?**

EXTEND YOUR VOCABULARY

TIP: Make a note of new idioms and the context they're used in. To help you remember them, group them according to their theme.

TASK: Complete the 'building' idioms below with the correct nouns. Check your answers in a dictionary.

bridge fort house tower wall

1 I'm going out for a minute. Could you hold the ____________ while I'm gone?
2 Alana was really funny in the school play. She brought the ____________ down!
3 Don't burn your ____________s with your brother. You might need each other's help one day.
4 The writing's on the ____________ for the chess club. We've got nowhere to meet.
5 Dave's been a ____________ of strength since my grandfather died. He's really helped me.

Page 42

ABSTRACT NOUNS

disappointment	honesty
failure	humour
fame	power
fear	regret
freedom	sadness
friendship	youth

GO BEYOND

1 **Look at the words. Think of a person or situation that defines what each word means.**
2 **Show your list to someone else. How similar are your choices?**

NEW WORDS IN UNIT 4

awe-inspiring	deforestation	iconic	shape (v)
barren	diversity	inner-city	spare no expense
barrier	downfall	majestic	thought-provoking
brochure	emblematic	masterpiece	wipe out
contemporary	fate	minimalist	wonder
cutting-edge	futuristic	settler	worship

WORDS & BEYOND

UNIT 5

Pages 50 and 51

USUAL AND UNUSUAL ADJECTIVES

alternative
exceptional
extraordinary
mundane
nondescript
offbeat
ordinary
out of the ordinary
predictable
remarkable
unpredictable
weird

EXTEND: MORE USUAL AND UNUSUAL ADJECTIVES

commonplace
odd
off-the-wall
run-of-the-mill

GO BEYOND

1 Write short sentences using six of the words. They can be about a person, film, book, place or something else.

2 Read your sentences to someone else. Do they agree? If not, give reasons for your opinion.

EXTEND YOUR VOCABULARY

TIP: Use a thesaurus to find words with similar meanings and vary your vocabulary. Then use a dictionary to understand the differences in meaning between the words – how formal they are, whether they have a positive or negative meaning, etc.

TASKS:

1 Match the words to the definitions. Use a dictionary for help.

1	a bargain	a	cheaper than many other similar things
2	affordable	b	much cheaper than its normal price
3	competitive	c	cheap and of poor quality (informal)
4	low-cost	d	relatively cheap, especially for air travel
5	tacky	f	cheap enough for ordinary people to buy

2 Find the differences in meaning between these words and expressions:

dear   a rip-off   exorbitant   overpriced   cost an arm and a leg

Page 54

VERBS TO DESCRIBE CHANGE

Go up	Go down	Change
increase	decrease	result in
grow	fall	turn into
rise	shrink	lead to
		transform (into)

GO BEYOND

Write sentences about these things using the verbs.

1 the price of mobile phones
2 the internet
3 the use of PCs
4 pollution
5 big cities
6 black clothes

NEW WORDS IN UNIT 5

a blast
affordability
airsickness bag
boundary
branding
consent
crisps
eligible
fake
hands-on experience
ideological
incurably
juxtaposition
marble
origin
outsider
philanthropist
pigment
quirkiness
storage
texture
trash
unconventional
wax figure

Pages 60 and 61

COMPOUNDS

Compound adjectives	Compound nouns
cutting edge	breakthrough
far-reaching	gene therapy
groundbreaking	genetic code
left-handed	upbringing
never-ending	
open-minded	

EXTEND: MORE COMPOUND CHARACTER ADJECTIVES

absent-minded
big-headed
short-sighted
thick-skinned

GO BEYOND

1 **Write at least one noun that you can use after each compound adjective, eg *never-ending nightmare*.**
2 **Write at least one adjective or verb that you can use before each compound noun, eg *exciting breakthrough*.**

EXTEND YOUR VOCABULARY

TIP: As you read and listen to English, be aware of different ways to form compound words. Use them to experiment with forming new words. Then look in a dictionary to see if they exist.

TASK: Complete the definitions with a compound. Use a word (or form of a word) in the definition and a word in the box.

free (x2) friendly intensive proof ready

1 An opportunity that doesn't involve risk is ________ .
2 A bottle that a child can't open is ________ .
3 Food that contains no fat is ________ .
4 Food you can heat in an oven with no preparation is ________ .
5 A device that's easy to use is ________ .
6 Work that requires a lot of people (labour) to do is ________ .

Page 64

THREE-WORD PHRASAL VERBS: PEOPLE AND COMMUNICATION

be up to
check up on
get away with
get through to
get up to
grow out of
live up to
look down on
look up to
stand up for

GO BEYOND

1 **Write a sentence about each of these people using different verbs from the list:**
- you
- a friend
- a member of your family
- someone famous

2 **Read your sentences to someone else. Explain why you wrote them.**

NEW WORDS IN UNIT 6

asymmetrical
asymmetry
awe-inspiring
be a mirror image of
bias (towards)
blueprint
cell
complex tasks
compromise
cultural pressures
cure (for)
DNA
external
field (of work)
filter
fist
gene
genetic
hemisphere (of brain)
internal
molecule
natural tendency
organism
perspective
pose a threat
put yourself in somebody's shoes
REM sleep
right-handedness
speak too soon
sponge
subconscious
symmetrical
symmetry
transplant
valid

WORDS & BEYOND

Pages 72 and 73

FILM WORDS

aisle	remake
auditorium	row
cinemagoer	session
credits	spoiler
dubbed	subtitled
foyer	trailers

EXTEND: WORDS WITH MORE THAN ONE MEANING

credit	row
dub	trailer

GO BEYOND

1. **Draw a simple plan of a cinema you know and label the parts.**
2. **Choose the option you prefer. Then explain your choices to someone else.**
   a subtitled or dubbed?
   b opening or closing credits?
   c front, middle or back row?
   d matinee (afternoon) or evening session?

EXTEND YOUR VOCABULARY

TIP: Make a note of the words with the same spelling but with different pronunciation and meaning.

TASK: Match each pronunciation of the words to the correct meaning. Check your answers in a dictionary.

1	close /kləʊz/	shut
	close /kləʊs/	near
2	console	try to make somebody feel better
	console	gadget for playing games
3	desert	leave somebody alone
	desert	area of dry land
4	live /laɪv/	not recorded
	live /lɪv/	be or stay alive
5	minute /mɪnɪt/	60 seconds
	minute /maɪnjuːt/	very small

Page 76

ADJECTIVE + NOUN COLLOCATIONS

heavy cold, heavy rain, heavy traffic
strong accent, strong contender, strong smell
complete disaster, complete surprise, complete waste of time
final decision, unanimous decision, wrong decision
mysterious circumstances, normal circumstances, special circumstances
fatal illness, serious illness, long illness

GO BEYOND

Imagine you're writing your autobiography. Write at least three sentences about your life. Include a different collocation in each one.

NEW WORDS IN UNIT 7

ace	irritating	patron	sing along (to a song)
consent	jump the queue	rattle	slurp
continuous (take)	lip-sync	ruin	transporter
fantasy world	massive	screening	unwrap
humble	out of line	seating	wrapper

Pages 82 and 83

WORLD TRADE

cargo/freight	railway
commerce	retailer
goods	ship (v)
industry	store (v)
manufacture (v)	transport (v)
motorway	warehouse

EXTEND: WORD BUILDING

accommodation	resident
location	storage

GO BEYOND

1 **Choose three nouns from the list. Think of a place near you where you can see each one.**
2 **Choose two verbs from the list. Think of a place near you where the activity takes place.**

EXTEND YOUR VOCABULARY

TIP: Some words have a number of different nouns, verbs and adjectives in their word family. Some can also form part of a compound. Use a dictionary to explore word families and discover new ways to use familiar words.

TASK: Complete the definitions with the correct form of the word *ship*. Check your answers in a dictionary.

1 the business of carrying goods, especially by ship ________
2 a company that builds ships ________
3 goods that are bought and then shipped together to the customer ________
4 an accident in which a ship is destroyed (wrecked) ________
5 a ship with sails ________
6 a place where ships are built or repaired ________

Page 86

BUYING AND SELLING

bill (n)	exchange rate (n)
charge (n, v)	export (n, v)
cost (n, v)	import (n, v)
currency (n)	purchase (n, v)
delivery (n)	tax (n, v)

GO BEYOND

1 **Answer the questions.**
a What's the currency in your country and neighbouring countries?
b What's the exchange rate between your currency and the US dollar?
c What things does your country import and export?
d What was the last thing you purchased? What did it cost?
e Why do people have to pay tax on their income?
2 **Ask someone else the questions. Compare your answers.**

NEW WORDS IN UNIT 8

abolish	drive out of business	labour-intensive	shipping containers
breathtaking	exhibition hall	(un)load	speedy
budget	expenses	locavore	steel
carbon footprint	(a) handful of	mystery shopper	trade fair
consumerism	horn	overnight	tribute
convention	hub	revolution	trucking
customs	income	savings	

WORDS & BEYOND

Pages 94 and 95

PREFIXES	EXAMPLE WORDS
co-	collaborative, cooperate
dis-	disagree, dislike
inter-	interact, interview
mis-	misbehave, mistrust
multi-	multitask, multilingual
non-	non-stop, non-fiction
pre-	preconception, prefix
re-	rename, reuse

EXTEND: MORE PREFIXES

anti-	anti-war, anti-establishment
post-	post-hippy
pro-	pro-freedom
out-	outdo
sub-	subculture

GO BEYOND

1 **Write one sentence using as many of the example words as you can.**
2 **Compare your sentence with someone else's. Who managed to use the most example words?**

EXTEND YOUR VOCABULARY

TIP: English uses a large number of prefixes to build words. Knowing them can help you guess the meaning of new words – and build your own.

TASK: What prefix can you use to complete each group of words? What does the prefix mean? Check your answers in a dictionary.

1 ______-detached house, ______-skimmed milk, ______-professional
2 weather ______ cast, the ______ seeable future, in the ______ ground
3 ______ attack, ______ intelligence, ______ act, ______ productive
4 ______ function, ______ formation, ______ nutrition
5 ______ curricular activity, ______ terrestrial, ______ ordinary, ______ sensory perception

Page 98

IDIOMS

at the end of the day
be barking up the wrong tree
be the tip of the iceberg
be water under the bridge
cross that bridge when we come to it
get it off your chest
get the wrong end of the stick
in the heat of the moment
look on the bright side
there's / see light at the end of the tunnel

GO BEYOND

Choose two idioms and draw a simple picture to illustrate them. Then write a sentence including the idiom under each picture to show what it really means.

NEW WORDS IN UNIT 9

assignment	indeed	rush	speechless
beforehand	misinterpret	self-obsessed	the elephant in the room
consultant	label (v)	secure	willing
digital native	quote somebody	sit upright	

Pages 104 and 105

PHRASAL VERBS: LANGUAGES AND LEARNING

break down
catch on
come across
die out
end up
get across
get by
keep up
look up
make up
pick up
try out

GO BEYOND

1 **Choose four phrasal verbs from the list and use them to make four predictions about you or the world around you.**
2 **Show your sentences to someone else. Discuss whether your predictions will come true or not.**

EXTEND: INTRANSITIVE PHRASAL VERBS

break down
catch on
die out
get by

EXTEND YOUR VOCABULARY

TIP: Some compound nouns and adjectives are formed from phrasal verbs. For example, 'breakthrough' (see Unit 6) comes from the phrasal verb 'break through'. Make a note of related nouns when you learn a phrasal verb.

TASK: Complete the second sentence with a compound noun based on the phrasal verb in the first sentence. Check your answers in a dictionary.

1 Our car broke down on the motorway. We called a __________ truck.
2 A minibus will pick us up at 9 o'clock. The __________ point is in front of the school gate.
3 A lot of new businesses are starting up here. Most __________ are in the IT business.
4 Grow up! It's time you started behaving like a __________ .
5 I was brought up to respect others. I'm proud of my __________ .
6 I like to work out every day. I go to the gym for my daily __________ .

Page 108

COLLOQUIAL PHRASES

bloke (UK), guy (UK, US)
chill (out) (UK, US), kick back (US)
cool (UK, US), awesome (US)
crash (out) (UK, US), hit the sack (UK, US), get some 'Z's (UK, US)
dosh (UK), dough (UK, US)
How's it going? (UK, US) What's up? (US)
I'm off (UK, US), I'm out of here (UK, US)
mate (UK), buddy, dude (US)
No worries. (UK, US), No problem. (UK, US)
shattered (UK), beat (US)
ta (UK), cheers (UK)
the loo (UK), the men's room (US)

GO BEYOND

Write a conversation between two friends using as many of the phrases as you can. Keep the sentences as short as possible.

NEW WORDS IN UNIT 10

acquire
appalling
convention
credit
derogatory
eavesdrop
geek
genuine
hyperpolyglot
imply
insult
make a quick exit
misrepresent
nerd
offend
originate
proficiency
sarcasm
species
under threat
warrior

IRREGULAR VERBS

base form	past simple	past participle
agree	agreed	agreed
be	was/were	been
become	became	become
begin	began	begun
bite	bit	bitten
break	broke	broken
bring	brought	brought
build	built	built
buy	bought	bought
can	could	been able to
catch	caught	caught
choose	chose	chosen
come	came	come
cost	cost	cost
cut	cut	cut
do	did	done
drive	drove	driven
eat	ate	eaten
fall	fell	fallen
feel	felt	felt
find	found	found
fly	flew	flown
forget	forgot	forgotten
get	got	got
give	gave	given
go	went	gone
grow	grew	grown
have	had	had
hear	heard	heard
hide	hid	hidden
hurt	hurt	hurt
keep	kept	kept
know	knew	known
learn	learnt/learned	learnt/learned
leave	left	left

base form	past simple	past participle
lend	lent	lent
let	let	let
lose	lost	lost
make	made	made
mean	meant	meant
meet	met	met
must	had to	had to
overcome	overcame	overcome
pay	paid	paid
put	put	put
read	read	read
rise	rose	risen
run	ran	run
say	said	said
see	saw	seen
sell	sold	sold
send	sent	sent
set	set	set
shrink	shrank	shrunk
sink	sank	sunk
sit	sat	sat
sleep	slept	slept
speak	spoke	spoken
speed	sped	sped
spend	spent	spent
stand	stood	stood
take	took	taken
teach	taught	taught
tell	told	told
think	thought	thought
throw	threw	thrown
understand	understood	understood
wear	wore	worn
win	won	won
write	wrote	written

UNIT 2 READING

Page 18, Exercise 5

Taro accepted the turtle's invitation. He jumped onto its back, and they plunged deep into the sea. It was the first time Taro had been so far underwater. Before long, they reached the bottom of the ocean. For a minute Taro couldn't believe what he saw. There were fish of all colours, shapes and sizes swimming among the pink and blue coral. Everything was like a dream.

Soon they reached the gates of the Coral Palace where the queen was waiting for Taro. Her name was Otohime and she wore a long, white robe and a golden crown. As she moved, her dress, which was covered with hundreds of pink shells, swayed in the water.

Otohime spoke in a soft voice. 'Welcome, Taro-san! We would like to thank you for rescuing my loyal turtle. Please follow me.' Taro followed Otohime through the palace until they finally came to a huge room filled with beautiful furniture and treasure. In the centre of the room there was a long table with the strangest food Taro had ever seen. Taro sat at the table and ate from golden plates until he could eat no more. As he ate, tiny fish danced for Taro and the queen while a group of lobsters played beautiful music.

Taro spent many days at the Coral Palace. Each day was a new experience, which ended with an amazing feast and an evening of entertainment. For a while Taro forgot his friends and family above the sea.

UNIT 4 GRAMMAR 1

Page 41, Exercise 6

Situation 1: Weather forecasts for this weekend don't agree. Some say it'll be hot and dry. Others say it'll be cold and wet.

Situation 2: Astronomers have spotted a giant asteroid. There's a 50% chance that it will hit Earth next year.

Situation 3: The first mobile phone call was made on 3 April 1973.

UNIT 5 LANGUAGE & BEYOND

Page 56, Exercise 1b

BIG BRANDS LIKE TO TARGET TEENS FOR SEVERAL REASONS:

–The younger you are when you start using a brand, the longer you'll continue buying the brand.

–You probably like to do the same things as your friends. So there's a far greater chance they'll buy the same brand as you.

– Parents often give their teens money. It's often easier to persuade a teen to buy something than an adult.

UNIT 8 LISTENING AND VOCABULARY

Page 86, Exercise 7

1 Who pays your phone bill? Do you have a mobile internet connection? Have you ever had to pay a really big phone bill? How much was it? What happened?

2 Have you ever had to change money or pay for something in another currency? What was the situation? What currency did you change or use?

UNIT 10 IN THE PICTURE

Page 105, Exercise 8

My English survey

1 How easy do you find it to ***keep up*** / ***pick up*** new vocabulary?

2 How often do you ***look up*** / ***break down*** words you don't know?

3 Do you think you'll ***get across*** / ***end up*** using the languages you've studied?

ALL STUDENTS

UNIT 7 GRAMMAR 2

Page 77, Exercise 5

Choose one of the film situations and write a short conversation for the scene. Include examples of the future in the past.

Thriller: You're both on a secret mission to find a stolen case but something has gone wrong with the plan. What went wrong? What's in the case? What are you going to do?

Horror: Student A has been conducting secret experiments. Student B has just discovered the secret and wants an explanation. What was the experiment? Why was it a secret?

Science fiction: It's the year 2165 and creatures from another planet have come to Earth. What did people think when they first arrived? Why did they really come? What happened?

UNIT 2 READING

Page 18, Exercise 5

Then one day Taro felt a great longing for his family and friends and decided to return home. So the next time he saw the queen, Taro said, 'Thank you for your kindness but I must return home.' Otohime brushed away her tears and said, 'I am sorry you are leaving, Taro.'
Then Otohime gave Taro a jewel-encrusted chest and said, 'This will bring you great luck if you keep it. But you must never open it. Do not forget my words, Taro-san. It will only bring you luck if you keep it unopened.'
Holding the precious chest in his hand, Taro got on the turtle's back and they sped to the surface of the sea. When he arrived at the gates of his village, Taro was surprised to see that everything had changed and there were no familiar faces. No-one knew Taro's family apart from some old men who had heard their grandparents speak of them.
Taro walked back to the seashore, sat on a rock and stared out to sea. Suddenly he remembered the chest the queen had given him. Taro forgot her warning and opened it. A cloud of white smoke appeared and surrounded Taro. When it disappeared, he had become an old man with hair as white as snow. Taro had been under the sea for many years. Now time had caught up with Urashima Taro.

UNIT 4 GRAMMAR 1

Page 41, Exercise 6

Situation 1: Due to a technical problem, the internet will stop working for the whole of the coming weekend.
Situation 2: New evidence suggests that all ice at the Arctic might have melted ten years from now.
Situation 3: The first low-cost airlines started up in the 1970s. Since then, their growth has been spectacular.

UNIT 5 LANGUAGE & BEYOND

Page 56, Exercise 1b

ADVERTISING COMPANIES USE DIFFERENT METHODS TO SELL TO TEENS.
–They try to make you feel special even though they are selling to hundreds of thousands of people.
–They try to sell you a rebellious teen image even though it's been carefully developed by adults.
–They encourage you to use social media to help market their products.
–They try to get your personal data so they can continue selling to you.

UNIT 6 GRAMMAR 1

Page 63, Exercise 4a

5 The eye turns light into electrochemical impulses.
The only visible part of your brain is located here.
The eye, where the only visible part of your brain is located, turns light into electrochemical impulses.
Q: WHAT PART?

6 Dolly was the first mammal to be cloned from an adult cell.
Her name became famous around the world in 1997.
Q: WHAT MAMMAL WAS SHE?

7 This technique works by stimulating our bodies to produce antibodies.
It has saved millions of lives.
These antibodies can fight a particular disease.
Q: WHAT TECHNIQUE?

8 This organ is one of five body parts.
The body parts have no obvious purpose.
The organ's located in your intestines.
Q: WHICH ORGAN?

UNIT 8 LISTENING AND VOCABULARY

Page 86, Exercise 7

1 Do internet service providers charge a lot for a home internet connection where you live? How fast do connections tend to be? Do you know if local and national calls are included in the cost of the service?
2 Have you ever purchased anything online? Was it imported from another country? If so, how quickly was it delivered to your house? How much did they charge for delivery?

UNIT 10 IN THE PICTURE

Page 105, Exercise 8

My English survey

5 How well do you think you'd ***get by / get across*** in an English speaking country?
6 If you could ***come across / try out*** a new language, which would you choose?
7 Will you ***keep up / die out*** your English when you leave school?

ANSWER

UNIT 7 GRAMMAR 2

Page 77, Exercise 3b

a) a Segway
b) a Wii console

STEP-BY-STEP PROJECTS

Download more information from www.macmillanbeyond.com

MAKE A KAMISHIBAI STORY

- Find a variety of magazine photos or draw pictures – *landscapes, people, objects* ...
- Use the pictures to create a story. Write the story in note form on the back of the pictures.
- Tell your story to other students, showing them the pictures.

Units 1 & 2

WRITE A 'HOW TO' MANUAL

- Choose something you know how to do or make – *make a paper plane, cook a dish, revise for an exam* ...
- Make a list of things you need to complete the task.
- Write a set of instructions, including illustrations.

Units 5 & 6

CREATE A START-UP

- Decide what type of business you want to start up – *hairdressing, app development, catering* ...
- Think about what's going to make your business different from the competition.
- Present your start-up idea to investors.

Units 3 & 4

DUB A FILM

- Choose a short scene with several characters from a local film or TV series – *soap, action film, drama* ...
- Translate the dialogue into English.
- Speak and record the English version of the scene.

Units 7 & 8

INVENT A LANGUAGE

- Choose the kind of language to invent – *universal language, Martian, simplified English* ...
- Make a list of basic vocabulary, including greetings.
- Teach some of your language to the class.

Units 9 & 10

Macmillan Education
4 Crinan Street
London N1 9XW
A division of Macmillan Publishers Limited

Companies and representatives throughout the world

ISBN 978-0-230-45593-1

First published 2015

Designed by emc design ltd
Illustrated by John Batten (Beehive Illustration) p76; Peter Cornwell pp21, 43, 86; Tom Croft p111; Nigel Dobbyn (Beehive Illustration) pp18, 29, 53, 91, 98; Mark Duffin pp38, p82–83 (main image); Sally Elford (banner icons) pp6, 16, 26–27, 28, 38, 48–49, 50, 60, 70–71, 72, 82, 92–93, 94, 104, 114–115; Tony Wilkins pp47, 50, 64, 118.
Cover design by emc design ltd
Cover photographs by Getty Images/Bill Varie, Alamy/Tetra Images
Picture research by Emily Taylor

The authors would like to thank all the team at Macmillan in the UK, Mexico, Poland, Spain and the rest of the world for everything they've done to make Beyond possible. Special thanks to our commissioning editor, managing editor and our publisher for their endless hard work and encouragement. We'd like to thank Studio 8 for their creative work on the drama group videos and EMC for coming up with the Beyond design concept. We'd also like to thank all the teachers and other individuals who have contributed to the course whose names appear on this page. Finally, we'd like to thank our friends and families for all their support.

The authors and publishers would like to express thanks to all those who contributed to the development and formation of Beyond. In particular, we would like to thank the following teachers, contacts and reviewers: Cristina Moisén Antón, Argelia Solis Arriaga, Krzysztof Bartold, Paweł Bienert, Agnieszka Bojanowska, Samuel Gómez Borobia, Ma. Eugenia Fernández Castro, Jolanta Chojnacka, Elsa Georgina Cruz, Dominika Dąbrowska, Barbara Dawidowska, Galina Dragunova, Monika Drygiel-Kobylińska, Mauricio Duran, Natalia Evdokimenko, Maria Teresa Velázquez Evers, Marciana Loma-Osorio Fontecha, Monika Fromiczew-Droździńska, Patricia García, Axel Morales García, Miguel Angel Rodriguez García, Aleksandra Gilewska, Joanna Góra, Ewa Górka, Daphne Green, Agata Helwich, Bethsabe Ruiz Herrera, Robert Jadachowski, Patricia Guzmán Luis Juan, Anna Kacpura, Ruth Kanter, Regina Kaźmierczuk, Katarzyna Konisiewicz, Maria Koprowska, Bogusława Krajewska, Aldona Krasoń, Joanna Worobiec Kugaj, Joanna Kuligowska, Tadeusz Kur, Maria Kwiatkowska, Josefina Maitret, Javier Majul, Claire Manners, Laura Elena Medina, Carmen García Méndez, Iwona Mikucka, Talhia Miranda, Claudia Rangel Miranda, Armando Nieto, Joanna Nowak, Anna Nowakowska, Ewa Nowicka, Anastasia Parshikova, Paloma Carrasco Peñalba, Ma. Del Carmen Fernández Pérez, Joanna Płatos, Louise Emma Potter, Maria Teresa Portillo, Juan José Gómez Ramírez, Aida Rivera, Gabriela Rubio, Gabriela Bourge Ruiz, Irina Sakharova, Małgorzata Sałaj, Patricia Avila Sánchez, Jessica Galvan Sanchez, Miguel Angel Santiago, Karol Sęk, Barbara Sibilska, Tatiana Sinyavina, Agnieszka Śliwowska, Vlada Songailene, Ángela Siles Suárez, Beata Świątkowska, Ewelina Szmyd-Patuła, Agnieszka Szymaniak, Juliana Maria Franco Tavares, José Luis Vázquez, Irma Velazquez, Małgorzata Walczak, Dariusz Winiarek, Justyna Zdunek, Zofia Żdżarska, Dominika Zięba, Marzena Zieleniewska, Anna Zielińska-Miszczuk, Robert Zielonka.

The authors and publishers would also like to thank the following schools who allowed class observations – MEXICO: Centro de Formación Escolar Banting, Centro Escolar Las Águilas, Colegio América, Colegio Axayacatl, Colegio Donato Bramante, Colegio Edgar Morin, Colegio Francés Nueva Santa María, Colegio Gesi Secundaria, Colegio José Martí S. C., Colegio San Agustin, Colegio Sir Winston Leonard Spencer Churchill De México, Colegios La Salle Boulevares, Cristian Fernández de Merino, Erasmo De Rótterdam, Escuela De Ruán, Grupo Colegio Rosario Castellanos, Instituto Atenea, Instituto Crisol, Instituto Cultural Americano Mexicano, Instituto Manuel Acosta, Instituto Oriente Arboledas, Instituto Zaragoza, Liceo Americano Francés, Liceo Ibero Mexicano, Liceo Mexicano Japonés, Secundaria Simón Bolívar. SPAIN: IES Anselmo Lorenzo, IES Camilo José Cela, IES Complutense, IES Joaquín Turina, IES Laguna de Joatzell, IES Luis García Berlanga, IES Manuel de Falla, IES Máximo Trueba. POLAND: Gimnazjum nr 30, Gimnazjum nr 104 Warszawa Wawer, Gimnazjum nv120, Gimnazjum nr 141, Gimnazjum nr 145, Gimnazjum, ul. SZKOLNA 4, Publiczne Gimnazjum w Wiązownie, ZSP w Jazgarzewie. TURKEY: Ahmet Şimşek Koleji, Anabilim Koleji, Büyük Çamlıca Koleji, Doğa Koleji, Kirimli Fazilet Olcay Anatolian High School, Modafen Koleji, Sakıp Sabancı Anadolu Lisesi.

The authors and publishers would like to thank the following for permission to reproduce their photographs:
Alamy p116, Alamy/AF Archive pp26, 44(tr), Alamy/Galina Barskaya p61(2), Alamy/Jamie Carstairs p107(bl), Alamy/ClassicStock pp94(b), p95(f), Alamy/CuboImages srl p39(tr), Alamy/Phil Degginger p84(cr), Alamy/DesignPics Inc pp20(louis), 22(tr), Alamy/David J Green Studio p7(envelope), Alamy/Olaf Doering p87(tl), Alamy/Ted Foxx p52(Marek), Alamy/Robert Fried p60(5), Alamy/Garry Gay p50(a), Alamy/Mandy Godbehear p31(bl), Alamy/Elly Godfroy p51(c), Alamy/Guy Edwardes Photography p17(b), Alamy/Mark Hayes p36, Alamy/Hero Images Inc p95(j), Alamy/Peter Horree p14(br), Alamy/D. Hurst p52(francesca), Alamy/Ikon Images p143(tl), Alamy/Image Asset Management Ltd p44(tmr), Alamy/ImageBroker p105(tr), Alamy/ImageSource pp22(tcm), 61(7), Alamy/Ivy Close Images p17(d), Alamy/Patrik Jandak p61(6), Alamy/John Joannides p51(e), Alamy/Juice Images p56, Alamy/Gergely Kishonthy p31(tl), Alamy/Art Kowalsky p39(bl), Alamy/Lordprice Collection p44(tl), Alamy/Edmund Lowe p105(cr), Alamy/Steve Mayes p52(background), Alamy/MBI p72(b), Alamy/Innis McAllister p7(NYC), Alamy/MCLA Collection p17(e), Alamy/Mint Images Limited p10, Alamy/Mulrooney Oxford UK p39(tl), Alamy/Chris Noble p62, Alamy/OJO Images p51(i), Alamy/David Pearson p73(e-foyer) p74, Alamy/PhotoAlto pp51(d), 60(1), 143(bl), Alamy/Photodreams1 p105(tm), Alamy/Photofusion Picture Library p95(e), Alamy/Photos 12 p80, Alamy/Picture Partners p110(d), Alamy/The Print Collector p44(tml), Alamy/Radharc Images p14(tr), Alamy/Paul Raftery p16-17(library), Alamy/Ray Roberts p7(Houdini), Alamy/RubberBall p61(4), Alamy/Stockbroker p95(I), Alamy/StockbrokerXtra p95(g), Alamy/Nik Taylor p52(stephen), Alamy/Tips Italia Srl a socio unico p21, Alamy/Travelib History p94(a), Alamy/UK Stock Images Ltd p34, Alamy/Colin Underhill p107(bcm), Alamy/View Pictures Ltd p73(e-exterior), Alamy/Steve Vidler pp39(tml), 58, Alamy/Liam White p48, Alamy/Wonderlandstock p12(choosing colours), Alamy/www.BibleLandPictures.com p16(br), Alamy/Rawdon Wyatt p107(tm); **BananaStock** p64; **Brand X Pictures** p20(linda); **Corbis**/Horace Bristol p18, Corbis/Robert Ghement/epa p71, Corbis/Inspirestock p108, Corbis/JLP/ Jose L. Pelaez p110 (c), Corbis/Klaus Mellenthin/Westend61 p51(f), Corbis/Pauline St. Denis p51(j), Corbis/Stephen Welstead/LWA p61(3); **Eyevine**/Emily Berl/The New York Times p106(tr); **Ford Images**/Wieck p7(ford); **Getty Images** pp94(c), 118, Getty Images/Clive Andrews p107(tcm), Getty Images/Art Media/Print Collector **© Succession Picasso/DACS, London 2014** p54(b), Getty Images/Peter Cade p88(tm), Getty Images/Culture Club p7(Carroll), Getty Images/Gregorio Cunha/AFP p53, Getty Images/Digital Vision pp42, 143(cr), Getty Images/Jonatan Fernstrom p66, Getty Images/First Light p102, Getty Images/Flickr Open p143(tr), Getty Images/Flickr RM/Sergio Amiti p39(br), Getty Images/Izabela Habur p95(d), Getty Images/Frazer Harrison p105(tl), Getty Images/Noel Hendrickson p142(bmr), Getty Images/Kemter p28, Getty Images/Ron Levine p87(bm), Getty Images/Zoran Milich p46(tr), Getty Images/OJO Images p12(tl), Getty Images/Leonardo Patrizi p110(a), Getty Images/PhotoAlto p77, Getty Images/PhotoAlto/Odilon Dimier p72(a), Getty Images/Picture Press RM p12(tr), Getty Images/Sturti p100(tm), Getty Images/Tetra images p110(b), Getty Images/Time & Life Pictures p84(tr), Getty Images/Universal Images Group Editorial pp19, 54(c), Getty Images/WireImage/Nick Harvey p30(cl), Getty Images/David Woolley p87(br); **ImageSource** p60(cr, br); **Glow Images**/Laurne Bourdais p78; **The Kobal Collection**/Paramount p104(cr), The Kobal Collection/Columbia Pictures p6(tr); **PhotoDisc** p8, Photodisc/Getty Images p22(tl); **Proceedings of the National Academy of Sciences/**"Ragini Verma, PhD, Proceedings of the National Academy of Sciences, (http:/www.uphs.upenn.edu/news/News_Releases/2013/12/verma) p63; **SuperStock** p104(belgium, brazil, canada, ireland, new zealand, singapore, spain, switzerland, uk); **ThinkStock** pp6(cr), 27, 49, 95(h), 104(malta), 115, ThinkStock/AbleStock.com p51(h), ThinkStock/AbleStock.com/NA p32(br), ThinkStock/Design Pics RF p51(b), ThinkStock/Digital Vision p24(background), ThinkStock/Getty Images/Hemera p143(br), ThinkStock/Getty Images/Hemera/Robert Mizerek p73(b), ThinkStock/Getty Images/istockphoto pp7(elizabeth, padlocks), 12(car crash, girls chatting), 14(cl), 17(a,c), 16(cr), 22(tm), 29, 31(cr), 32(tr), 38, 74, 54(d, a), 70(a,b,c), 74, 96, ThinkStock/Getty Images/iStockphoto/Apiruk p88(tcr), ThinkStock/Getty Images/iStockphoto/Jim Blubaugh p39(bcl), ThinkStock/Getty Images/iStockphoto/CynthiaAnnF p61(8), ThinkStock/Getty Images/iStockphoto/Lijuan Guo p39(bmr), ThinkStock/Getty Images/iStockphoto/HappyToBeHomeless p40(background), ThinkStock/Getty Images/iStockphoto/Joel T p51(g), ThinkStock/Getty Images/iStockphoto/Dic Liew p73(f), ThinkStock/Getty Images/iStockPhoto/MajaPhoto p46(bottom), ThinkStock/Getty Images/iStockphoto/mariusz_prusaczyk p41, ThinkStock/Getty Images/iStockphoto/photoncatcher p73(c), ThinkStock/Getty Images/iStockphoto/VitalyEdush p39(tcr), ThinkStock/Getty Images/seewhatmitchsee p7(webpage), ThinkStock/Getty Images/Stockbyte p20(gregory), ThinkStock/Getty Images/Wavebreak Media p40(inset), ThinkStock/Hemera p100(br), ThinkStock/Hemera Technologies p70(d), ThinkStock/Jupiterimages pp30(cr), 68, ThinkStock/Mike Mols p142(br), ThinkStock/Stockbyte p61(9).

Commissioned photography by Studio 8 Limited pp13, 23, 35, 45, 57, 67, 79, 89 and 101.

The author(s) and the publishers are grateful for permission to include the following copyright material:
Excerpt from the Macmillan Reader entitled 'Middlemarch' © Macmillan Publishers Limited, 2007, Published by Macmillan Publishers Limited. Used by Permission. All Rights Reserved.
Excerpt from the Macmillan Reader entitled 'Moby Dick' © Macmillan Publishers Limited, 2007, Published by Macmillan Publishers Limited. Used by Permission. All Rights Reserved.

Printed and bound in Thailand
2019 2018 2017 2016 2015
14 13 12 11 10 9 8 7 6